THE EVERYTHING® COUPONING BOOK

Dear Reader,

As a child, I always wanted to be a teacher, never a writer. Things changed and I ended up in the accounting field, which worked out well for a while because after having children, I became a stay-at-home mom. While home with my children, I discovered the online world. I met amazing people and found information I had no idea was out there, including how to use coupons. Once I learned how much money could be saved with coupons, I knew I wanted to share my knowledge with as many people as I could.

Being a teacher was bound to happen eventually, because in August 2008 I began writing my blog *www.KouponKaren.com* where I teach people how to use coupons, find sales, save money, and even make a little extra money. Over the years it's grown into a full-time occupation, and now I blog on a daily basis. I decided to write this book because there are so many people out there who could really benefit from learning about coupons and using smart saving tips to make their hard-earned dollars go farther.

Sincerely,

Karen Wilmes, a.k.a., Koupon Karen

Welcome to the EVERYTHING® Series!

These handy, accessible books give you all you need to tackle a difficult project, gain a new hobby, comprehend a fascinating topic, prepare for an exam, or even brush up on something you learned back in school but have since forgotten.

You can choose to read an Everything® book from cover to cover or just pick out the information you want from our four useful boxes: e-questions, e-facts, e-alerts, and e-ssentials.

We give you everything you need to know on the subject, but throw in a lot of fun stuff along the way, too.

We now have more than 400 Everything® books in print, spanning such wide-ranging categories as weddings, pregnancy, cooking, music instruction, foreign language, crafts, pets, New Age, and so much more. When you're done reading them all, you can finally say you know Everything®!

QUESTION

Answers to
common questions

FACT

Important snippets
of information

ALERT

Urgent
warnings

ESSENTIAL

Quick
handy tips

PUBLISHER Karen Cooper

DIRECTOR OF ACQUISITIONS AND INNOVATION Paula Munier

MANAGING EDITOR, EVERYTHING® SERIES Lisa Laing

COPY CHIEF Casey Ebert

ASSISTANT PRODUCTION EDITOR Melanie Cordova

ACQUISITIONS EDITOR Ross Weisman

SENIOR DEVELOPMENT EDITOR Brett Palana-Shanahan

EDITORIAL ASSISTANT Matthew Kane

EVERYTHING® SERIES COVER DESIGNER Erin Alexander

LAYOUT DESIGNERS Erin Dawson, Michelle Roy Kelly, Elisabeth Lariviere, Denise Wallace

Visit the entire Everything® series at *www.everything.com*

THE
EVERYTHING®
COUPONING
BOOK

Clip your way to incredible savings!

Karen Wilmes
Creator, KouponKaren.com

Aadamsmedia
Avon, Massachusetts

*This book is dedicated to my parents, Angela and Jack
Cimino, for believing in me and encouraging me to always
follow my dreams. And to my husband, Steve, for showing
me that I can do anything I set my mind to do.*

An Everything® Series Book.
Everything® and everything.com® are registered trademarks of F+W Media, Inc.

Published by Adams Media, a division of F+W Media, Inc.
57 Littlefield Street, Avon, MA 02322 U.S.A.
www.adamsmedia.com

Contains material adapted and abridged from *The Everything® Meals on a
Budget Cookbook* by Linda Larsen, copyright © 2008 by F+W Media, Inc.,
ISBN 10: 1-59869-508-8, ISBN 13: 978-1-59869-508-3.

ISBN 10: 1-4405-3142-0
ISBN 13: 978-1-4405-3142-2
eISBN 10: 1-4405-3357-1
eISBN 13: 978-1-4405-3357-0

Printed in the United States of America.

10 9 8 7 6 5 4 3 2 1

Library of Congress Cataloging-in-Publication Data
is available from the publisher.

This publication is designed to provide accurate and authoritative information with regard to
the subject matter covered. It is sold with the understanding that the publisher is not engaged
in rendering legal, accounting, or other professional advice. If legal advice or other expert
assistance is required, the services of a competent professional person should be sought.
—From a *Declaration of Principles* jointly adopted by a Committee of the
American Bar Association and a Committee of Publishers and Associations

Many of the designations used by manufacturers and sellers to distinguish their products are
claimed as trademarks. Where those designations appear in this book and Adams Media was
aware of a trademark claim, the designations have been printed with initial capital letters.

*This book is available at quantity discounts for bulk purchases.
For information, please call 1-800-289-0963.*

Contents

Acknowledgments

I would like to thank my family for allowing me the time to write this book, and my daughters Holly and Allison for inspiring me to always be the best I can be. I also want to thank the KouponKaren.com readers who come back every day wanting to learn about saving money and inspiring me to find the best deals I can each week. If it weren't for them, I would be talking to myself!

I would like to thank my friends and family who cheered me on and helped me along. Their support helped more than they will ever know! I would also like to thank my acquisitions editor Ross for giving me this opportunity and for answering all my questions throughout the writing process. Writing a book isn't as easy as writing a blog. And finally, I'd like to thank Adams Media for giving me the chance to share my knowledge of saving money and using coupons. It's been a fun journey, one I will never forget.

The Top 10 Things You'll Learn about Using Coupons

1. **Why You Should Use Coupons.** Using coupons can help you get the most from your hard-earned money.

2. **How Coupons Are Like Money.** When making purchases, the more coupons you use, the less money you hand over.

3. **The Different Types of Coupons and Where to Find Them.** Coupons can be found in more places than the Sunday paper. Once you know where to look, you'll see them everywhere.

4. **How to Get Items for Free.** With the right combination of coupons, sales, and store incentives, you can easily identify items and get them for free.

5. **Tips for Shopping for Organic Foods on a Budget.** Organic foods do occasionally go on sale, but if you plan your shopping trip carefully, the money you save on other items can go toward the purchase of organic foods.

6. **How to Organize Your Coupons.** From a shoebox to an envelope or a binder, there are many different ways you can organize your coupons.

7. **How to Plan Your Shopping Trip.** Plan your shopping trip to maximize your couponing success. Go to the store with a plan and you're guaranteed to save every time.

8. **How to Build a Stockpile.** Building a stockpile of the items you use all the time means you'll never run out and be forced to pay full price.

9. **How to Save Money Online.** You can save money on every purchase you make online, whether it's by sale, mark down, coupon code, free shipping, or cash back.

10. **How to Coupon with a Little or a Lot of Time.** Even if you have a little bit of time or money, you can still use coupons to save money.

Introduction

USING COUPONS IS A great way to stretch your hard-earned dollars, especially if they are limited. Coupons can not only get you items you need, but also can help supplement a savings account to save for items you want. There seems to be a stigma for using coupons—that only poor people use them—but actually that's not the case. Anyone can use coupons and no one should be looked down on if using them. Some people may also think that there are only coupons for processed, unhealthy foods. While there are an abundance of coupons for those types of products, there are also coupons for a lot of other items. If you can't find a coupon for something you want, then you can use the savings from other items to purchase those things. There is always a way to save; you just need to find it.

Coupons can be scary at first if you don't know anything about them. There is a lot more to it than just getting a Sunday paper and clipping coupons. The savings can be pretty big if you use them properly and combine them with other saving opportunities, which are explained throughout the book. One of the keys to being successful in using coupons is to have a good organization system. If you can't see what you have, then chances are you aren't going to use them. If you spend hours clipping and sorting coupons, and then don't use them, then you've wasted valuable time. This book explains several ways to keep yourself organized so you can spend the least amount of time couponing and still get the greatest savings.

Building a stockpile is a great way to help you save on last-minute purchases, and you don't even need a lot of room in order to have a successful stockpile. You can use even the smallest spaces to put a stockpile of items you use regularly. This will ensure you never pay full price for items again. Building a stockpile may be easy, but maintaining it may not be. You'll learn key factors in maintaining your stockpile to get all your money's worth.

You may already use coupons but you want to take your coupon usage to the next level by using more coupons. This book will help teach you all the different kinds of coupons that are available and how to use them combined with other savings opportunities. The stores have incentives to get you to shop there and when you use them in tandem with coupons, you will save so much more. You'll learn about all the available saving options and how to combine them with coupons.

If you don't want to use coupons but want to save money, you still can, and this book will show you how. If you like to shop online, there are so many ways you can save money not just with coupon codes, but with discount websites. You can own designer-brand clothes and accessories at a fraction of the cost, if you know where to look. You can even make money sharing these deals with your friends.

What it all comes down to is this—almost anything you buy, you can save on with just a little bit of research. And once you know what you're doing, it will take even less time. There are savings opportunities all around you; this book will help you see them and use them.

CHAPTER 1

Introduction to Couponing

Couponing is becoming increasingly popular. The economy hasn't been thriving for a few years and many people are struggling just to get by with the basics. Coupons can help stretch a budget in ways that can help any family. Using coupons isn't rocket science, but there is a right and a wrong way to use them. Once you understand coupons and how to use them, you can expect to save up to 50 percent off your grocery bill—if not more—each time you shop. The result isn't just a lower grocery bill; using coupons can also help you get those things you want, but may not have been able to afford. It just takes a little time to learn and then you'll be off on a savings adventure.

Why Should You Use Coupons?

This is a question that everyone should be asking themselves, not just those who are strapped for cash. Coupons are all around you, available to use all the time. Why wouldn't you use them? If you were looking through a magazine and found a dollar bill tucked in between two pages, what would you do? You would probably take it and use it next time you went shopping, right? Then why not grab the coupon that's in the magazine instead of a dollar bill and use it next time you go shopping? Believe it or not, it's the same thing. Coupons are just like cash. You hand them to the cashier when making a purchase, in addition to your payment. So treat them like cash and use them!

ESSENTIAL

Don't be embarrassed to use coupons. It doesn't mean you are poor; it means you are a smart shopper and you want to stretch your hard-earned dollars as far as you can. No matter your financial situation or your reason to use coupons, it should be something you are proud of doing.

Reduce Debt and Save for Vacations with Coupons

How many times have you thought that if only you had a little bit more money each week, you could pay off your credit card faster or perhaps just pay cash so you didn't have to charge things you need? You do work hard for your money, so wouldn't it be great to be able to splurge and buy something you didn't need, but wanted instead? Everyone should treat themselves from time to time, but when your credit card bill is already through the roof, you may feel guilty buying something and adding to that balance.

You may simply just want to afford a babysitter so you could have a date night with your spouse. After a long week, getting out and just enjoying yourself is a nice reward, but not when you can't afford it. But what if you could? What if you did have just a little bit more money every week for things like this? Guess what? Using coupons may just be the key to accomplishing all those things, including reducing your debt or even saving for a vacation.

Believe it or not, coupons work like cash even though they aren't actual money. The creditors won't take them to pay bills, of course. But if you use them at the stores where they are accepted, you'll have the cash to pay those creditors. Wouldn't that be nice? Just think—coupons could help get you out of debt; coupons could help pay off your car; coupons could help get your family to Disney World. If you save $50 each week combining sales and coupons, in one year you'll have $2,600. If you save $75 each week, in one year you'll have $3,900. Those numbers look nice, don't they?

If you are a one-income family, it's almost like pulling in a second income with the money you're saving using coupons. Yes, it does take time out of your day to plan shopping trips and then complete them, but if it's the only thing you can do, it's like you are getting paid to do it.

Save on Everyday Purchases

Coupons aren't just used to purchase items in grocery stores and drugstores. There are so many other ways to use coupons in your everyday life to help save money. Chances are, you do something every day that you could have saved on by using a coupon. Every time you hand over cash for something, whether it's a service or an item, you should be thinking "Could I have saved money by using a coupon?" And guess what? You probably could have.

Do you have a job that requires you to wear dress clothes every day that need to be dry-cleaned or cared for when washing? If so, there is a good chance you can get a reduced price on your dry cleaning with a coupon. Did you wash your car today? You probably could have used a coupon to receive a discount on your car wash. And if you went out to lunch, you may have been able to save a few dollars on the meal as well. That's three opportunities you could have had to save money.

Of course you may not be able to use the same dry cleaner you always do, or you might have to stop at a different car wash, and even have to eat somewhere else. But if you had the option to go to one place and pay full price or go to a different place and get a discount, then why not go to the place where you're going to save money? It's almost a no-brainer and some might think, "Why wouldn't you just do it?" It will just take you a few moments to find out if you have a coupon or if you can get your hands on one to use. And if you save an average of 10 percent each day you use coupons, it will add up over time to a nice savings.

A History of Couponing

Coupons have been around for a long time. The first coupon issued was in 1884 by the Coca-Cola Company. They mailed coupons to customers, and also included coupons for a free drink in magazines. Coca-Cola Company gave stores or restaurants free syrup to cover the cost of the free drinks. It's estimated that one in nine Americans received free drinks between 1894 and 1913. The next coupon wasn't issued in the United States until 1909 when C. W. Post printed coupons for breakfast cereals and other Post products. Then coupon usage grew during the Great Depression in 1930, and by 1940 big chain grocery stores began to offer coupons to win customers over from smaller local markets. And that is when the competition began!

If coupons have been continually used over the years, obviously there is a reason. The reason is they help you save money. If people weren't really saving money, then coupons would no longer be issued. The companies aren't going to spend the money to print them if no one is using them.

The first coupon from C. W. Post was for one cent off Grape-Nuts cereal. Who knew when they issued that coupon that Grape-Nuts would still be on the shelves 100 years later?

Why Issue Coupons Instead of Lowering the Price?

Coupons are issued not only to help you save money, but also to help advertise an item. If you see an item on a coupon and you see it all the time, it's going to stick in your head and you may buy it or even just talk about it. Word of mouth is another great way to advertise, and it's free!

Of course companies could just lower the price of their product, instead of offering coupons, but they make money on items that they issue coupons for. How? Well, if you purchase an item because you had a coupon for it, and then you really like it, are you going to buy it again? Probably. Will you only buy it if you have a coupon? Possibly, but not all the time, and that is what companies are counting on. Yes, there are some people who will only buy items they have coupons for, but not everyone uses coupons and some of those who do, don't use them every time they shop. Even the most extreme coupon user will purchase an item from time to time without a coupon.

Lowering the price of an item instead of issuing coupons means everyone gets that low price, not just those who clip coupons. So you can look at it as a reward from the manufacturer for taking that extra step.

How to Approach Couponing

Couponing can be fun if you approach it in your own way. You can use coupons to any degree that you'd like. If you only want to use them at the grocery store, you can. If you want to use them only on health and beauty items, you can. You don't even have to use a coupon each time you shop. That's completely up to you. Though once you start, you may not want to stop. There is a lot to learn about using coupons but anyone can do it. You don't have to be a woman or a mom—couponing is for whoever does the shopping. Don't be intimidated by coupons. If you begin with an "I can do it!" attitude, then you can!

Always Look for a Sale Before You Shop

If you seriously want to save a lot of money, you need to be on the lookout for every opportunity you can find to save money or use a coupon. You shouldn't pay full price for anything before you've thought about whether you can save on the purchase. However, coupons aren't available for all items so the best you may be able to do is purchase some things on sale. That's okay too because you are still saving money.

QUESTION

Should I apply for the store credit card to save on my purchase?
Department stores may offer you an incentive to apply for their store credit card. It could be an instant savings or a coupon off your next purchase. It can be very tempting to apply for the credit card just to get the savings. Unless you are planning to pay the balance when you get your bill, it's probably not a great idea. The interest rates on these credit cards are extremely high and the money you save by getting the card will probably be eaten up by interest if you don't pay the balance in full.

This means that impulse shopping will have to stop and you need to be able to have the self-control to not buy an item until you can save on your purchase. If you do a little research first, you may find it on sale somewhere. And if not, you just have to hold out until it is on sale or you come across a coupon for it. Most things go on sale at one time or another and it won't hurt to wait a little while for it.

Try Different Items and Stop Being Brand Loyal

Using coupons is going to pose a big challenge to some, especially those who are brand loyal. If you always use one brand or always shop at one store, you need to toss all that out the window. This is a time in which all brand loyalty needs to be pushed aside. That doesn't mean that you can't buy the brands you like or shop at the stores you like. It just means that you will have to sometimes purchase another brand or shop at a different store. You will have to shop where the sales are and buy the items that are on sale and/or for which you have a coupon. It may be hard at first, and some members of the family may resist it for as long as they can, but eventually when you see the money that you are saving, it will be easier.

Do some comparison shopping so you can see exactly how you can save. If one brand you like to use is always $1.00 more than another brand and that other brand has a coupon for an additional $.50 off, then the total difference is $1.50 saved. If you purchase this item twenty times in one year, you will save $30 by switching one item. Imagine if you did this with ten items. That's a savings of $300 in one year, which may equal a car payment. When you look at it that way, it may not be so bad to change brands. Do some research and see exactly how much of a difference you can make just by changing the brand of products you use.

One Step at a Time

If you've never used a coupon before, it can seem overwhelming—and it may be, at the beginning. Start slow and try to be organized. It will take time to develop a system that works for you. If you try to do it all at once, it is also possible to get discouraged and frustrated and not succeed at all. Take baby steps and learn as you go; then you can easily save money every single time you step foot into the stores.

Tackle one store at a time and one type of coupon at a time. Once you learn the basics, you can apply them anywhere. You are relearning how to shop and spend money, which could lead to big changes for you. Once you start using coupons and saving money, you won't know why you ever paid full price for anything, and you won't want to anymore either! You'll be proud to share your newfound knowledge of saving money with everyone.

ALERT

You may be tempted to use your savings on additional items that aren't on your shopping list. It's easy to convince yourself that since you saved money, it's okay to buy something else. While this is fine to do from time to time, it won't get you anywhere in the long run. Use your savings toward something you need, rather than something that you simply want, until you are in a better financial situation.

Start Slow

Gathering coupons and shopping at three or four stores a week is too much to take on when you first start. Once you get the hang of couponing, you can add more coupons and stores to your shopping trips. How can you do this? Grab a Sunday paper and only use the coupons from that paper's inserts on your shopping trip. Yes, there are so many more coupons that can be used, but until you get the hang of it, just use the ones in the Sunday paper. It's unrealistic to think you can go from saving nothing to saving 100 percent the first time you shop. Starting slow will teach you the basics for becoming a successful coupon user.

Explore the systems throughout this book and find something that works for you. Don't go by what works for your friend, or your sister, or your neighbor, because that may not work for you. And if what you try doesn't work after a little while, try something else. It will be a trial-and-error phase and it may even seem like a part-time job, but it's a job that pays when you take home bags of groceries and only pay 50 percent of the regular price. Get help from everyone in the house. Even the kids can help and you'll be teaching them how to budget their money at a young age. If you don't start slow, it can be easy to become frustrated and give up—and that won't save any money, will it?

You Can Do It!

You can do this. It doesn't take a special person. You don't need a college degree or have to be the president or CEO of a company to have the smarts to use coupons. Anyone who shops can learn to use coupons. Just think about how wonderful it will feel the first time you put all your groceries on the counter at the store, hand over your pile of coupons to the cashier, and pay at least 50 percent less than you did the week before. You've learned how to save money for your family. You are contributing to the household finances by using coupons.

Couponing Etiquette

There is a right and wrong way of doing everything, including using coupons. Don't try to cheat the system. You will lose in the end. Don't take advantage of a cashier who doesn't know what he is doing. Some of them aren't properly trained or they don't really care. If you take advantage of that, you'll lose in the end. Retailers are out to make money, not lose money. Abusing the system will result in the use of coupons being limited and even eliminated. Follow the rules and play right and you'll be successful.

One important rule in couponing: Do not clear the shelves. You have every right to stock up but don't take everything, even if you have the coupons. Be sure to leave some for the next person. That person may need only one and if you took them all, they get nothing. Try to put yourself in their shoes; imagine if every time you went shopping, the items you wanted were gone. It's very frustrating. Remember what your mother taught you; treat others the way you want to be treated. That works in couponing too!

The Drawbacks of Extreme Couponing

Extreme couponing is real, but it is not for everyone. In fact, it's only for a select few. Extreme couponers purchase an overabundance of items, some they may not even need. They use these items to help them save on other items perhaps with incentives from the store or overage from another item. These types of shopping trips need to be planned out meticulously and change from week to week or sale to sale. It's not the type of shopping trip that everyone could do, nor would do, every week. Everything needs to fall into place—the sales, the stores, the coupons, and the deals all need to work out, to save an extreme amount of money. Unfortunately sometimes couponing etiquette is violated while making these extreme purchases, by using the wrong coupons on the wrong items.

Getting thousands of dollars of products for free each time you go to the supermarket isn't possible. Filling twenty-five carts with food, unless you have a family of twenty to feed, isn't something that can be done every day. And you definitely won't get that all for free each time you shop. You have to think about what's going on behind the scenes when you see someone spend $10 and get $2,000 worth of products.

- Where did all those coupons come from?
- What products were on sale?
- What items did they make money on using sales and coupons?
- Did they use the proper coupons?
- Did the store offer incentives for purchasing certain products?

You must take all those things into consideration when looking at an extreme couponer's shopping trip.

Coupons Aren't Always Free

An extreme couponer probably purchased a lot of newspapers to get so many coupons. Which means the coupons weren't free. The total cost of the shopping trip must include what they spent acquiring the coupons. Besides buying extra newspapers, there are ways online for you to get more coupons. There are coupon-clipping websites where you can pay a fee to get more coupons. You aren't paying for the actual coupon, since that is illegal, but you are paying for the service of clipping, sorting, and mailing them to you. But these aren't free; you are paying a price for them in some way, shape, or form. This price must be included in the total cost as well.

What Did Those Items Cost?

Most of the products that an extreme couponer purchases were probably on sale since that's the way you'll get an item for the best price. However, were they all part of a weekly sale or were there some items on clearance or just marked down to sell? Produce and meat products may have been marked down to sell that day and aren't being purchased at full price. That can make a big difference on purchasing certain items. Knowing how the items were priced is very helpful when trying to figure out how someone scores such a great deal.

Of course depending on the price of the item and what coupons you have, it's possible to get an item for free and even make money on a purchase. That money can then be applied on another item as *overage*. When this happens, you are lowering the price of another item. Chances are, an extreme couponer will use this strategy to lower the price of other items.

Use the Right Coupons and Shop Store Incentives

Depending on how accurate the registers and coupons are, the coupons used may have been for specific items or sizes of items that were not purchased. When someone is using a lot of coupons, it's easier for one that doesn't belong to slip by. For this reason, the bar codes on coupons are being changed so the manufacturers can code the coupons in more detail to ensure that the proper items are purchased when using a coupon.

Store incentives can also help lower the total purchase price. If the store offered incentives with some purchases, the extreme couponer probably had to complete several transactions to get all those incentives.

You can apply store incentives toward another item to lower the total purchase price. For instance, if you purchase three items, you may receive a few dollars off your next purchase. Or if you spend a certain dollar amount, you'll receive a coupon off your next purchase. When making multiple transactions, you can apply these accordingly and roll them into other transactions, therefore lowering your out-of-pocket total.

ESSENTIAL

The time spent on an extreme shopping trip is another thing you need to account for. Don't forget how much time goes into planning these shopping trips. The extreme couponer spends hours upon hours planning his trip, finding the coupons, calculating his costs, and mapping out his shopping trip. And then there is the time it takes to shop and check out.

Can You Save Like an Extreme Couponer?

Can you save up to 90 percent on a shopping trip? Yes, you can occasionally, but not every time you shop. Do you need to purchase 1,000 items to save that much? No. With careful planning you can be an extreme couponer and save up to 90 percent at times without buying 100 cans of tomato sauce or 1,500 toothbrushes. But please don't expect to shop like that all the time and get everything for free. You will have to pay things; you'll just be paying less than full price.

CHAPTER 2

What Is a Coupon?

The *Merriam-Webster's Learner's Dictionary* defines a coupon as "a usually small piece of printed paper that lets you get a service or product for free or at a lower price." Coupons are like money. If you hand over $10.00 in coupons at the time of a purchase, then $10.00 in cash stays in your wallet. Once you learn how to use coupons, you'll be amazed at how easy it is, and how much money you can save. Knowing how to use a coupon properly *and* the best time to use it makes it a lot more valuable than just a "small piece of paper."

Anatomy of a Coupon

Before you can use a coupon properly, it is helpful to fully understand all its components. There is a lot of information found on coupons, for both the consumer and the retailer. The consumer needs to know how much the coupon is for, which products it's for, and how many items need to be purchased to use the coupon. They also need to know how long they have to use the coupon and exactly how they can use the coupon in a transaction. The retailer needs to know all those components along with where to send the coupon for redemption and what they will get in exchange for the coupon. If you can't find all this information on a coupon, then it may not be real and the store may not accept it.

Here is a list of the important information you can find on a coupon and what it means:

- **Value and Quantity.** The value stated is what will be discounted when the coupon is used. This amount will automatically be deducted when the register reads the bar code. There will be a quantity that you'll need to purchase in order to use the coupon. If it says $1.00 off of two boxes, you must purchase two boxes to use the coupon. The quantity and the value are coded within the bar code.
- **Picture.** Each coupon will have a picture of the product along with a description of the product. Sometimes the coupon may be for a family of products but will only show one item in the picture. If you read the entire description, you'll know what you can purchase with the coupon.
- **Description of Product.** You may only be able to use the coupon on a specific size of an item or a particular product within the family of products. Read the actual description written on the coupon to figure this out. You may have a coupon for Tide but it says it's only good on Tide Plus Bleach. If that's the case, you cannot use the coupon on regular Tide. You may also be restricted to use it on one particular size. For instance, if the manufacturer does not want you to use the coupon on the trial size, then it will say "not valid on trial size." (Trial sizes and travel sizes are usually the same thing.)
- **Expiration Date.** Most coupons will have an expiration date, but if there is no expiration date, it will state that somewhere on the coupon. This date is the last day that you can use the coupon. Make sure

that you do not accidentally cut off the expiration date when clipping the coupon. If you do, you won't be able to use it.

- **Note to Consumer and to Retailer.** The note to the consumer is to explain how to use the coupon and the note to the retailer explains where they can send the coupon and what they will receive for a handling fee when redeemed. You may only be able to use one coupon per transaction or per household. If this is the case, the note to the consumer will explain. The retailer is actually paid for each coupon they submit. They will receive the face value along with a handling fee, which is stated on the coupon. If this information is not on the coupon, it is not a manufacturer coupon.

- **Bar Code.** The bar code has lots of information that is read by the cash register. It was made to speed up the process when checking out. The cashier no longer needs to input the value of the coupon. All that information can be read from the bar code, including the dollar amount, the product, the expiration date, and the quantity.

QUESTION

What if I accidentally cut off the expiration date on the coupon while clipping it?
If you accidentally cut off the expiration date of a coupon while clipping it, then you've voided the coupon. The expiration date is needed to make it valid. The store needs to know how long a coupon can be used, or they cannot accept it. If they could, then there would be no need for an expiration date in the first place.

The Numbers on the Coupon Bar Code

Each number on the bar code means something to the store's computers, as do the numbers on the UPC code on the product. The first number will tell the register whether it can be doubled or not. Some coupons can be doubled according to store policies. If the coupon cannot be doubled, it will state that on the coupon and the bar code will begin with a nine. If the coupon can be doubled, it will begin with a five. This will be read by the cash register and if your store doubles coupons, the register will double them according to the way it's coded.

The second set of numbers is the manufacturer code. This number identifies the product so the register will know if you purchased that product. The next set of numbers is the product code. From that number the register knows how much the coupon is worth, when it expires, and how many items you need to purchase to use the coupon.

The *Extreme Couponing* television show has shown the misuse of coupons, which results in companies losing hundreds of thousands of dollars. Because of this, they are reworking the bar codes on coupons to make them more accurate so the registers can identify what you are purchasing. This will avoid the misuse of coupons and hopefully speed up the checkout process.

The Big Two: Store and Manufacturer Coupons

There are two types of coupons: manufacturer coupons and store coupons. They are slightly different and you can usually tell which one is which. The best part of the two-coupon system is that because they are different, they can be used together to maximize your savings! Doing this will get you better prices on products and really help stretch your budget. But before you can do that, you need to understand the differences in the two types of coupons.

Manufacturer coupons are those coupons that are issued by the manufacturer themselves and can be used at any store that accepts manufacturer coupons. These are the most common coupons that you'll find and they will always have a bar code on them. The manufacturer will reimburse the store the face value of the coupon along with a small handling fee. Manufacturer coupons can be found in the Sunday newspapers, in stores, online, and many other places.

A store coupon is a coupon issued by a specific store and can only be used at that store. Store coupons will usually have the store name printed somewhere on the coupon. There may or may not be a bar code on it, though generally there is so the register can read the coupon rather than having the cashier manually enter it. The bar codes of store coupons may look extremely different from the bar codes on manufacturer coupons, which is also another indicator of the type of coupon that it is. Manufacturer coupon bar codes consist of all numbers and the store coupon bar code may have a mixture of numbers and letters.

ALERT

Store coupons do have expiration dates. However, some stores are a little more lenient on adhering to those dates. Check with your local store because it's possible that they may honor their own coupons for a little while after they expire. This may be on a store-by-store basis, but it doesn't hurt to ask. Having a little more time to use a coupon can sometimes help you to save a lot more!

Manufacturer Coupons + Store Coupons = More Savings!

If you have a store coupon and a manufacturer coupon for the same item, you are in luck because you can use them both in the same transaction! Store coupons are special in that they can be combined with manufacturer coupons. This allows you to really reap the savings and sometimes even get items for free or close to free. You can use one store coupon and one manufacturer coupon on one item, in the same transaction.

For example, if you have a manufacturer coupon for $1.00 off one box of Cheerios cereal and you also have a store coupon for $.50 off one box of Cheerios, you can use both coupons and save a total of $1.50 off one box. Now the best way to do this is to pair it up with a sale. If the Cheerios are normally priced at $4.49 and are on sale for $2.99, you can use both the store coupon and the manufacturer coupon and pay only $1.49 for the box of Cheerios. That's a savings of $3.00 off the regular price. If you usually buy Cheerios at full price, you'll save a lot of money over the course of a year by using coupons like this.

Where to Find Store Coupons

Store coupons can be found in several places. The easiest thing to do is ask at the store if and where you can find any store coupons. You could even call customer service and ask if they have a mailing list. Sometimes when you apply for a store credit card or even use your own credit card at the store, they will mail you store coupons from time to time. Those are usually a surprise and sometimes just for loyal customers.

Lots of times you'll find a store's coupons right in their weekly ad. It may be a coupon just to get a sale price, or it may be an extra savings that you can use that week and sometimes even longer. Check the expiration date and if it doesn't expire before the end of the week, clip it and file it for use later, especially if you have a manufacturer coupon to pair up with it. Hold out for a sale to get the best deal.

Some stores issue store coupons at the beginning of the month. Others issue them at the end of the month for the following month. Check next to the weekly ad in the stores to see if they have a place for store coupons. Also look by the register when checking out and even the pharmacy counter to see if they are kept there. Some stores have printable store coupons, which you'll find on their websites.

Proper Usage

If you are going to use coupons, you must use them properly. The coupon itself is filled with lots of information and once you understand it, you'll know exactly how you can use the coupon. Within the note to the consumer on each coupon you will see a few different versions of the wording for how to use the coupon. It may say "Limit one coupon per purchase," "Limit one coupon per transaction," "Limit one coupon per person," or "Limit one coupon per visit/day/household." They all have a slightly different meaning and can be confused very easily. You will find that even some cashiers aren't always sure what they mean.

Here is a list to make it easier for you to understand:

- **Limit one coupon per purchase** means you can only use one coupon per item you purchase. If you are purchasing one shampoo, you can only use one coupon for that item. If you are buying a second shampoo you can use another coupon for the second one because that is another purchase.
- **Limit one coupon per transaction** means you can use only one of those coupons per the entire transaction. If you are purchasing two shampoos of the same kind, then you can only use one coupon for that particular shampoo in one transaction. In order to use both the coupons, you would need to make a separate transaction.
- **Limit one coupon per person** means only one of those coupons can be used by one person. It doesn't matter how many transactions you make, you can still only use one coupon. If you are shopping with a spouse, technically you can make separate purchases and

each use one of those coupons since it's limited per person, not per household.

- **Limit one coupon per household** means that out of all the people living in your home, you can only use that coupon once.

It may also be broken down even further stating only one per person, per visit, per day, per household.

ESSENTIAL

If the value of the coupon exceeds the value of the item, then you get the product for free and may even make money on the purchase. The cashier should deduct the full value of the coupon because the store will receive the entire value of the coupon from the manufacturer. The problem with this is most stores will not give you cash back, so you'll have to purchase another item to eat up the overage.

Read the Wording

The manufacturer puts a picture on the coupon to easily identify what the coupon is for. The only problem is that sometimes they put a picture on the coupon that may not go along with the wording on the coupon. Therefore always read the description of the coupon to know exactly what it's for.

For example, you may have a coupon for $1.00 off the purchase of Tide and the picture on the coupon may be that of a bottle of Tide Free & Gentle but the coupon wording will say "good on any Tide detergent." That means that you can purchase the regular Tide or even Tide Total Care. You don't need to just purchase Tide Free & Gentle. On the other hand if the wording said "good only on Tide Free & Gentle," then that is the only product you can use this coupon on.

Use Two Coupons with a Buy-One-Get-One-Free Sale

You can use one manufacturer coupon per item you purchase. That means if you are purchasing two of the same item and they are on sale buy-one-get-one-free, then you can use a coupon for each item, including the item you will be getting for free. Why can you do this? Because you are purchasing and taking home two items. The store just happens to be discounting one item completely.

For example, Purex detergent is on sale buy-one-get-one-free and they are priced $9.89 each. You have two $2.00 coupons good on Purex detergent. You purchase two, use two of the coupons, and pay $5.89 for both of them with a final cost of $2.95 each.

Regional Coupons

If you shopped across the United States in one day, your head would be spinning because of all the differences in prices from place to place. Not so much for neighboring states, but more for different regions. This is because the cost of living varies across the country, so the prices within the stores need to adjust accordingly. This theory passes along to the coupons you'll find in each state as well. Sale prices will differ, as well as the values on manufacturer coupons.

In the Northeast you may receive a coupon for $1.00 off when you purchase two of the same item, but in the Midwest the same coupon may only be for $.50 off when you purchase one item. The West Coast may have the same coupon but for $.75 off when you purchase two items. This is what they mean when they say coupons are regional. The values of the same coupon may vary from region to region within the Sunday inserts.

Finding the Better Coupon Value

How can you get your hands on a regional coupon that will save you more? If it happens to be from a neighboring area, you can purchase a local paper to find it. You can also find an online coupon-clipping website, which may have the coupon value that you're looking for, or you could even check eBay. Otherwise there isn't much you can do; it's just the way the coupons are distributed.

Coupons that you find online won't depend on your location, unless the site you are getting your coupons from asks for your Zip Code. If that's the case, then they will feature coupons that are for either products sold in your local stores, or values that are more in tune with the prices in your region. But no one says you can't put in a Zip Code for another city or state to see what other coupons are available.

The Subcategories of Coupons

There are different types of coupons offering different types of discounts. The most common coupon you'll find will have a value of a dollar amount or less off a specific product or group of products. Others you may come across are coupons for a free product without a purchase, a free product when you buy another product, and a percentage off your purchase.

QUESTION

Can coupons be sold?
Coupons cannot be sold. As stated on coupons, they are void if sold, purchased, transferred, or exchanged. There are websites, including eBay, where you can purchase coupons. However, you are not actually purchasing coupons but rather paying for the service of having the coupons clipped, sorted, and mailed to you.

The coupons that offer you a specific dollar amount of savings can differ in amounts depending on what the coupon is for. If it's a coupon for an expensive product, the value may be pretty high and if it's for a less expensive product, the value may be quite low. The value will also differ according to how many items the coupon is for. You could have a coupon for $.50 off the purchase of one box of cereal or it may be $1.25 off the purchase of three boxes of cereal. Whatever the value is, you will receive a discount of that amount when you purchase the product indicated on the coupon. The only exception to this rule is if your store doubles or triples coupons. Then you will receive more than the value listed on the coupon according to their rules on doubling and tripling coupons.

Free-Product Coupons

A coupon for a free item is one that normally comes directly from the manufacturer. Occasionally you may get one in the Sunday inserts, but a printable coupon for a free item is usually a counterfeit coupon. (Yes, there are such things as counterfeit coupons.) A coupon for a free item will look like a regular manufacturer coupon with all the same components. The thing that will be different is it will have a maximum value for the product indicated, and usually a box for the cashier to write in the cost of the item. If the item costs more than the maximum value, then the store will only give you the maximum value and you will have to pay the rest. You are also responsible for paying any tax on the item according to your state tax laws.

Be careful when you find a coupon for a free product. Most companies won't make a coupon for a free product available for you to print yourself. It doesn't mean it won't happen, it's just rare. If you find a coupon that you aren't sure is real, check the website address that it's hosted on. If it's hosted on the company website then it's probably real. A free-product coupon that comes in the form of a PDF file is almost always counterfeit. PDF files can be printed over and over so a manufacturer wouldn't issue a coupon for a free item in that format.

Buy-One-Get-One-Free Coupons

There are two types of free item coupons: one that you don't have to make a purchase for and one that you do. The one you have to make a purchase for is referred to as a buy-one-get-one-free coupon. To get the free item you must buy one other item first. It may be the same item as the free one or it might be a different item. Sometimes you may have to purchase two of one item to get the free one. It will tell you on the coupon exactly what you need to purchase in order to get your free item.

Buy-one-get-one-free coupons enable you to purchase two of the same items but only pay for one of them. There will also be a maximum value the store will give you for the product indicated on most of these coupons. Some stores will even let you use a buy-one-get-one-free coupon with a buy-one-get-one-free sale; that way you'll receive two free items. Check your store's coupon policy for more information on how they handle the combination of buy-one-get-one-free sales with the coupons.

Percent-Off Coupons

Department stores are known for offering percent-off coupons. These coupons will deduct a specific percentage off the entire purchase price or off the price of one item. It will be clearly stated on the coupon how you can use it and where you can use it. These are normally store coupons rather than manufacturer coupons. Of course there may be limitations on what you can buy with the coupon, so be sure to read it for any exclusions.

CHAPTER 3

Where Can You Get Coupons?

More and more companies are issuing coupons to make their products more enticing so you will purchase them. Of course you won't find a coupon for every product you purchase, but you will for a good amount of them. Once you begin your journey of coupon usage, you will find them in places you never noticed them before. Many people think that the only place to find coupons is in a newspaper. But in reality, coupons can be found in so many different places—you'll be amazed at where you may find your next one.

Newspapers and Printed Material

The local weekend newspaper is a great source to gather coupons. Each week you will find at least one coupon insert in the Sunday paper, with the exception of some holiday weekends. If there are going to be some good coupons that weekend, you can purchase an extra copy of the newspaper to get more coupons. Some dollar stores even sell them for $1 each. Of course getting a subscription to your local paper will save you a lot in the long run since buying newspapers every weekend can add up. But if you're using your coupons, then it's not really a waste of money.

You can find coupon insert previews during the week before the inserts are issued on several websites including *www.KouponKaren.com*. This preview is a great tool in gauging if you want to purchase the paper or not, and if you'd like additional copies. Coupons do vary by region, so you may not get every coupon listed, but if you use it as a guide it can be helpful.

You may even be lucky enough to find a Saturday edition newspaper that has the coupons for that weekend—a day early. You'll even save money since it will cost less than the Sunday edition. These vary from place to place and if the Saturday edition has coupons, then the Sunday edition may not. It's rare to come by, but check your local stores on Saturdays to see if you're one of the lucky few to get this nice little bonus on the weekend!

ALERT

Always check the newspaper before you leave the store to see if the coupons are there. Sometimes the coupon inserts go missing and you don't want to end up with that newspaper, especially if you are only purchasing it for the coupons. It's always best to check first so you're not disappointed when you get home.

Coupons in Magazines

Magazines are another great source for finding coupons. Magazines include coupons for products that they advertise and for products that relate to the magazine's articles, as well. Always check the magazine thoroughly before tossing it in the recycle bin. If you find a magazine that tends to have a lot of coupons that you use each month, you may want to consider getting a subscription to save on the purchase price. It's always more expensive to purchase a magazine at the newsstand than through a subscription. Even if you spend $20 for a one-year subscription, as long as you use at least two $1.00 coupons from the magazine each month, you'll be ahead.

All You Magazine

All You magazine is a great place to find coupons. The magazine is full of coupons each month on all sorts of products. You can purchase *All You* magazine only at Walmart or by subscription. There's a very good chance that the first two issues will pay for a one-year subscription, just in coupon savings.

Find Coupons Online

Most people get their daily news online and are purchasing fewer newspapers. Manufacturers realize this, so in order to be sure that you'll get their coupons, they have begun to offer them online. The coupons can be found in several places but the first place you should look is on their website. If there is a particular product that you use, check the company's website to see if they have any printable coupons available. If they do, then you should be able to easily locate the coupons on the main page or at least a link to them. Look for an area labeled "special offers" or "coupons."

It's a great idea to also sign up for their e-mail alerts; then you'll be notified of new coupons as they are available. Because coupon prints are limited, it's best to be one of the first to know of the coupon to have the chance to print it.

Check the Couponing Blogs

There are many blogs out there dedicated to helping you save money with coupons. They also help you save time by highlighting the new coupons as they become available—every day! Do some research and find a site or two that you like and follow them so you'll be notified each time they find a new coupon. (Google is a great place to start your research. If you do a simple search for "using coupons" or "coupon blog," you'll find a great list.) Any way you can save time in couponing is worth it. You may even get coupons that are hard to find on these blogs. Some of them work closely with companies and are able to offer you coupons that you can't find anywhere else.

ESSENTIAL

When signing up for online newsletters, use an alternate e-mail address so as not to fill up your in-box. You can get free e-mail addresses from Gmail, Yahoo!, Hotmail, and more. This way all your personal e-mails won't get buried and you'll have all your newsletters in one spot.

Search for Coupons on Google

One of the best ways to find a coupon you are looking for online is to do a Google search for it, along with the words "printable coupon." You'll find an abundance of sites that will tell you where to get the coupon. Be sure to check the date, as Google is known for pulling up older posts. And always remember that printable coupons have a limit; once that limit is met, the coupon is no longer available. But that doesn't mean it won't come back again. Even if you found an old coupon, check to see if it has reset and you can still print it. (Hint: If you are able to print the coupon again, then that means it's been reset.)

Look for Coupons in Stores

You don't even have to take any coupons with you when you go shopping because you can find some as you walk the aisles in the stores. There are several types of coupons that you'll find in stores to make your shopping trip even easier. These coupons can mostly be found right near the product that they are for, and are put there for promotional reasons. It doesn't matter why they are there, it's just helpful that they are!

If you really don't want to search for coupons before you shop, you can just use the ones you find in the stores, but you won't save very much and you can't count on what you'll find. However, any money saved is, well, money saved. For someone who doesn't normally use coupons, looking for in-store coupons at your grocery store is a great way to begin to get an understanding of how coupons can lower your grocery bill.

Those Blinking Machines Have Coupons

Blinkies are coupons that are in those little machines that are hanging off the shelves and sometimes blink as you walk by, or even play music. They are the machines that your kids love to grab coupons from because once you take one, another one will come out. Luckily there is a slot where you can put the coupon if you choose not to use it. You can find these hanging on the shelves near the product the coupon is for. Ideally they have it there in the hopes that you'll use the coupon that day and purchase that product.

A few facts about these coupons: they almost always say "Do Not Double," so even if they are under the double maximum for your store, they will not double. They may be good on a single quantity or more and sometimes they have very long expiration dates, which is always nice! If the expiration date is long and you decide to grab one for later use, be sure to only grab one and leave some for the rest of the customers.

Don't Miss the Tear Pads

Tear pads are exactly as they sound—pads of coupons that you tear off. You can find these in a few different places. They may be attached to the shelf next to the product, which makes them very easy to use. They can also be found on displays in the aisles and even at the registers. You may find tear pads at grocery stores, convenience stores, and even gas stations. Tear pads are all around, so be sure to keep an eye out for them.

If you find a tear pad, try to resist the urge to take more than one, or the entire pad for that matter. If you take an extra coupon to use at a later date, that's fine, but don't take more than that. Let other people have a chance to also reap the savings from the coupon.

Coupons on Products

Peelies are coupons that are found directly on the product; you can peel them off and use them on that purchase. Some stores may prefer that the cashier peels them off when you make the purchase and other stores may not care. It's always best to check with your store for their policy. But do not take the coupon off the product if you do not intend to use it at that time.

Before you toss any packaging in the garbage or recycle bin, be sure to check it well. There may be a coupon on the packing or even loose inside the package. It's best to open the box all the way to see if it's printed inside. Sometimes these coupons will be for higher values than what you'll find anywhere else. The manufacturer is hoping that you'll purchase the product again and use the coupon. Of course their long-term hope is that you'll like it so much, you'll continue to purchase it with or without a coupon.

Catalina Coupons

Have you seen those little printers at the registers that print out coupons? Have you ever wondered what those were called? They are Catalina machines and they print coupons that are referred to as Catalina coupons. There are various reasons why you'll receive these coupons. Sometimes they may be triggered by purchases you make and give you a coupon for a competitor's product. Lots of times you'll receive a coupon for an item that maybe you haven't purchased in a while in the hopes you'll purchase it again. If you are scanning a store card, then your purchases are being tracked, which is how the machine can produce coupons that are tailored to you and your spending habits.

QUESTION

What do I do if my Catalina doesn't print out?
If your Catalina doesn't print out at the end of your transaction, the first thing you want to do is make sure you've purchased the proper items (for example, if the expected coupon was listed in the store ad or perhaps next to the item on the shelf, but then the coupon doesn't print for you at checkout). It's very easy to pick up the wrong item because some deals may be for very specific products. Once you've verified that you have the proper items, you'll need to call the Catalina company to get your coupon. The stores don't have the ability to print the coupons.

Catalina coupons are usually manufacturer coupons, which means they can be stacked with store coupons to help you save even more. Occasionally you may receive a store coupon from a Catalina machine. It will tell you right on the coupon which one it is. You may even receive a coupon toward your next in-store purchase. These are usually triggered by a purchase you made and can be used for almost anything. If there are any restrictions, it will be printed on the coupon. The restrictions may vary by store.

Wine Tags

Does your grocery store or drugstore sell wine? If so, have you ever noticed a tag hanging from the neck of the bottle that perhaps was really a coupon? Those are called wine tags and at times, they can be pretty good coupons. They are rare, but you may be lucky enough to find a coupon that will allow you to save on a produce or meat purchase.

The idea behind wine tags is that if you purchase that bottle of wine, you now have a coupon to use on a food purchase. Sometimes the item the coupon is for may match the type of wine to complete a meal. However, the coupons aren't there for you to take without purchasing the bottle of wine; they are for those customers who actually buy the wine, so don't steal the wine tags.

Get Them Direct!

Companies receive letters, calls, and e-mails every day about complaints, so why not send them an e-mail and give them a compliment? They may even send you coupons as a thank-you for reaching out to them. It's worth a try and at the same time, you have the opportunity to give feedback on your favorite products, even if that feedback is as simple as "thanks for making a great product my family loves."

Contact Companies for Coupons

To begin, make a list of the products you use most and truly love. Then find a way of contacting the companies. You can give them a call, write them a letter (and mail it to them), or send them an e-mail. You can find a contact page on the manufacturer's website, which will include phone numbers, e-mail addresses, and even sometimes mailing addresses. Choose the way that's easiest for you to make contact.

When you have a few minutes, choose a few companies and send them some feedback. You want to tell them how and why you enjoy their products. Feedback like this is valuable to them and something they are always open to hearing. And don't be afraid to tell them something you don't like about the product. They need to know that as well. If you choose to e-mail them or contact them through their website, be sure to include your mailing address. If you are filling out a form on their website and they don't have a spot for you to enter your address, include it with your note so they at least have it. Before you finish, be sure to ask them to put you on a mailing list for coupons.

Make a List and Follow Up

Keep a list of companies that you contact and ask them how often you can request coupons. Some of them may allow you to contact them more than once a year, and others not. On your main list of companies you are contacting, note when you first contacted them and when you can contact them again. Of course if you have a reason to e-mail them, you're always welcome to. They won't reject your feedback, but they may not send you more coupons. This isn't a way of obtaining a lot of coupons, but it's a nice way of getting some free-product coupons or high-value coupons. And once you're on their mailing list, they may send you more!

ESSENTIAL

Most companies will send you coupons for their products, or their family of products. Sometimes you'll receive a nice high-value coupon that you don't normally find anywhere else. But even better, you may get a coupon for a free item! If you can, collect all the free-item coupons you receive, making sure to note the expiration date, and then use them in one transaction for an almost-free shopping trip!

Keep track of what coupons you receive and when you receive them. It might even be a good idea to follow up with the manufacturer and let them know you received the coupons. Perhaps they will be grateful enough to even send you more!

Creative and Uncommon Places

You may find coupons in places you least expect. And as you begin to use them, you'll find that you will either notice them or automatically look to see if you can find them, no matter where you go. And don't be afraid to tell people you know that you use coupons so if they get some they don't want, they can pass them along to you.

Scope Out the Doctor's and Dentist's Offices

Always keep your eye open when you visit your doctor's office. Take a look around at the literature they have in the waiting room, at the check-in window, and even in the exam room. There may be coupons for products that you can purchase over the counter that your doctor may suggest to you. Pediatricians and obstetricians get coupons for formula and even free samples. If you don't see any, ask your doctor. They may have them but just not out on display.

The dentist is good for giving you a free toothbrush, floss, and even toothpaste. She may also have coupons for oral hygiene products. Look around and don't be afraid to ask. The companies send coupons, along with free samples, to dentists so they will share with you and you'll hopefully become a customer and purchase these products all the time. If your dentist has coupons or samples, she will be more than happy to share them with you.

That's What Friends Are For

It is great to have a couponing buddy who can help and share with you. But other people you may know might not be as excited about using coupons. They may catch on after they see all the money you are saving with coupons, but until then, ask them to pass along their Sunday inserts or magazines once they go through them and take out what they want (if they take anything at all).

Your coworkers may also be a great resource for coupons. You can form a group in which you all share the coupons you aren't going to use each week. If you think this may be something they are interested in doing, ask everyone to bring their coupon inserts in on Monday, then each take turns clipping them either while on lunch break or at home that night. Not everyone uses the same products, so it's a great way to get more coupons for the products you use and also to help someone else save on products they use.

ALERT

You may hear about people "dumpster diving" to get coupon inserts. Before you dive into any dumpsters, you better check with the recycling center to make sure you can actually do this. You may think you are recycling by using the items, but the recycling center makes money on the weight of the recyclables. By taking their inserts, you are taking their profits. They may frown upon this, and in reality, it's stealing.

Send for Free Samples and You May Get Coupons Too

When you see an offer for a free sample, it may be worth more than you think. Lots of companies include coupons with their free samples in hopes that you'll purchase their product after trying it. Lots of times the coupons that are included with free samples are higher value or better value coupons than you'll receive anywhere else. Since it doesn't cost you more than a few minutes to request the sample, it's well worth your time.

CHAPTER 4

Printable Coupons 101

Gathering coupons can be a lot of work—too much work for some. If you don't want to go through the hassle of getting a weekend paper, you can still use coupons. Some of the easiest to get your hands on are printable coupons. With printable coupons you don't have to look through an entire insert of coupons you don't want just to find the ones you do want. Instead you search online for the coupons that you will use by going directly either to the company websites or to the many websites that host coupons. Even if you only use printable coupons, you can still save a lot of money.

Common Printable Coupon Sources

If you are lacking time, having coupons located in one place online would be helpful. Sadly, there isn't one central location for all printable coupons, but there are a number of websites that have a vast assortment. These websites update their lists often—sometimes daily—which means there is great variety from month to month. These popular sites are:

- *www.Coupons.com*
- *www.RedPlum.com*
- *www.SmartSource.com*
- *www.CouponNetwork.com*
- *www.BettyCrocker.com*
- *www.Pillsbury.com*
- *www.EatBetterAmerica.com*
- *www.BoxTops4Education.com*

The coupons found on these websites are manufacturer coupons and can be printed directly from the websites on either a PC or a Mac. Anyone who has access to a computer and printer can print these coupons no matter where they live. However, some websites will require you to enter your Zip Code in order to better serve you with coupons from your area. This is helpful with store coupons.

FACT

When you print coupons for the first time, you'll be asked to download and install a coupon printer, which is the printer software. This is required as it's the only way your computer will know how to print the coupons properly. There are a few different programs, depending on which website you print from; therefore you may be required to download a few of them.

Print Them Before They Are Gone

The best time to find some of the hottest coupons is the first few days of the month. The coupon websites restock coupons at the beginning of the month and lots of times introduce new ones. The hot coupons don't last long, so it's best to make a habit of checking your favorite printable coupon sites during the first week of the month. If you see one you think you may use, print it and file it for future use. Printable coupons come and go without warning. Each coupon has a set "print amount" and once that is reached and all coupons have been printed, they disappear from the list. The coupons can reappear anytime within the month, but there is no way of knowing when—or even if—they will. This leaves you with two options: You can print the coupons you think you may use when you find them, or wait and take a chance that they will still be available when you want to use them.

Most coupons will not expire immediately. The expiration dates on average are about thirty days from date of print. Some coupons will reset after the beginning of the month and then you can print them again the following month. Some coupons come back from the previous month, and sometimes there are a whole bunch of new coupons.

Use a Coupon Database

A coupon database is a great place to find lots of coupons, especially printable ones. If you don't have time to search all the different websites for coupons, a coupon database may be what you need. A coupon database is exactly what it sounds like—a database of coupons. You type in the coupon you are looking for and you'll find a list of available coupons including printable coupons. The link to the printable coupon will be right there for you to quickly click over to and print out.

You'll want to find a coupon database that is maintained often enough so the newer printable coupons will be there and the old ones will be deleted. Of course at any time of the day a coupon can be released and even maxed out. Most databases have an option for you to report a coupon to them so they can either add it to their list or remove it if it's no longer available. There are several coupon databases available to use, including one on *www.KouponKaren.com*. These databases are free to use and many coupon blogs will have one. If you can't locate a coupon database on a website, you can do a Google search for "coupon database" and you'll find a list of sites that have them available to use. If you find one that you have to pay for, don't pay. This is something that can easily be found for free on another website.

Printable Coupon Dos and Don'ts

In terms of printable coupons, there are a few things you want to make sure you are doing correctly to get the full benefit of the coupons. And conversely you also want to make sure you don't do anything that is wrong and could get you into trouble.

Most coupons are available to be printed at least two times per computer or IP address. Of course there are exceptions and you may only be able to print a coupon once, but always try again until it tells you that you've printed it the maximum times allowed. You can either go back to the original source of the coupon or hit the back arrow button twice to reprint. It's perfectly fine to print the coupon as many times as it will allow you to. The manufacturer is aware you may purchase more than one item and they want to encourage this by allowing you to print more than one coupon. Of course if you don't want more then one, don't print it. Since coupons prints are limited, you want to be sure to leave it for someone who can use it.

ESSENTIAL

Check back often during the month on those items you use most to see if you can print the coupon again. If you are buying more, you may as well save each time you can! Some coupons reset during the month, which means you can print it again.

Don't Waste Paper Printing Coupons

Try to print as many coupons as you can at once to avoid wasting paper. Coupons.com is one of many websites that will allow you to print three different coupons on a page, if at least three are selected. You should make it a rule to print them in quantities of three to fill up an entire sheet of paper. If you just print one, you may print out an ad or a recipe to go along with the coupon or the rest of the page will be blank. If you have no choice but to print one coupon at a time and it prints on the top of the paper, turn the paper around, put it back in your printer, and print another one on the other side of the page. Then you'll have two on a sheet.

You can also save paper by using scrap paper when printing coupons. The backside of the coupon does not need to be blank. It still works the same as if you printed it on a new sheet of paper.

Share Your Almost-Expired Coupons

If you find you have some printable coupons that are going to expire before you have a chance to use them, share them with your friends and family. Then the cost of printing the coupon isn't completely wasted and someone you know will be able to reap the benefits of the coupon. The manufacturer planned on that coupon being used, so why not give it to someone? You could also leave the coupon in the store near the product for someone else to use.

Check the Store's Coupon Policy

Before you use a printable coupon, be sure to check with your store on their policy for accepting printable coupons. There is a chance your store may not accept this type of coupon due to misuse or some other sort of problem. You'll want to know ahead of time before you spend time planning your shopping trip. And even though you don't need to print coupons in color for them to be accepted, the store may have a policy on only accepting them in color, again due to a problem they might have had with the misuse of coupons.

Printable Coupon Don'ts

The most important thing you must remember about printable coupons is that you cannot make a photocopy of them. It is against the law to photocopy a coupon whether it's a printable coupon or not. Each coupon is coded with a unique code. The manufacturer will know if the same coupon has been redeemed twice and the code can tell them what IP address it came from. They will no longer allow you to print coupons from your IP address if they catch you doing this. Why is it illegal? They have a budget for their coupons and when people misuse them, it costs the manufacturers thousands if not millions of dollars. The result of this will be that eventually they will discontinue coupons for their products.

You also want to be sure not to get printable coupons wet, as the ink will run and not be readable anymore, and therefore your coupon will be void. The paper that regular coupons are printed on can hold up a little better when wet, so while you shouldn't get those wet either, they won't become unusable like printable coupons can.

You want to also make sure before you print the coupon that you have plenty of ink in your printer. If you are sending a bunch of coupons to the printer at the same time and you run out of ink, you have just lost that print opportunity.

Color Versus Black and White

A coupon does not need to be printed in color to be accepted. Black and white coupons are just as good; they just don't look as pretty. Most coupons will print a watermark that you'll be able to see in the background of the coupon. This will still show up in black and white or color. You will also notice that there is a dot-scan barcode near the expiration date, which shows the store it's a legal coupon. If you make a copy of the coupon, these watermarks will not show up. Unfortunately, because people abuse coupon usage and try to present copies of coupons, some stores will not accept a coupon unless it is printed in color ink. Check with your stores to find out their policy on accepting black and white printable coupons. This may be on a store-to-store basis and not companywide.

ALERT

Printable coupons are usually for a set dollar amount off the product. Very rarely will you find a printable coupon for a free item. If you do, there is a good chance that the coupon may not be legitimate. If you come across a printable coupon that is for a free product, you may want to verify with the company that issued it if that coupon is real.

Setting Your Printer to Black and White

Printing coupons can be costly when it comes to printer ink. When printing a document, you have the option of using just black ink before you hit print. This option is not available when printing coupons. Once you hit print, the coupon is automatically sent to your printer and bypasses the print screen. If you use a PC, you can set the default on your printer to always print in black and white thus saving your color ink, which is always more expensive then black ink. For most computers you can find this option in the settings of the printer itself. The following steps will work on most PCs to change the default ink to black and white:

1. Go to the Control Panel in your computer.
2. Select Hardware and then Devices and Printers.
3. Locate the default printer and right click and select Printing Preferences.
4. Select "Print in black and white" and then Save.

Once you follow these steps, your printer will automatically default to using the black ink cartridge unless you tell it otherwise. Using only black ink will save you a lot when printing coupons since the pictures on the coupons are always in color. It may not look as pretty but you are looking to save money, not to have the best-looking coupons in line at the grocery store.

Finding Deals on Printer Ink and Paper

Because you're printing all these coupons, you'll likely run out of ink quickly. Some ink cartridges can be costly, so the question comes up fairly often "Am I really saving money?" First of all the answer is yes, because if you counted how many coupons you can print from one ink cartridge, chances are the value of the coupons far exceeds the cost of the ink. Of course that's if you use them all. But even if you didn't, you probably are ahead. But there are ways you can save money on ink cartridges too. The office supply stores offer incentives to recycle your empty cartridges. They will give you a couple of dollars back in exchange for your empty ink cartridge. Then they will properly recycle the container. The money usually comes in the form of a voucher that you can then use in the store. The company will mail it to you at a later date, perhaps at the end of the quarter. Check with your office supply store for more details.

The voucher may not be instant savings, but you'll eventually receive it and then use it toward anything in the store, including printer ink. Some stores might have programs that allow you to receive rebates back for your purchases, including ink. If you participate in both those programs, you may save up to 15 percent off your ink cartridges. Look for details in the store or online.

Office supply stores run deals on other items, besides printer ink and paper. If you purchase these items, you can use the savings toward the price of printer ink and paper. You may receive a full rebate on a purchase and sometimes instant savings. Think of it this way—the money you save on one item you can put toward the other item.

The paper in my printer jammed. Can I reprint that coupon?
Before you print a coupon, be sure the printer is turned on and the paper is loaded properly. Once the coupon has been sent to the printer, you may not be able to print it again. If the paper jams in your printer or something else happens to interrupt the printing, then you just lost that coupon. You may be able to print it one more time because some coupons are set for you to print twice, but you will only get one coupon, instead of the opportunity to print two.

Refilling Ink Cartridges

Some ink cartridges can be refilled with a special kit that costs a fraction of the price of a new ink cartridge. Bonus: you are recycling the old cartridge as well, which means less waste in the landfills. The kits don't always work perfectly, as the cartridges aren't made to be refilled. But if you are only printing coupons and the occasional letter, this may work well for you and you could save up to 75 percent filling them yourself. Some stores even fill them for you, like Walgreens. Then there is no mess. Or purchase them online and save even more.

If your ink is still costing too much, consider purchasing a new printer that has an ink cartridge with a lower price point. You may have to invest a little bit up front but you will save in the long run between the savings from the ink cartridge and the coupons you print. Do some research to find out how much the cartridges cost and how many sheets you will get per cartridge. Look for those that have high yield print cartridges. When you find a printer you like, wait for a sale, or check Craigslist, eBay, yard sales, or even consignment stores. You don't need to purchase it brand-new.

Overages

There are times that if you shop right, your coupons will exceed the value of the products. One example of this is if you catch the item on sale or on clearance and you have a coupon for it. The store should give you the value of the coupon because that is what they are going to get back from the manufacturer. If this happens, you can apply the overage to another item in your transaction. Some stores will adjust the coupon down to the cost of the item and give it to you for free. Overage is nice of course. It's always best to check your store's policy on overage on a coupon.

The most common time you'll catch an overage with a coupon is when you find the item on clearance. If you catch something that is 75 percent off the regular price, and it's not a very high-valued item, there is a good chance it will be less than the coupon you are going to use. For example, you come across a clearance deal for toothpaste that is normally $3.49 and is now 75 percent off and is on clearance for only $0.88. If you have a $1.00 coupon, then you'll receive an overage of $0.12. You'll just need to be sure that you are purchasing an additional item to "eat up" the overage because the store may not give you cash back.

Redeeming and Troubleshooting

Printable coupons work the same as other coupons and have the same rules. But because you print them yourself, there can be imperfections that can lead to problems when redeeming. How many times have you been in line at a store and have had to wait while someone is trying to use a coupon and holds up the line? It happens for various reasons that sometimes cannot be avoided. The computer systems aren't always set up to be very coupon friendly and will beep when you try to use a coupon, even when using it properly. This happens more often with printable coupons than others. There may be nothing wrong with what you are doing; it's just a problem with the register.

Unfortunately some stores won't let you use a coupon if the register won't accept it. If this happens to you, you have three choices: Stand there and argue, purchase it without the coupon, or leave without the product and deal with it afterward.

If you have a pile of coupons to use and you notice the person behind you has only a couple of items to check out, you may want to let them go before you. It will lower your stress level while checking out, especially if you worried about having a problem with any coupons you are using. You'll also feel good knowing that you did a good deed.

If you decide to stand your ground with the cashier or manager until you get your way, first make sure you have the proper item. Check the size, scent, or flavor because the coupon may be for something very specific. You may also be required to purchase more than one item to use the coupon and the cash register knows you didn't. Or the coupon may be expired. If you know you have the correct product and are using the coupon correctly, then calmly explain why you are using the coupon and why you believe you are using it properly. The cashier may still refuse the coupon even if you are buying the right product, simply because the register won't take it, but at least you tried. If that doesn't work and it's for a product you need, you can purchase the product without the coupon or leave without making the purchase and then call the store's corporate office when you get home. It's possible that the store employees, including the manager, don't understand or have not been properly trained on coupon usage and then corporate can deal with that. If there is a problem in the store, they need to, and should want to, know about it. You may also find that some stores simply have strict rules for coupon usage. This can be the result of the misuse of coupons.

Problems Redeeming Printable Coupons

Computer systems are smart, but not always helpful. Since you are printing these coupons at home, it's very possible that the bar code on the coupon may not scan because it's slightly smudged or worse yet, it my have printed flawlessly and still won't scan. After several struggles the cashier may be successful, but this may result in a line behind you and potentially angry customers. If the cashier is unable to scan the coupon, the store should still accept the coupon and enter it in manually. Whether they scan the coupon or not, they can still redeem it. As long as the cashier enters the coupon as a manufacturer coupon, it should be fine.

Problems Printing Coupons

At one point or another you will probably have some problems printing coupons. You may experience the coupon-printing program not working, or it mysteriously disappears from your computer and you have to reinstall it, several times. If that continues to happen, you may want to check the settings on your antivirus software. The firewall may be blocking the program from working properly or even installing properly. If that still doesn't help, you can contact the company who is issuing the coupon for further trouble-shooting. Some programs won't work with certain versions of Windows or on a Mac. Eventually they should catch up with this and create a fix for it, so be sure to run your computer updates.

FACT

If you cannot print a coupon or you simply do not want to download the printer software, you may be able to request that the coupon be sent to you. Click the "help" button on the bottom of the web page. You will then be able to input your mailing address to receive the coupon by mail. Unfortunately, you will only receive one copy of the coupon, even if the print limit is two.

Another common problem with printing coupons is the website you're printing from. They could be experiencing problems, which are also out of your control. However, the most frustrating problem with printable coupons is when the website tells you that you've already printed the coupon and you know you haven't. Unfortunately there is nothing you can do about this either. You receive this notification because either the link you are trying to print the coupon from is coded so it can only be printed once or you might have printed it a while ago and the coupon has never reset for you to print again. Most coupons can only be printed two times per computer until the manufacturer resets the coupon; sometimes they never reset them.

CHAPTER 5

E-Coupons 101

E-coupons are manufacturer coupons that are loaded onto your grocery card before you shop. E-coupons can be the easiest coupons to use as you don't need to clip, organize, file, store, or lug anything to the store, except for your store loyalty card. Everything is stored and tracked by your card and once you register all your grocery cards with the e-coupon websites, you just load the coupons to your card, shop, scan your card, and collect your savings. E-coupons are mostly for brand-name products, but occasionally you'll find one for a store product. Just be sure to have your grocery card with you at all times to use your e-coupons.

The Mechanics of E-Coupons

Before you can begin to use e-coupons, you must apply for a loyalty card at your grocery store. It's a very simple process; you can apply at the store and sometimes even online. Once you apply, you'll receive a card for that store, which you will then hand to the cashier each time you shop. They will scan the card and you'll receive the sale prices for that shopping trip. Most stores have it set up that the only way to receive the sale price is with the card. If you forget your card, most stores will scan a store card so you get the sale prices. You will receive a card the size of a credit card and also a small card you can put right on your keychain so you won't forget it.

Load E-Coupons onto Your Loyalty Card

To get the e-coupons onto your loyalty card, you'll need to load them yourself. They aren't automatically there. To do this, you'll need to sign up with an e-coupon website. Then you simply add your shopping cards to your account online. If you aren't sure if your stores accept e-coupons, check the website for a list of the stores that do participate.

Before you go shopping, sign into your e-coupon account and add the coupons you want to use to the store card. If you'd like, you can add all the coupons if there is a slight chance you'll use them. You may find an unadvertised sale while at the store. It's easy to miss something in the weekly ad and you never know when you'll find something on clearance or in the markdown bins.

When you give your loyalty card to the cashier, she will scan your card before you pay and if you purchased any items that match up with the e-coupons on your card, the coupons will be deducted from your total purchase.

ESSENTIAL

All e-coupons are manufacturer coupons and cannot be used along with paper manufacturer coupons. It's either one or the other. Using them both would be against the terms of service for using coupons. If you have a store coupon, that is fine. This is one of those things you need to regulate yourself, as the registers don't know that you are using two manufacturer coupons.

Easier Than Paper Coupons

Since the stores require you to have a loyalty card to get the sale prices, this has to be one of the easiest ways to use coupons. E-coupons are manufacturer coupons and work just like paper coupons; you will have to purchase a specific product, possibly a specific size, and they have expiration dates. Once the coupon expires, it is no longer available on your shopping card.

The downside of using e-coupons is you can only use one per card. But for those people who don't stock up on items, it's a nice savings with little time invested. There is nothing to sort through, they are paperless so there is less trash, and you are saving on ink and paper. E-coupons cannot be doubled or tripled; they are used at face value only.

Using E-Coupons

E-coupons can only be used once per shopping card. After the e-coupon is used, it will no longer be available on your shopping card and you will not be able to load another one onto your card. This is a disadvantage of using e-coupons. With paper coupons you can use more than one coupon and purchase several items to stock up. With e-coupons, you do not have that option. So they aren't a good source to use for stockpiling, but you will still save money.

You can load coupons from various e-coupon websites onto your cards, as long as they are accepted at the store. A list of stores that accept the coupons will be on the e-coupon websites. To save the most, try to use an e-coupon along with a sale. Each type of e-coupon may work differently. It's always best to read each website carefully to make sure there are no surprises at the store.

Where to Find E-Coupons

E-coupons are loaded onto your grocery card from e-coupon websites. These are sites that host the e-coupons much like printable coupon sites. The manufacturers work with the websites to offer the coupons and with the stores to redeem and accept them. If you do a basic Google search for "e-coupons" you will easily find them. You can also look on your grocery store's website. Chances are, if they accept e-coupons, they will have that noted somewhere on the website. After all they really want you to shop at their store. If they make it easier for you, there is a better chance that you will.

If you have minimal time to search online for e-coupon websites, ask at the store if they participate in any e-coupon programs. You can check with the cashier while checking out, but it's possible they won't know, so your best bet is to stop by the customer service desk to inquire. If they still can't tell you, ask them to make a phone call to the corporate offices or ask for a copy of their coupon policy.

ALERT

Once you add e-coupons to your card, you may not be able to remove them until you use them or they expire. If you add two of the same coupons from two different sites, you cannot choose which coupon to use if you only purchase one item. This creates a problem when they are two different values. The register will randomly select which one to use and you have no control over it.

Check Coupon Blogs for E-Coupon Updates

There are many coupon blogs like *www.KouponKaren.com* that will list the sites that offer e-coupons and even tell you when there are new coupons that you can add to your store card. If you follow these sites and either sign up for their e-mail newsletters or add them to a reader, like Google Reader, then you'll be notified of anything new and any changes. This way you avoid having to check the individual e-coupon sites, which saves you time.

Pair E-Coupons with Sales to Save Even More

Like paper coupons, you want to use e-coupons when you can get the most bang for your buck. That means the best time to use them is with a sale. Since you can only use e-coupons at certain stores, this may be harder than it seems since not all stores have the same sales all the time. The coupon blogs are another great place to check because they will let you know when there is a sale that you can use the e-coupon with. This is very helpful because you can't possibly remember every single e-coupon that is available. You would need to check the e-coupon sites each time you make your shopping list, but if there is a site that can tell you that there's a coupon available, then it's a nice timesaver for you!

E-Coupon Websites

The only way to get e-coupons onto your card is by visiting the e-coupon websites and loading the coupons onto your card. There are several websites that offer e-coupons, which means you may find some of the same coupons repeated on these sites. They may be the same value, or some may offer a better variety than others. If you are going to use e-coupons, check all the sites to find the best ones for you. If you want to purchase multiples of the same item, try to locate another coupon on a different website for more savings. If you don't use them, then they will just disappear when they expire.

Cellfire E-Coupons

Currently, Cellfire coupons are accepted at over 3,500 grocery stores across the United States. You can check their website to see if they currently work with your grocery store. They add more stores all the time. Cellfire coupons are updated on a bi-weekly basis and when you visit *www.cellfire .com*, you can see what's available. Cellfire also has nongrocery coupons that can be saved to cell phones. When you visit *www.cellfire.com* on your cell phone, you can download the app that works with your phone. Once you download the cell phone app, you will have access to coupons for other savings including department stores, restaurants, and entertainment. You can search for them with your Zip Code, which means if you are out of town, you can see what's available where you are. Once you find a coupon you want to use, simply show your mobile coupon to the cashier to receive your discount. Cellfire will track your savings online and show you how much you've saved using Cellfire coupons.

Shortcuts E-Coupons

Shortcuts.com is similar to Cellfire. You sign up online at *www.shortcuts .com* and add your grocery store cards to your account. Then browse the coupons and select the ones you want and add them to your card. Shortcuts also has printable coupons in the same place to save you time. These printable coupons are not the same as the e-coupons; they will be different and cannot be used with the e-coupons. But it will save you from having to look elsewhere for printable coupons. Shortcuts also offers cash-back savings and online coupon codes to help save even more when you shop online. Having all these resources in one spot online is great for a busy person who still wants to save money.

ESSENTIAL

A great tip for using e-coupons is to print a shopping list from the e-coupon website and take it with you to the store. Then you'll know at all times what you have loaded on your card. There are so many coupons that it can be hard to remember exactly what you have on your card at all times. If you can remember without a list, then you have super powers!

P&G eSaver

P&G eSaver are e-coupons that Proctor & Gamble offers to its customers to make coupon clipping easy. Like Cellfire and Shortcuts, P&G eSaver e-coupons are only accepted at certain grocery stores. Once you open an account at *www.pgesaver.com*, select the coupons you'd like to add to your card. Then when the cashier scans your card, the coupons will be deducted from your purchase total.

E-Coupons Are Not Always Instant Savings

Another form of e-coupons are ones that aren't instant; you will receive the savings at a later date. They work the same as other e-coupons; you have to purchase a certain product to receive the savings, but you won't get the savings at the time of the purchase. You still will be required to buy a specific product within a certain time period, as the coupons will expire. Once you purchase the product, the store will report your purchase and you'll receive the savings in an account online.

These types of coupons may change throughout the month or may only be available until all savings have been taken advantage of. Like paper and printable coupons, there may only be so much in the company's budget for the program, and when it's used up, the coupons will disappear. So if you find an e-coupon you'd like to use, try to use it as soon as you can so you don't lose out on the savings.

Upromise

You may have noticed a Upromise sign on the shelves at the grocery store, but never knew what it was about. Upromise is a savings program for college and is also an example of an e-coupon that isn't an instant savings, as it doesn't come right off your total when purchasing the qualifying items. Instead the value of the e-coupon will be deposited into your Upromise account. Then the money is put toward college savings. It's a great way to get a jump-start on saving for college and you don't really have to do too much to save the money. Just shop as you normally do and when you purchase a Upromise qualifying product, you get the savings.

Upromise is super simple to use and can be used along with manufacturer coupons for additional savings. To begin you'll have to sign up for an account at *www.upromise.com*, which is free and easy. Once you open your account, just add your grocery and drugstore cards to your account. Then whenever you purchase a participating product, the money will be deposited into your account. To find a list of participating stores, check the website.

ALERT

You can only use one e-coupon per shopping card but if there are two sites with the same e-coupon, you can load both onto your card and use both when you purchase two items. If you only purchase one, the register will randomly select one e-coupon to use.

Once you've added your cards to your account, there is nothing more to do. Why? Because there are no coupons to load onto your cards. You will be able to see a list of participating items, but you don't need to take any action other than purchasing the products. The stores will report any items purchased to Upromise without you doing a single thing. Be prepared, though—it can take several weeks for your purchases to be credited to your Upromise account, as the system of reporting is a little slow.

Another way to earn money with Upromise is by using your credit card to make certain purchases. There is a place in your account where you can register your credit card numbers. When using your registered credit card to make purchases at participating stores, restaurants, and gas stations, money will be deposited into your college fund. More free money for college because you don't have to buy anything particular! This is probably one of the easiest ways to start saving for college.

Extended family members can help save for college too! If you don't have children in college but someone in the family does, open up a Upromise account and have the money deposited into someone else's account. Grandparents can even split the amount among all their grandchildren.

SavingStar

SavingStar can be used at over 24,000 stores nationwide and works similar to Upromise because you don't receive instant savings but instead the money is deposited into your SavingStar account. Unlike Upromise, you do need to activate the savings in your account before you shop. Then after you make a purchase, the stores will report to SavingStar what was purchased according to your store loyalty card. Once they receive the reports, the money is deposited into your SavingStar account within seven to thirty days.

QUESTION

What if I don't receive credit for my purchase with SavingStar?
It may take up to thirty days for you to receive the credit in your SavingStar account. You must hand over your store card in order to receive any credit. If you forget your store card, they cannot credit you. It's best to keep your receipts until after the credit shows up in your account. If you don't see it within thirty days, contact SavingStar customer service.

The money will accumulate until you withdraw it and they offer you several options to receive your savings, which is really nice. When your SavingStar account reaches $5.00, you can request a PayPal payment, a deposit into your bank account, or a gift card. It's a little more work than Upromise but still fairly easy. Once the savings are activated on your card, there's nothing left to do until you are ready to withdraw your money.

The e-coupons on SavingStar are limited, so you'll want to check the account a couple of times a month to see what's available. If you think you'll use them, activate them in your account before they expire. Otherwise you may lose out on the savings.

Coupons on Your Cell

Think about how nice it would be if every time you shopped at your favorite store, you had a coupon to use. Guess what? If you have your cell phone with you, you can! And it's very simple. Department stores understand that everyone is carrying cell phones now and they also want you to keep shopping at their stores, so they offer another form of e-coupons: text coupon codes.

If you have a coupon for store A, chances are you are going to shop there instead of Store B, right? But if you leave that coupon at home or in the car, then it's not very helpful. But what if you could keep your favorite coupons where you store all your favorite friends? That is where cell coupons come into play. You can receive text messages with coupon codes right to your phone from your favorite stores! Then when shopping, just whip out your phone and give the cashier the coupon code and you'll save right then and there. It is that easy.

Some e-coupons can also be accessed from your phone for even easier use. Target has e-coupons that you can receive on your phone that the cashier can just scan from your phone. Once you sign up for the Target e-coupons, you'll receive an e-mail reminder to use them right before they expire.

Sign Me Up!

You need to sign up with the stores to receive text message coupons on your cell phone. It's a very simple process that you can do right from your phone. There are several ways to find out who offers text coupons. First, check online at your favorite store's website to see if they have information for signing up for text coupons. If you're at the store, look for signs at the register. If you can't locate anything, just ask the cashier when checking out or call the company. You can find a phone number on their website and most times on the receipt as well.

To start receiving coupons you will be given a number and a phrase or word you will need to text. The number isn't like a regular phone number and will probably be about 5–6 digits long. You'll need to text something specific to that number to sign up. Once you sign up, you'll receive coupons right to your cell phone whenever they are available. Be sure to watch the expiration dates because they will expire, just like paper coupons. You can opt out at any time from receiving these text coupons. Each time you receive a text coupon, there should be some information on how to stop them in the future.

ALERT

There is no charge to load an e-coupon to your store card or cell phone from the e-coupon websites and they are free to use. But be aware that if you don't have unlimited text messages on your phone, you'll be charged for text coupons according to the text message rates with your cell phone company. If you have unlimited text messages, then these texts won't cost anything additional.

Use a Coupon Every Opportunity You Get

Using a coupon is always going to save you money. You can use text message coupons as a gauge for when you should shop. If you only shop when you have a coupon, then you are guaranteed to always save. If you always have your phone with you, you will always have access to any available coupons. If you don't have a coupon, then you shouldn't shop. A good goal would be to use a coupon every time you shop, whether for groceries or appliances or anything else. And remember, a sale is a great way to save when you can't use a coupon.

CHAPTER 6

Using Coupons

At this point, you probably have a nice stash of great money-saving coupons and it's time to put them to good use. Having them and using them are two different things and you want to use them properly to get the most bang for your buck. It would be fantastic if everything you purchased could be paired up with a coupon, but that won't always be the case. However, if you are not brand loyal, it is possible to utilize coupons on up to 75 percent of the items you purchase once you learn the ropes.

Planning Ahead

Never go to the store without a plan. If you have a plan and stick to it, you are certain to spend less money. Preparing for your shopping trip will take time, especially the first few attempts. However, within a short time you'll develop a system that works for you. There are scores of tools online to help prepare for your shopping trip. Weekly store match-ups, which you can find on many blogs, can be a huge help in planning. The blogger lists the items on sale along with where to find the coupons to save the most money. Most times, the top deals will be highlighted so you can see what you'll find at a quick glance. Decide on the stores you shop most and skim through the blogs to locate the deals for those stores that week.

Shop for Sale Items Only

Wouldn't it be wonderful if you received a price cut on all items you purchase every time you shopped? Well, guess what, you can! Of course it takes lots of preparation and you will need to have everyone in the household on board. You may also have to be resourceful in the kitchen. If these things are possible, it can happen.

The technique to get there? Every time you shop, purchase sale items only. Yes, you read that accurately: Only buy items that are on sale. This may be easier said than done for some since various geographical regions have more options to shop than others. That said, if you start out slowly, you can be successful almost anywhere you live. You may have to think outside the box from time to time, but look at it as a fun challenge.

FACT

The sales you find online may not match up with your store. This is because sales are regional and blogs usually list the store sales according to one region. It's best to scan your store ad before heading to the store to make sure the sale you want is happening at your store.

Begin each week by scanning the ads for what's on sale. The front page of most ads will have the items that are priced the best. Make a list of the things you need, not "want," that are on sale at the various stores where you shop. Once you've compiled the list, check an online coupon database like the one on *www.KouponKaren.com* to see if any of the items you've selected to purchase have available coupons. Ideally it would be smart to only purchase those items on your list that you have coupons for, but that may not always be workable.

Get an Early Start

You may have the opportunity to begin your planning process even before the sales start. Some stores mail their weekly sale ad a few days before the sale begins. Ask if they have a mailing list they can place you on. The ad may also be accessible a few days early in the store. It never hurts to check. Additionally, you can find several store ads or simply the highlights online on an assortment of blogs a few days earlier. One way to get a jump-start on your shopping list is to do a Google search for the name of the store and the date the sale begins. For example, search for "Stop & Shop Sale Week of 5/16." If any of the highlights have been posted online, the sites will be listed.

If you decide to search for the deals online, you should glance at a couple of different sites as some may have a deal listed that others don't. There are several reasons for this, including regional sales, regional coupons, and the fact that some of the sales may be unadvertised. After you find a website or two that you like, bookmark them for faster access next time.

Following Sales Cycles

Have you ever noticed that cereal goes on sale a lot around the time school starts? And then again in the summertime? This happens with a lot of products and oftentimes there isn't even a reason for the sale; it's just part of a cycle. Sales do happen in cycles and if you follow along carefully and purchase items you use most when they are on sale, you may never have to pay full price again. Wouldn't that be nice! The manufacturers and the stores realize that certain items are used more often at different times of the year or month. To make it easier they put these items on sale to help you fit them into your budget.

Each month you will find certain events that coordinate with sales, including produce that is in season. Below you'll find some of the more popular items you can expect to find on sale throughout the year:

- January is National Oatmeal Month. You'll find various deals on Quaker products, along with some health food products. It's also a month most people make New Year's resolutions to become healthier, which means you'll find lots of deals on fitness equipment, including memberships to fitness clubs. Superbowl Sunday typically falls in January, which means you will find deals on party items like soda, chips, and other snacks. This is also the month that you can get great deals on Christmas holiday clearance items. Cold medicines typically are found at good prices during the month of January too, and since the expiration date is normally pretty far out on these items, now is the time to stock up to get you through the winter.
- February is National Canned Food Month. You'll find lots of great deals on canned food like vegetables, fruit, and tuna. These are staple items that you can easily stock up on, since they typically have a long shelf life. Valentine's Day will bring great deals on chocolate. And don't forget about the Chinese New Year, which means that soy sauce, teriyaki sauce, and other Chinese food items will be on sale to help celebrate.
- March is National Frozen Food Month. It's time to clean out the freezer and stock up on items like ice cream, frozen meals, frozen vegetables, and even breakfast items. With the warmer weather approaching in some areas, you are sure to find spring apparel and accessories beginning to show up in stores and on sale in March too.
- April generally brings the holiday of Easter, which means you can find many great deals on ham, which is an Easter dinner favorite, along with baking supplies. This is the perfect time of the year to stock up for baking until the next good sale, which is usually at the end of the year. If you bake often, you will appreciate the savings this month. If you have a deep freezer, then you can grab a few hams to use throughout the summer. And don't forget the after-Easter clearance sales, which will include many spring items as well. April also hosts Earth Day, which means you can score deals on organic food,

reusable items, and even energy-saving products. It's a great time to stock up on lightbulbs and also to think about replacing your old appliances with new energy-efficient ones. This is the month you'll find some of the best sales for those items.

- In May you celebrate Memorial Day. Everyone loves to have cookouts, which means you'll begin to find great deals on condiments, dips, sauces, and dressings, along with hot dogs and hamburgers. These products tend to be on sale throughout the summer months, but generally begin in May. May also brings Cinco de Mayo, which means you'll find sales on chips and salsa.
- June is National Dairy Month. You can find great sales on items such as eggs, milk, cheese, butter, yogurt, and more! It's also the month leading up to the 4th of July, so toward the end of June you find more grilling items and condiments on sale once again.
- July is National Ice Cream Month. The best prices on ice cream can be found this month. Even though it's the middle of the summer, you will also begin seeing the back-to-school sales. Even if you don't have a child in school, it's a great time to stock up on household office supplies.
- August is the second phase of the back-to-school sale but this time it's for lunch box items. There are great deals on lunchmeats, snack items, breakfast items—especially cold cereal—and the lunch boxes themselves. It's also the time when you'll find lots of cleaning products on deep discount. It must be a good time to give the house a thorough cleaning after the kids are back in school. You can also find great deals on patio furniture, since the stores really don't want to stock these for the upcoming seasons.
- In September the back-to-school clothing and school supply sales are still in full swing. You'll also find great sales for baby stuff this month.
- October is National Seafood Month so expect sales on—you guessed it—seafood. It's also Halloween and the candy sales are back. Have a fall birthday party? Stock up on candy for the piñata while it's on sale. In addition, it's the beginning of the baking season, so you'll begin to see great prices for flour, sugar, and other baking products. There will also be plenty of sales on canned and fresh pumpkins too!
- By November the baking sale is in full swing and probably the best deals since Easter can be found. Stock up now because these prices may not

be back until April. You will find a big savings on staple baking items and also an abundance of coupons. Thanksgiving is also in November, which means you can score great deals on turkey, stuffing, boxed potatoes, cranberry sauce, and all the Thanksgiving meal fixings. Some of these staples have a long shelf life, so stock up when you find a great price even if you don't have a coupon. Winter apparel and accessories also begin to go on sale, along with blankets for the cold season.

- December will wrap up the baking sales and continue with the holiday food sales through the end of the month. Paper goods are on sale throughout the month, which comes in handy with so many people having holiday parties. You can also use them throughout the year, so stock up if you find a good price.

Besides all the obvious items that will go on sale each month, everyday items will be on sale in cycles as well. For example, your grocery store may have whole chickens on sale about every five weeks. They may also have frozen vegetables on sale every four weeks. If you watch the sales of the items you use most, you'll see the pattern. Once you know the pattern, plan to shop for those items only when they are on sale as often as you can by stocking up with enough to get you through to the next sale. This may take a little time before you notice the patterns, but when you find a great sale, be sure to make a note of when it happens.

ESSENTIAL

Amazon.com is a great place to score some hot deals on grocery items all year long, and they are delivered right to your door. Some of the deals only last a few hours but if you look for items you use regularly, you may find them dirt-cheap. However, with Amazon you are buying either in bulk or a large size. Amazon also has clipless coupons, which you can look for on the item page.

Request Rain Checks

It's impossible for the stores to keep everything in stock at all times. They try their best, but they can't predict the exact amount they will sell. For this reason, many stores offer rain checks on some items. If an item that is on sale that week sells out before the end of the sale, they will offer you a rain check, which allows you to purchase the item at a later date at the sale price. If you have a coupon, you will also be able to use it at the time of your purchase as long as the coupon has not expired.

How do you get the rain check? Some stores will have the cashier issue it at the register when you check out, while others issue them at the customer service desk. Check with the cashier and if he or she can't help you, then you can stop and grab the rain check on your way out the door. It will only take a few moments. It will help if you have the sales ad with you to assist the employee.

What Is on the Rain Check?

The rain check will include all the information the cashier will need at the time of your purchase in order to honor the sale price. The items needed are the product name, size, sale price, and the quantity that you can purchase. At times there will be limits on how many items you can purchase with a rain check and most times you will have to purchase them all in one transaction. Rain checks may or may not have an expiration date and that will vary by store. If you purchase fewer items than you are allowed according to the rain check, the cashier may or may not give it back to you to use again. That also differs from store to store.

QUESTION

What if I lose my rain check?
You must have the rain check with you when you make your purchase in order for the store to process it. If you lose the rain check, then you lose the opportunity to purchase the item at the previous sale price. File away the rain check with your coupons so that it will be handy when you're ready to use it. The store likely doesn't keep a record of who receives rain checks; therefore they have no way of knowing if you had one.

Troubleshooting with Rain Checks

There is nothing worse then getting to the store not only to find out that the item you want is not in stock, but that the store will not issue a rain check for that item. Unfortunately, there isn't much you can do about it. If this is the case, most times it will be noted in the sales ad or on the shelf where the item is kept that no rain checks will be issued. It's possible that there were limited amounts available or the store doesn't plan on getting that particular item back in stock again. This happens a lot with seasonal sales; once they sell out, that's it.

How can you overcome this? A number of stores will restock the shelves before the sale is over, even if there are only a limited number of items. They may still have more in the back, or they might be getting a second shipment in before the sale is over. Shipments can come in anytime during the week. Check with the person in charge of the department and ask if they expect to restock before the sale is over and if so, when? If they can supply you with this information, try to return at that time. Your best bet—if you know ahead of time that they will not issue you a rain check—is to shop the day the sale begins for the best chance of getting the item you want.

Make a Grocery Price List

Knowing how much everything costs at the stores that you shop at regularly will save you a lot of money over time. By knowing the regular price of the items that you use most, you'll recognize when you catch an excellent deal. This goes back to the idea of only buying items when they are on sale. Some stores may discount certain items lower than any other store. If you know this, you can plan to purchase individual items only at those stores.

A grocery price list can be a great tool to use when making your weekly or monthly menus. While browsing the ads, use your price list as a guide to whether or not the sale price is really the best price. The items in the ad are there to get you into the store but sometimes they can be deceiving. The prices listed may only be a slight discount some weeks, but when it says "On Sale," people tend to automatically assume that it's a terrific price. Having a price list handy will help you determine whether it really is a good price and if not, you can skip right over that item unless you really need it.

Constructing Your Grocery Price List

The items you use most should be the first things you account for on your grocery price list. Your kitchen cabinets are the best place to start since most items you use often will be there. Start a list; include these items and then go through and add anything you know you buy, but don't have on hand at that moment. Make two columns after each item, one for the regular price and one for the sale price. Then tuck the list into your coupon binder and take it with you the next time you go shopping. As you grab the items off the shelves, add the regular price to your sheet and if it's on sale, then add the sale price too. Or you can list the sale prices as you go through the weekly ad while making your shopping list. If you find that the sale price differs from one store to another, add a third column where you can note the sale price and label that column with the store name. If you shop regularly at more than one store, continue to add columns until you've listed them all. You can also include the drugstores in this list or make a different one for those stores. As you buy new items, add them to the grocery price list and eventually you'll have a database of everything you purchase, along with the prices.

A grocery price list is also a fantastic way to keep track of sales cycles. Just note the dates that you find the items on sale and over time you'll see a pattern. Keeping all of this in an Excel spreadsheet is helpful, but if you don't have access to a spreadsheet, a simple notebook can be just as effective. Hopefully you acquired it on sale during the back-to-school sale season!

ESSENTIAL

If you are strapped for time and you need help constructing your weekly shopping list, get a one-subject notebook to gather the deals you find each day while scanning the ads or the blogs. Then when it's time to shop, you have everything you need right there. You can even toss the coupons in between the pages as you find them.

Stacking Coupons

"Stacking" coupons is a term for using more than one coupon on an item. That being said, this does not mean using more than one manufacturer coupon on one item. It means using coupons that are not "like" types of coupons on one item. Store coupons and manufacturer coupons are an example of this. You can only use one manufacturer coupon per item—but if you have a store coupon for that item, you can use it along with the manufacturer coupon and stack them for more savings. In other words, if you have a Target coupon for Pantene and you have a manufacturer coupon for Pantene, you can use them both on one item, in one transaction.

For example, Pantene shampoo is on sale at Target, two for $7.00. You have a $2.00 Pantene Target store coupon and you have a $2.00 Pantene manufacturer coupon. Both are for when you purchase two Pantene items. If you shop at Target you can then purchase two Pantene products and use both coupons in one transaction and your final cost will be $3.00 for both, or $1.50 each. That is an example of how to stack coupons. Can you see how great the savings can be? Not all stores offer store coupons, but you should take full advantage of those that do!

FACT

The best time to buy an item is when you can purchase it at its cheapest. When you find coupons for the items that you use most often, it is best to hold on to them until you find a sale. You may be tempted to use it right away, but before you do, ask yourself two questions: "Do I need this right now?" and "Is it on sale?" If you can't answer "yes" to at least one of those questions, then it's best to hold on to the coupon until the item is on sale.

Box Stores and Wholesale Clubs

You can use coupons at Walmart, Target, and even some wholesale clubs like BJ's. If you're not sure if the store you are shopping at accepts coupons, ask before you shop. The box stores and wholesale clubs sometimes have regular prices and sale prices better than you will find in the grocery stores and they may accept coupons. Not just store coupons, but manufacturer coupons too. And when you stack the two together, you'll save even more!

Walmart does not have store coupons, but perhaps they may in the future. They honor manufacturer coupons, and some Walmarts will even double coupons now. Check with your local store and ask about their coupon policy. Target issues store coupons that you can find online at *www.target.com*. They change weekly; usually on Sundays. Their store coupons can be stacked with sales and manufacturer coupons to save you even more.

Using Coupons at BJ's Wholesale Club

BJ's Wholesale Club has a fantastic coupon policy that most people are not aware of. BJ's offers store coupons that are mailed to members' homes and are also available at the store. Along with these store coupons, they allow you to stack manufacturer coupons for even more savings. However, it gets even better. BJ's packages items in bundles of more than one of the same item. In some instances you can use more than one coupon on one bundle. How can you tell? If the items that are bundled together could be divided and sold separately, then you can use a coupon for each item in the package. The way to know is by looking at the items and if they each have their own bar codes, then they can be broken down and sold individually.

For example, if there are four boxes of toothpaste bundled together and they each have a UPC bar code of their own, then you can use more than one coupon for the toothpaste. If the coupon is for a single item, you can use four. If the coupon is for two items each, then you can use two of them since you'll be purchasing four items. If you happen to have a store coupon for that bundle of toothpaste, you can use that coupon too.

You may find a bundle of four Colgate toothpastes at BJ's Wholesale Club and you have four $1.00 Colgate manufacturer coupons along with one $2.00 BJ's Wholesale Club Colgate store coupon. Combine these five coupons and save $6.00 off this bundle of Colgate toothpaste.

This policy can be found online at *www.bjs.com*. However, some stores may have to adjust the coupon policy, so it's always best to check with the local store before shopping.

CHAPTER 7

Organizational Strategies

Once you have your coupons, you need to organize them or you won't use them. After all, if you saw a pile of coupons, would you really want to go through it looking for what you need? Probably not. There are numerous ways you can organize coupons, but what works for one person may not work for someone else, so try a few different ways until you find a system that works for you. Spending time clipping, sorting, and filing coupons is time-consuming and it's not for everyone. But if you become an organized couponer, and stay organized, you will succeed.

Clip and Sort

The oldest and most common way of organizing coupons is by clipping them each week when your inserts arrive and then sorting them into a little accordion coupon holder, which you can pick up at your local dollar store. Most people begin this way, but the more you get into couponing, the harder this system can be to maintain. Sorting 100 coupons each week can become very time-consuming.

Set a Coupon Clipping Schedule

The best way to stay organized if using the clip-and-sort method is to pick a day in the week and put aside some time to sit down and clip all the coupons you think you may use. Then immediately put them into your coupon holder by department or whatever way you like to file. If you don't come up with a regular schedule, you'll end up with a pile of inserts and may feel completely overwhelmed. That overwhelmed feeling can result in you either tossing them all in the trash or waiting so long that the coupons you wanted to use have expired. That won't help you save money, especially if you purchased extra newspapers to get more coupons.

Enlist the family to help you cut coupons and even sort them. Little children can help match like pictures if you have several of the same coupons. They can even lay them out for you neatly so you can see what you have. If they are old enough to cut well, you can have them cut the coupons while you sort them. Make it a family affair and then they will learn along with you and it may help them budget their money better in the future.

Help! I'm Running Out of Room

Once you really get into using coupons, you may find that the small accordion file isn't big enough to hold all your coupons. This may seem hard to believe at first, but between the insert coupons, printable coupons, and all the others, you'll end up with a lot of coupons. Your file will be overflowing, which will slow down sorting, filing, and using.

If you outgrow the small file, it may be time to re-evaluate how you're organizing coupons. At this point you need a system that will accommodate a lot of coupons. One option is to move to a bigger accordion folder, perhaps one from the office supply store that is used to sort checks. But even if you do that, it may not be long before you need something even bigger to house all your coupons.

Box Systems

Using a box to sort your coupons is a great way to handle a vast amount of coupons. And it's also a cheap way to do it because you can use something as simple as a shoebox and spend nothing on it. A fishing tackle box, toolbox, and even a sewing box will all work as well. If you have something hanging around collecting dust, it's a great way to put it to use.

Whatever you decide to use must be strong enough to hold a lot of coupons, especially if you plan on transporting it back and forth to the store each time you shop. Now that you have more room, you can also store your scissors in the box for quick finding. Remember, time is money!

Organizing Your Coupon Box

To organize the box you choose for coupons, you'll need some index card separators or cut-up cardboard to divide and label the coupon sections. You'll want to separate the coupons by type so you can sort them and find them easier. If you use cardboard, you'll just need a marker to write the categories you want to use. To begin, it's best to make a list of how you'd like to sort them. They can be in very general categories like cleaning products, pet food, canned goods, and condiments. Or you could break them down even more by dog food, cat food, canned vegetables, frozen vegetables, cookies, crackers, etc.—you get the picture. By making a box system, you have the control to make the categories however you see fit for your shopping trip. This is one advantage over using something premade.

Putting Together Your Coupon Box

Once you have your categories figured out, use a marker to label each divider with a category. Make sure you measure them to be a height appropriate for the box. You'll want to make sure the top of the divider is higher than the coupons so you can see them in a glance.

Once they are labeled, put them in an order that makes sense to you. This could be alphabetical order, order of aisles at your favorite stores, grouped by type, or whatever you like. As long as it makes sense to you, it will work. Customize it as much as you'd like to make it as easy as possible. Using coupons doesn't have to be hard, so don't make it complicated.

Be sure to keep up with clipping, sorting, and filing each week so you don't get behind. It's best to set aside time to clip and sort your coupons every week. Don't let them pile up or you'll never get to them. It's best to clip them as soon as you can and immediately sort them into your box using the dividers you set up with categories. Then, when you are looking for coupons, you know where to find them.

ALERT

> Don't forget about store coupons! It will be helpful to make a section for store coupons since you'll be collecting those as well. Easy access to them means they will get used. You can make one section for all store coupons or break them down by store. Again, whatever works for how you shop. Personalize it to your needs.

Some people like taking their entire coupon box to the store just in case they need something. If that works for you, great, but having all of your coupons with you may be confusing, especially at first. It's very easy to become frustrated while learning something new, so it's best to pull what you need beforehand. If you must take the box with you "just in case," you can always keep it in the car. That way you will have access to it if necessary.

Using a Coupon Binder

The binder system is great for those who want to see exactly what they have at all times. This system makes locating coupons very easy. However, this method can be time-consuming when filing your coupons. Each system has its advantages and disadvantages.

Constructing a Coupon Binder

You will need to purchase some supplies to make a coupon binder. It may mean a small investment, but it's also possible that you have some of these items on hand. Or if you plan ahead, you may be able to score deals on everything you need to construct your coupon binder. The basic supplies needed are a three-ring binder, some pocket pages, and page dividers. The three-ring binder can be something you recycle from another project. As far as its thickness, that really depends on how many coupons you plan on storing in it. You can start small and then work your way to a bigger one if needed.

The pocket pages are the most important part of the binder system, after the coupons themselves. They are what will store the "meat" of your binder, so you should think about what kind of pages you want to use. There are a few different styles to accommodate different coupons. The most popular size is the one they market for baseball cards, which are called trading card pocket pages. Each sheet has nine pockets to a page. There are others that have bigger pockets, but this style will fit most of your coupons.

Nice sturdy pocket pages are a must so they hold up well over time. How many you need will depend on how many coupons you collect. When purchasing them, keep in mind that one coupon will go in each pocket. But if you have four of the same coupon, then you'll put all four of them in that one pocket. So as you see, you will need a lot of pocket pages, but first you need to figure out which ones will work best for the coupons you collect.

Choosing Pocket Pages for Your Binder

Each size pocket page has its advantages and disadvantages. You want the coupon to fit inside the pocket without having to fold it, as often as possible. When you start folding the coupon, it gets bulky and the pocket will not hold as many. So it's best to start out with a variety of pocket pages to see what you need. Unfortunately, they are sold in packs of pages, but not in an assortment. You may want to find a friend who is also building a coupon binder and split the purchase with her. Then you won't be left with extra pocket pages you may not need. Be sure to check eBay and Craigslist to see if anyone is selling odd sheets, to avoid having to purchase an entire pack.

The bigger, six-pocket pages are great for those slightly larger coupons that you may have to fold to fit into the smaller pockets. Depending on what store they come from, they may also hold rain checks easier. Don't forget to file your rain checks with your coupons so you can use them! You can fold longer coupons in half and store them in the six-pocket pages too, but if you have a lot of them, it will get bulky pretty fast.

Finally, you'll need some divider pages. The basic three-ring binder divider pages or something similar will work. These will help by dividing the coupons into sections so it's easier for you to locate them. You'll need as many divider pages as you feel you will use. You could choose to skip these, but they will make finding your coupons a bit faster. And of course, it's more organized.

QUESTION

What about the oversized coupons, rain checks, and rebate forms? The four-to-a-page photo pocket pages may be perfect for larger items. If you tend to collect a lot of longer coupons, these pages may house them better than the smaller pocket sizes. If not, you can use currency pocket pages, which have three long pockets the size of a dollar bill. Just make sure the place you house your rain checks and rebates is somewhere you can see them so you don't forget about them!

Putting It All Together

Now that you have everything you need, it's time to put your coupon binder together and use it! You'll first want to make a list of categories that you'd like to use. These will be the categories that you write on the divider page tabs. This can be tailored to your needs, but they can be as simple as canned goods, paper goods, health and beauty, frozen foods, and any other category you choose. You can break them down into even more specific categories like canned vegetables, baby food, dog food, shampoos, and so on. It's your binder, so make it work for you.

You may need to adjust the categories from time to time depending on the coupons you find. If you start off with generic categories, you may find after a while that breaking them down more specifically will be a timesaver.

Once you have the divider pages in place, put the pocket pages in between the divider pages. Since you don't know how many you need in each section, you will have to move them around as you add coupons. If you'd like, you can wait and add these as you put the coupons in the binder. Of course some sections will need more and others less.

Now it's time to add coupons. Each pocket should contain the same or "like" coupons. For example, for canned goods put each kind of canned good coupon in its own pocket. Canned pasta sauce will go in one pocket, canned vegetables will go in another pocket, and canned beans will go in another pocket. This way you see exactly what you have when you flip through your binder. If you put all the canned item coupons in one pocket, you won't know what's underneath, and chances are, you won't use them all. The pockets will also get bulky pretty fast.

Putting Your Coupon Binder to Use

Once your coupons are sorted and filed into your coupon binder, it's time to start using them. Each week when you make a shopping list, you will be able to easily locate and identify the coupon that you want to use. You first look for the appropriate section and then find the coupon you want. You'll also be nicely organized if you decide to bring the binder into the store. It will fit easily in the front of the shopping cart and your coupons will be tucked into the pocket pages so they won't fall out during transit (which would be a nightmare after all the time you spent sorting them!).

FACT

According to Inmar—a company that tracks coupon usage throughout the United States—65 percent of coupons used in 2010 were for food items. That increased by 3 percent in the first quarter of 2011 due to the stores offering more in-store coupons and promotions.

Whole Coupon Insert Method

Keeping the entire coupon insert until they need the coupons is the perfect way for busy people to organize their coupons. The idea behind this is you don't clip a coupon until you need it. And of course that means there is no sorting and filing of coupons either. There can be huge advantages to this system; however, you still need to be organized for it to work. Otherwise you'll have piles of coupon inserts sitting in the house and again, this can lead to you getting discouraged with coupon use.

The whole coupon insert method is a timesaver because not only are you not cutting coupons ahead of time, but you are also not cutting coupons you *may* use. If you don't use them, the time spent cutting is lost. But this way if you don't use them, you haven't wasted any time. For someone who doesn't have the time—or the desire—to cut, sort, and file coupons, this is the way to go.

Sorting Your Coupon Inserts

If you choose the whole coupon insert method as a way of organizing your coupons, then you'll need two things: an accordion file that fits at least 8.5" × 11" papers, and a pen. That's it! The process is very easy and will take very little time each week. When you get your coupon inserts, you will need to bunch them together into like kinds. For instance, if you purchase an extra paper and have two Smart Source coupon inserts, put one inside the other so they are bunched together. Once you do that, write the date of the insert right on the front page. If you aren't sure of the date, look along the spine of the coupon insert to find it. Then you file the inserts by date in your accordion file. Now you are done filing your coupons away for the week.

QUESTION

How do I know what coupons I have when using the whole coupon insert filing system?
There are a few ways you can find what coupons you have when you file coupons by whole inserts. Before you file them away, you can make a list of the coupons in the insert that you might use. Put the date of the insert on the top of the sheet. Of course that's the long way. You can also use an online coupon database like the one on *www .KouponKaren.com* to search for coupons, which will tell you the name and date of the coupon insert containing the coupon.

Stay Organized While You Shop

If you walk into the store with a big mess of coupons in your hand, you are going to end up walking out of the store with the same big mess of coupons in your hand, and not use a single one. Couponing is much easier when you have a plan. Walking into the store organized gives you a greater chance of succeeding.

If you plan on shopping at several stores, make a separate list for each store and attach the coupons to the list that you are using for that store. You could also use an envelope for each store. Write your list on the outside and then put your coupons inside the envelope so you don't lose them. Use a different envelope for each store; this way you can just grab it when you go shopping and everything you need will be there.

FACT

You don't need to purchase envelopes to keep your coupons organized while shopping. You can use the ones you get with junk mail for free. Also, if you pay bills online, you can use the envelopes you receive to send your payments in, as well. It doesn't matter if there's writing on it; use the other side to write your list.

Separate the Coupons You're Using

Be sure that however you take your coupons with you, that you separate them from the rest of your coupons so you know what you are using. If you bring your entire filing system with you, keep those you are using separate from the rest. If you use the box system, put the coupons you are using for that shopping trip in the front of the box. If you use the binder system, have a spot in the front of your binder for coupons for that shopping trip.

Once you purchase a product that you have a coupon for, move it to a separate spot from the rest of the coupons, ready to give to the cashier. You could fold them and put them in your pocket, but then you'll have a mess at the register. You could have a separate section within your coupon filing system for coupons to present to the cashier. You could also have a separate envelope for coupons that were "used" or "in your shopping cart." Or you could simply move them to the back of the pile of your coupons. Any one of these options is fine; just be sure to have a way to keep the ones used separate from the ones you want to use, or the rest of your coupons. Find a way that works for you, and stick to it.

Leave the Bulk of Your Coupons at Home

The first thing you want to do until you are a seasoned couponer is to leave the bulk of your coupons at home or in the car. Only take in with you what you are going to use for that shopping trip. If you are planning out what you will buy before you shop, then you should also be pulling your coupons at the same time. Keep the coupons clipped to your shopping list so you don't leave them at home. If you take all your coupons into the store with you, you're going to be tempted to look at every deal to see if you have a coupon for it. If you've already set your budget and made your list, there really isn't much room left for last-minute purchases, even if the items were on sale.

Shop Alone, If Possible

If you can, shop alone whenever possible. Then you can concentrate on what you are doing and what you are purchasing. It's very easy to pick up the wrong item when using coupons. You may not notice the size requirement on the coupon and grab the wrong size. Then you find out when you're cashing out and the system won't take the coupon. Or perhaps you were supposed to purchase more than one item to use the coupon, but you were so distracted, you completely forgot. Now you have to get another item or forget using the coupon just to get out of there.

Make a Detailed List

If shopping alone isn't possible, which is the case for many people with small children, make sure your shopping list is detailed as to what you are buying and how many of each. This will let you avoid having to search through your coupons each time you pick up an item. Put the number of items you need to purchase right next to the product on your shopping list. Even if it's just one, note that. If you make a rule of putting the number of items you are purchasing for every item, you'll never have a doubt if it should be one or three.

Also make sure you note on your shopping list the size of the item that is specified on the coupon. If the coupon is for any size, then put that on your shopping list. Then you can decide what size you want when you get to the store. It's always possible that purchasing a full-price smaller size with your coupon is a better deal than purchasing the larger on-sale size with a coupon. You may not know this until you get to the store.

Clean Out Coupons Before You Shop

If you do decide to take all your coupons with you when you shop, make sure all the expired coupons have been cleared out beforehand to avoid having to sort through them while you're in the store. It will be hard enough finding the coupons you want to use while shopping; the more coupons you have to sort through, the longer it will take. If you clean out the expired coupons on a regular basis, you won't have them with you to either hold up the process of sorting or use them by accident. If you give the cashier an expired coupon, you'll then need to take more time at the checkout to search for one that is not expired.

You may also find that after clipping some coupons, you never purchase those products. It's possible that the item just never goes on sale the way a competitor's item does; therefore with or without a coupon, you just aren't going to purchase it. For example, you may clip coupons for several different types of laundry detergent, but one brand may never go on sale as low as the others. If you can always get the others for a better price, you aren't going to ever purchase the more expensive brand, so you might as well stop clipping the coupons. The fewer coupons in your coupon stash, the faster you can go through them when you are looking for something.

Dealing with Expired Coupons

One of the grueling parts of using coupons is getting rid of them when they have expired. If you are using any of the clip-and-sort methods, you'll need to go through each section at least once a month to pull out the expired coupons. Of course if you use all of them, there won't be any expired coupons left, but chances are, there will be some. This is a great task to pass along to some of the younger members of your family if possible. It's also an easy task to do while chatting on the phone or watching TV.

ESSENTIAL

If you find you have a lot of coupons that you don't use, find out if there is a place in your local library where you can leave them for someone else to use. This will help you avoid ending up with expired coupons at the end of the month that you never got around to using, and it gives someone else an opportunity to use the coupons and save some money.

Send Expired Coupons Overseas for Military Families to Use

Once you pull all the expired coupons out, you have a choice of what to do with them. You can toss them in the garbage or recycling bin, or you can send them to military personnel overseas, who can still use them up to six months after they expire. The commissaries overseas will take these coupons from military families. And since most of them are working on a budget, they are very appreciative of the coupons. It may be the only way they can get their hands on them.

There are several ways you can send the coupons to these families. There are many blogs online that organize and send the coupons overseas and there are many organizations that do as well. Check the website Overseas Coupon Program (*www.ocpnet.org*) for a list of bases and addresses where you may send coupons. They also have great tips on how to go about doing it. You can send them in a priority envelope that you can pick up for free at the post office and you don't have to pay extra overseas shipping, which is a nice perk. It will cost you a few dollars in shipping, so the more you send, the better, but either way it's a small investment to help those serving our country.

CHAPTER 8

Planning Your Shopping Trip

If you are going to succeed in using coupons on a regular basis, you must get into the habit of planning your shopping trip before you go. Getting in a good routine will take time at the beginning, but it will get easier as you get into the habit of planning. Without a plan, eventually you won't want to be bothered with using coupons because it will seem too hard. There are lots of resources online to help plan your trip. Coupon blogs will highlight the weekly deals at your local stores, including what coupons to use, and they can be extremely helpful in your planning process.

Weekly and Monthly Menus

Everyone does it at one point or another—you arrive home from a big shopping trip, after purchasing a large array of groceries, and then realize you are missing some items for "complete" meals. So what do you do? You run to the nearest store and buy what you need, regardless of the price, even if the nearest store is a convenience store. This is a big mistake when trying to save money. These stores are called convenience stores because they are just that—convenient. But they are not cheap! Now the coupons you've been collecting get left behind unused and you've purchased something full price when you didn't have to. How can you avoid this? Plan ahead by making a weekly or monthly menu. Once your menus are completed, you will see what you have, what you need, and when you need to buy it. If you plan your meals according to what is on sale, you'll save money and time since your meals are already planned for the week. To top it off, there will be no need for last-minute runs to the store where you may wind up paying full price.

Plan Your Week's Menus for Fewer Headaches

Weekly menus can also be helpful because other family members can help out during those times when you might be tempted to eat out. It can also be a timesaver for busy people after a long day at work. Do you really want to come home from work and figure out what to make for dinner and then possibly even have to defrost something? Probably not. But if you have your menu prepared ahead of time, you can plan accordingly before you leave the house that morning. If you prepare a chicken dinner with two side dishes and you purchase everything on sale, you would spend less than $20 for the entire meal for a family of four. A family of four can't even eat at a fast-food restaurant for that little. It's definitely better to be prepared and have food in the house.

Where to Begin

Building a database of recipes you use on a regular basis along with ingredients is a great way to start. Include even the simplest dishes just to have a quick reference. Begin by making a list of the recipes, including all ingredients. Keep the list in a place where you can grab it for a quick glance. It doesn't have to be anything fancy; even a folder kept inside a kitchen drawer or cabinet would work. Be sure to catalog your spices and condiments at the same time. It's easier to use items when you know you have them. You may even find items you forgot you had that you now know you might use. Be sure to include regular staple items, like sugar, flour, etc. You don't want to run out of those at the last minute!

FACT

Now would be a great time to find more frugal recipes—like the ones at the end of this book—to add to your weekly rotation. There are also many resources available online where you can find recipes to fit any budget. Some websites even have online recipe boxes where you can store all your favorite recipes for quick finding, like *www.allrecipes.com*. Challenge yourself to find new meal options. It can be fun!

How to Shop

Shopping properly is the key to saving money. The best way to approach this is to plan meals around what is on sale. Gather the ads for your favorite stores and look for the best prices on meats, produce, and staple items. Make a list and then plan your meals on just the items that are on sale and in your pantry already. For example, if a whole chicken is on sale, look through your database of recipes and find a way to use it. You may even be able to get two or three meals out of it. Another option would be to purchase more than one, freeze the spare, and use it the following week.

Next, look at the produce section and see what vegetables are on sale and how to incorporate them into your meals. Many people prefer to use fresh vegetables for side dishes. If frozen veggies or canned veggies are on sale, you could plan to use those in a stew or a soup. If bananas are on sale, stock up on those because they freeze well. Make smoothies or banana pancakes for breakfast or even banana sandwiches with peanut butter for lunch. They are both nutritious and delicious. You may have to be a little creative and think ahead, but it can be done.

Plan a Meal with Leftovers

While planning a shopping trip, think about what you can do with any leftovers, since there may not be enough for another complete meal. Think about how much food you throw in the garbage. If you added up that food, you'd be amazed at how much it cost you. With just a little bit of time and creativity, you can create an entire meal out of your leftovers. If you plan it right, or just get downright lucky, you may even have enough to make an entire meal out of four or five nights of leftovers. It's like free food! If you're new to cooking with leftovers, there are lots of websites with recipes just for common items that are left from meals, like *www.lovefoodhatewaste.com*. You can search through the recipes by the foods you have. They also have dishes sectioned off into categories like kid-friendly, lunches, freezing, and vegetarian.

QUESTION

What can I do with all these single-serving leftover meals?
If you freeze one or two portions of leftovers a week, then later in the month you can take a night off from cooking and have a potluck dinner. Give everyone in the family a choice from the leftovers in the freezer and just reheat the meals. Add a salad if needed and call it a meal. You'll use what you have and save money on a meal. It will almost be like a free meal.

Plan for Leftovers While Shopping

If there is a great deal on a roast or a certain cut of steak one week, think about ways you may be able to use it. Make the roast for dinner one night, and then one day that week you could use the leftovers for sandwiches for lunch or even a salad. A steak may come in big pieces and while you can ask the butcher to cut it up for you, you can also just cook all of it and then use the leftovers for another meal or lunch. You can grill the steaks one night and use the leftovers for another meal. You can make a stew and even fajitas with just a little bit of leftover steak. Either one of these options can be paired with a variety of leftover vegetables as well for a quick, easy, and affordable meal.

What about baking? Lots of leftover items can be used in baking, even if only to add some nutritional value. Have you ever put puréed baby food carrots into your meatballs or sauce for those extra vitamins? You can do the same with leftover vegetables. Toss them into the blender and purée them. Leftover carrots—frozen, canned, or fresh—can be turned into a carrot cake if you are expecting company that week. Not expecting company? Make it anyway and freeze it for that last-minute guest or for a treat one night for your family.

Plan for Leftovers Before You Even Eat

When the kids ask for an apple, don't give them the entire apple if you know they will just waste most of it. Cut up slices so if they don't finish it, you can put the last few slices in the freezer for next time you make pancakes and muffins. It will add more flavor to the pancakes or muffins while making them a healthier option, with no extra cost to you. You can do the same with peaches, bananas, pears, and berries. Fruit can be easily frozen for future use.

Making a List

How many times have you found yourself at the grocery store without a list? What is the usual result of that? You overbuy and can also underbuy. There is always something forgotten or something you purchased that you didn't need. This is especially true when shopping with a spouse or children. There is so much more temptation around, and it can be hard to say no to extra purchases. Interruptions during a shopping trip can also interfere with what you were supposed to get. But if you always shop with a list, eventually your family will get used to it and will not ask for extra items again.

Avoid Overbuying with a List

You could end up with seven jars of pickles that you paid full price for, because you forgot you had them and thought you needed them. The solution? Make a list before going shopping and you will be less tempted to purchase something you didn't need or want, or that's not on sale. If you've planned your menu, everything you need is on the list and that's it. Lists can also be helpful if you have a spouse, child, or friend shop for you because they will be certain not to purchase it if it doesn't appear on the list.

Your List Doesn't Have to Be Fancy

The list doesn't have to be anything fancy. You can easily use scrap paper, the back of expired coupons, and even old greeting cards. Anything you can write on, you can use. Saving money doesn't always have to cost money. You can even use recycled cardboard from product boxes before you toss it in the trash. This is another area where you can be creative. Do not go out and buy a notepad just for your list if you don't have to, but do buy it on sale if you do.

Some people are just more organized than others. If you want to get a little fancy, you can set up a premade list of all the items that you do purchase and work from that when planning your shopping trip. This method can prove very useful for the organized person. Set up a Word or Excel document of some type with four columns. The first column is for the product name. If you use more than one size of the item, list each size separately or leave space to input the size when making your list. The next column will be a place where you can note sale prices. This is a good way to make sure that the item is marked correctly and to save you time later if it rings up incorrectly when cashing out. It's also helpful for those times when there are different sizes on sale. Armed with this information, you can be sure you are picking up the right item.

ESSENTIAL

If you really want to be organized, make your list in the order of the aisles at your favorite stores. Then you'll have less chance of missing something on your list, and you will spend less time in the store. Taking the time to shop with coupons can require more time than you are used to, so don't waste any of it! Time is precious.

Then make a column where you can note if you have a coupon and how much the coupon is for. This will also serve as a way of noting how many items you will be picking up. You can indicate that the coupon is for $1.00 off two items and whether you have more than one coupon. This will help you avoid looking through your stack of coupons at the store. And finally the last column can be used for the final cost. If you want to know exactly what you are spending, this is a column you want to be sure to include. It will only take a moment to figure out the final cost—simply write in the sale price and subtract any coupons you are using. Perfect for the person on a tight budget. Once your list is complete, simply print one out each time you shop and fill in the items you're buying. Make sure you print it on scrap paper.

Staying Within Your Budget

If you have a list, it is easier to stay within your budget, especially when you know the prices of everything. You are only buying things from the sales ad, remember? If you've made the list according to your menu, there is no reason to purchase anything that is not on the list either. However, there is one exception: If you find a clearance item or something marked down that they want to sell fast and it's something you can use, by all means grab it, especially if you have a coupon for it. Never pass up a good deal. But make sure it fits into your budget and be sure to check the expiration date.

Adjusting Your Budget

You may need to adjust your budget from week to week or even month to month for several reasons. Not everyone is paid on the same schedule and this can affect how one shops throughout the month. You may find that during certain weeks you may need to spend more due to a special occasion like a birthday, holiday, or get-together. There may be times when you can plan far enough ahead for these occasions and not even feel a dent in your budget, but not always. Take a look at your upcoming events at the beginning of the month or perhaps a month in advance so you know where you need to spend your money. This is just another way to help avoid overspending whenever possible.

Finding the Right Stores to Shop At

You may have four choices of where to shop each week and they may even be within equal driving distance from your house. The decision of which one or which two to shop at each week can be grueling. Think back to your menu planning. If you look at all the ads for each store and see what's on sale, you can't go wrong.

It's best to begin with looking at a maximum of two ads if you are strapped for time; otherwise it could become extremely overwhelming and be another reason to give up. And no matter how good a sale is, if you only need one item at that store and it's completely out of your way, it's definitely not worth the sale. In the end you will not save any money at all.

Watch for High Prices and Coupon-Friendly Stores

There are lots of factors to take into consideration when deciding where to shop. Keep in mind a store's sale prices. If they are always high, you may want to skip that store entirely. Do they have a friendly coupon policy or do you spend a long time just convincing them to accept the coupons you know you can use? What kind of store incentives do they offer? If their incentives are great, you'll probably save even more in the long run. You may always have great success shopping at one store, but someone else may not. It depends on what you're buying, when you shop, and how you shop. So while it's great to find out from friends and family where they have the most success shopping, it's also great to figure out what stores work best for you, your family, your shopping needs, and your budget. The best way to figure it out is by trial and error. Just make sure it doesn't cost you too much during this process. If it seems like you could be spending less money, time, and aggravation elsewhere, you probably could.

Saving Gas and Price Matching

Trying to make your shopping list each week can be a big headache. One store might have a fantastic price on something that isn't priced that well anywhere else, and another store may have everything else that fits your menu that week. Now you need to decide whether it's worth it to drive to that store for that one item. The money you spend on gas to purchase all the good deals must be accounted for. Otherwise you may find that while you're saving at the store, the amount you spend on gas has gone up. Is that helpful? No, not really. If you plan properly you may even be able to cut the amount of money you spend on gas each month by avoiding those last-minute stops at the grocery store on your way home from work.

Want to save a trip to another store? Let's talk about price matching. What is it? It's when the store will sell you an item for the same price that another store has it on sale for that week. This can be so helpful in saving you time, energy, and gas. There are rules to follow when price matching and it's always best to prepare yourself by checking with your stores ahead of time. Not all stores price match. If you find yourself in a last-minute situation, call the stores to find out if they will price match and with which stores they will do so. Usually, the stores will need to be within so many miles of the store you want to price match from; there are guidelines and it can't just be any store.

You will want to ask them for their instructions on price matching. Some helpful questions to ask are "Do you accept coupons for items you price match?" "Is there a limit on how many items or how many pounds you will allow?" "Are there any restrictions on what you will price match?" Most stores won't honor percent-off sales or sales for store-brand items. They may not carry the same size or quantity as the store that has in on sale. So— while price matching can be helpful, it may not always be possible.

ALERT

Be sure to have the ad with you for the item you want to price match. The store will need proof of sale, and you can't assume they will have the ad themselves. It's always best to shop with your ads just in case you have a pricing issue even when shopping at the store the ad is from. But with price matching, you *always* need the ad.

Plan Your Shopping Around Your Weekly Errands

When trying to decide where to shop, think about whether you will be going by any stores during the week. Look at your calendar to see if you or another family member has any appointments that may fall in the area of one of the stores where you are considering shopping that week. Of course it won't help if the appointment is on Friday and you need the groceries earlier in the week, but if you know before you plan, you may be able to work around it. You might even have a friend or neighbor who works down the street from one store that has a great sale that week. You could always ask them to stop in and pick up what you need, and return the favor another time.

Transporting the Right Coupons

If you don't take coupons with you, you won't save money. But if you don't have them organized in an orderly fashion, chances are you are going to get frustrated and eventually leave them at home, on purpose! That isn't going to save you money either, and then all the time you've spent finding, cutting, and sorting coupons has just been wasted.

Do I take all my coupons with me?
There are advantages to taking all your coupons with you to the store each time you shop, but it's probably not a good idea for a new coupon user. It may be too overwhelming to have everything with you. You may find yourself stopping in every aisle looking to see if you have a coupon. In the beginning it may be best to leave them at home. If you see something you think you may have a coupon for, make a note and check when you get home.

The key to using them, and wanting to use them, each time you shop is to be organized at the store. It will make your life easy, especially if you are shopping with children.

Take Two Envelopes Shopping with You

There are so many ways to be organized while shopping with coupons, and it may take you a while to figure out what works best for you. But when you begin using coupons, one simple way would be to take two envelopes and label one "Coupons for This Shopping Trip" and one "Checkout Coupons." The first envelope is for the coupons you want to use and the other envelope is for the coupons you are actually using. Why two different envelopes? To help you take the proper coupons with you to the store and to keep organized while there. When you place an item in the shopping cart, take that coupon from the "Coupons for This Shopping Trip" envelope and put it in the "Checkout Coupons" envelope. If you do this throughout your shopping trip, when you get to the register you can just take the coupons out of the "Checkout Coupons" envelope and hand them to the cashier. This will avoid sorting through the coupons at the register and holding up the line because you can't remember if you purchased an item or not. The cashier will thank you, the person behind you will thank you, and you'll realize that using coupons isn't such a headache.

Have a Plan B

After spending all that time planning, cutting, sorting, and calculating, it's inevitable that your shopping trip won't go as planned. If you made a list from your weekly menu and now some items are out of stock, that can mess up your entire shopping trip. So it's best to have a Plan B when shopping.

This can be tough if you're on a budget. The best thing to do is shop the first day of the sale, which will provide a greater chance of getting all the products you want. But there's always the chance that the store didn't get that item in on time, or they had limited quantities and the five people that were waiting for the store to open grabbed them before you could. You'd be surprised how often that can happen.

So what could your Plan B be? It could be as simple as deleting that item off your weekly menu, finding a substitute, or biting the bullet and paying full price for something that would work in its place.

When making your shopping list, plan one alternate meal. It could be something that you can turn to each week in case something isn't available. Either have this meal already in your house, or plan to purchase it if necessary when you're at the store. It could be something as simple as pancakes and fruit for dinner. But if you know you have an alternative option, it won't be as stressful when you can't find the products you want.

Swap One Main Ingredient for a Like Ingredient

You can also avoid stress if you plan ahead for how you could easily replace a missing ingredient with something else. If the recipe calls for turkey, why not substitute chicken for it? If it calls for beef, consider using pork or even chicken. If they are all out of fresh broccoli, check the freezer for frozen broccoli. If you prepare yourself ahead of time to expect something to be missing, it will be easier to come up with something other than "Takeout Tuesday Night."

CHAPTER 9

Store Coupon Policies

You've collected all the coupons, you've organized them, and even planned your shopping trip. Now you need to know what each store's policy is on accepting coupons. Yes, not only are there rules for using coupons, but each store may have a slightly different rule about how you can use coupons at their store. Checking the store policy beforehand makes it easier for you to use coupons and avoid any problems. The coupon policy will explain what coupons the store accepts, what bonuses it may offer, and any purchase requirements to use the coupons.

Why Policies Are Important

Coupon policies can make your shopping trip smoother and can help you plan for the shopping trip as well. If you know the store's policy on coupons, you can plan your spending and know what to expect the total to be after coupons. You'll know what kinds of coupons the store will accept and how they handle the coupons they do accept. The store's policy will also tell you how they handle coupons with sales, so you will know if you can use coupons on certain sale items. If you are on a strict budget, or want to be, then knowing the coupon policy will help you stay on target.

You'll Know Where to Shop

If you had the option of shopping at a store that accepts coupons and one that doesn't accept coupons, then obviously you'll shop at the store that accepts coupons. But if you didn't know this and you shopped at the store that didn't accept coupons only to find out after you've completed your shopping trip and handed over the coupons you spent time pulling from your coupon binder, you probably wouldn't be very happy. If you read the store policy and knew this beforehand, you would have saved yourself a lot of time. Remember, time is money.

Stores Need Guidelines

The stores also need guidelines in place in order to avoid the misuse of coupons. Usually when there aren't any rules, things get crazy and people abuse the system. This can't happen when dealing with coupons because they are like money. If you could use any coupon on any product, then what would the purpose of coupons even be? That's not what the manufacturer has intended; therefore the stores need to adhere to their policies in order to be reimbursed for the coupons. To make sure this happens, stores need guidelines for the employees and the customers about how coupons can be used to ensure the stores don't lose money. As long as the guidelines are communicated to all involved, then coupon usage should go smoothly.

Common Guidelines in Coupon Policies

Different stores have different rules, and the same store in different parts of the country will have different rules. One coupon policy you'll find that varies from store to store across the country is the policy on double and triple coupons. Not all stores double coupons and those that do may have different maximum values for doubling coupons. You'll want to know if and how your store handles double coupons so that you'll know if you're scoring a good deal or an okay deal. They may only honor double coupons on certain days of the week or only some weeks and not all month. Some stores may double up to a value of $.50 and others may double up to a value of $.99. Knowing this will help in planning your shopping trip, so be familiar with your store's coupon policy.

Triple coupons have become rare and will also vary from store to store. It is helpful to know if you'll need a coupon that they've printed in their weekly ad for your coupons to triple. You will also want to know if there is a limit to the amount of coupons that will triple per transaction. To plan your spending, you need to know if they will triple up to $.99 or less. A $.50 coupon tripled now turns into a $1.50 coupon and a $.75 coupon now turns into a $2.25 coupon. This can mean a very nice savings, so it's important to know exactly how it's going to work before you go shopping. Keep in mind that the store may not triple coupons every day. There may be a certain day of the month that the store will triple coupons, and you may also need to spend a certain amount to get the triple value. This is important information you need to know before you shop.

Accepting Competitors' Coupons

Some stores take competitors' coupons and if they do, it will be noted in their coupon policy. It may not be specific as to what stores they will accept coupons from, but they might give you a mile radius you can go by. It's best to just give the store a call and find out exactly what competitor coupons they accept if they aren't listed in the coupon policy. If they accept store coupons, this can be an even bigger savings for you, especially if you don't have to travel to another store to get the additional savings.

Stacking Coupons and Getting Rain Checks

The store coupon policy will also outline the rules for stacking coupons in their store. Stacking coupons is when you use one manufacturer coupon and one store coupon on the same item. This is allowed because they are not both manufacturer coupons. Most stores will honor stacking coupons; if your store doesn't, they will state that in their store policy. The store coupon may not just be a coupon for a specific product, but it could also be for a dollar amount off your purchase. These are both coupons that will save you more money if you can stack them with manufacturer coupons. So it's good to know beforehand how the store will handle them.

Rain checks are important if the store runs out of items quickly during a sale. If the store offers rain checks, then you'll be able to get the sale price at a later date. Check your store's coupon policy to see if they issue rain checks and if there are any rules to follow when redeeming them, along with any restrictions. This will come in handy if there's a product you really want to get at the sale price. It's nice to know beforehand if you can expect to get a rain check if they are out of stock.

How Does the Store Handle Overages?

Handling overages when using coupons is definitely something that varies from store to store. An overage is when the value of the coupon is more than the cost of the item, so you get money back. Some stores will offer the overage, which you can then apply to another item, and some stores will adjust down the coupon to make the item free rather than give you the overage. This will vary greatly from store to store, and it also may be something that isn't very clear to the cashiers and even the managers. Be sure you know how your store handles overages so you can plan your shopping trip, and be prepared to have to teach the cashier as well.

Where to Find Store Coupon Policies

The first place to look for a coupon policy is online at the store's website. This would be the best place for them to keep the policy so that it can be accessed by anyone, at any time. You may have to do a little searching to find it as it probably won't be advertised on the front page. If you're having trouble locating it, look along the footer of the home page where the small print is and you will find links like "Contact Us" or "About Us." There may also be one that says "Coupons," which will lead you to a page that has more information on using coupons. If you can't find anything along the bottom of the page, try along the top. If you still don't have any luck and there is a search box, try typing in "coupon policy" and see if anything comes up.

If the store has store coupons or printable coupons that you can print directly from their website, then there is a good chance that somewhere on that page, there will be a policy on using these coupons. It may not be anything in great detail, but there may be some sort of guidelines and perhaps even the entire coupon policy.

Request a Copy of the Store Coupon Policy

If your store doesn't have the coupon policy on their website, then you should contact them to get a copy of the policy so you know the rules and can avoid any problems at the store. You can either call customer service, send them an e-mail, or if you'd like to do it the old-fashioned way, you can mail them a letter requesting a copy be sent to you.

ALERT

Even if the store has a copy of their coupon policy online, you should request a copy be mailed to you as well. Having a hard copy that came directly from the store that contains your name and address and is printed on their letterhead is more credible than something you print online. It may help avoid any hassles in the store since it's an official letter written to you and signed by someone of importance.

When requesting a copy of the coupon policy, you'll want to make sure that certain issues are addressed. You'll want to know their policy on double and triple coupons, competitors' coupons, price matching, stacking coupons, using coupons with sales, rain checks, and overages. These are the more common issues that will arise while shopping and using coupons. Once you receive this letter, make a copy and take it with you while you shop and have it handy if questioned about your coupon usage.

Keep a Copy of the Coupon Policy with You

When you obtain the coupon policy of the stores you shop at most, it's best to print out copies and keep them either in your coupon binder or somewhere you can grab them easily and take them into the stores with you, just in case you need them. Not all cashiers and managers are properly trained on coupon usage, and some even think it's cheating to use coupons. If you have the coupon policy handy when shopping, you can take it out and show them exactly what their store policy is. You may be more knowledgeable on the subject than the store employees. Believe it or not, they may not even know there is a coupon policy until you show them.

What Do You Do with It?

Once you find the store's coupon policy, make sure you read it thoroughly so you know how they handle coupons and what limitations the store may have. If you are a big coupon user, you'll want to learn it so you don't have to keep referring back to it. If there is a big difference from one store to the other, after shopping with them and using coupons for a while, you'll learn who allows what. Don't assume that the employees will know the store's coupon policy, because some may not.

The store employees, including the manager, should know the store's coupon policy, right? Well, that may not always be the case. It may be up to you to tell them what the policy is. The best thing you can do, to avoid any confusion or problems while at the checkout, is to have a copy of the coupon policy with you. Then, if there are any questions or they deny you the use of a coupon, you can whip out the coupon policy to show them that what you're doing is acceptable according to their store.

Managers Have the Right to Override the Policies

You must keep in mind that managers will sometimes have the authority to override the coupon policy, which means even if the policy says you can do something, you still may not be able to. The manager may have to alter the policy to fit his or her store's need. Meaning, the store may have had a problem with coupons in the past, and therefore it needed to change the policy just for that store. It's unfortunate when this happens, but there isn't much you can do about it.

If a store tells you that you can't use a coupon the way the coupon policy says you can, check with corporate to make sure that store is an exception to the rule, just to make sure that the manager isn't trying to make up his own rules, or just doesn't understand the policy. It will only take a phone call, which is an easy enough thing to do.

Teaching the Cashiers the Coupon Policy

There is nothing worse than getting to the cash register after shopping a well-planned-out shopping trip to be turned down when trying to use your coupons. It's extremely frustrating, especially if you've done your research on using coupons at that particular store. For someone who doesn't like confrontations, this could halt your coupon usage. Then all the time you've spent learning, collecting, sorting, and organizing has been wasted. Don't let that stop you; be prepared for this to happen at any store, at any time, and learn how to overcome this obstacle.

ESSENTIAL

A good portion of cashiers are high school students, and unfortunately they probably don't really care about what coupons you are using. So it may be up to you to school them in coupon usage. Be prepared to tell them why you are using a coupon and if you have the coupon policy with you, then show them the rules according to the store.

You may have to teach the cashier the coupon policy if they aren't aware of how to use coupons in their store. Chances are, if they don't use coupons themselves, they may have no idea how to use them. It also could be as simple as them not having learned the policy because either they were not trained on it, or they just haven't been working there long enough to learn it. Some stores may have a very high turnover rate for cashiers, which will mean there's always a new person at the register.

Using Store Policies to Your Advantage

If you know your store's coupon policy, then you'll save as much as you can each week. Saving money doesn't happen just by using coupons. There are so many other ways to save along with using coupons and you want to learn as much as you possibly can so you can save the most.

If your store doubles coupons, you want to know when and how so that you can plan to use your coupons on the days they are doubled to save even more. If they price match, you want to know so you can avoid a trip to another store. Being able to use a competitor's coupons at your favorite store is going to save you much more money, especially if that coupon is a store coupon and you can stack it with manufacturers' coupons. Knowing what your store will and will not allow will save you money in the end.

QUESTION

How often do stores change their coupon policies?
The store could update their coupon policy at any time. They may have a regular schedule of going over their policies to be sure they are not losing money or customers, due to the current policy. They may only change the policy when they have a problem or see a need to. It's best to check every six months to see if there are any changes. If you have a written copy directly from the store of their coupon policy, you want to make sure you receive an updated copy at least once a year.

Save Time by Knowing the Rules

Knowing the store's coupon policy can also be a huge timesaver while shopping. If you know what the store's coupon policy is, you won't waste your time bringing coupons and planning deals that you won't be able to complete. The store may have a limit on how many items can be purchased when on sale, so if you dig out coupons for ten items, but they have a limit of four items when on sale, you just wasted a lot of time finding those coupons. Being prepared will always save you time.

Dealing with Difficult Employees

One of the biggest reasons people don't coupon very often is the hassle they receive at the stores while using coupons. Not everyone misuses coupons; there are a lot of people who spend time figuring out exactly what coupons they can use and how they can use them properly. These people know what they are doing, so being told they can't do something is very frustrating and embarrassing. At one point or another it will happen to you, so be prepared for how to handle it before you shop.

The best way you can avoid this is by making completely sure that you are using the proper coupons on the proper products. It's very easy to get confused or to miss something. Make sure you read the wording on the coupon and don't just go by the picture. If the picture is different on the coupon than what the coupon actually says, be prepared to explain to the cashier why you can use that coupon.

Remain Calm at All Times and Don't Make Enemies

The best way to get anything is to remain calm and to not cause a scene. If you are a problem, they may not let you back in the store again. It's hard sometimes to stay calm, but do the best you can. Explain to the cashier why you are using the coupons you are using as best as you can. If he still won't let you use them, then ask for the manager and do the same thing with her. If that still doesn't work, you're better off leaving the store and calling the main office when you get home.

Making enemies at your local stores isn't the best way to go about it. If they don't like you because you use coupons, then there is nothing you can do about it. But if you give them a reason not to like you, then shopping there isn't going to be easy. If that is the only store in the area, you'll miss out on a lot of deals if they won't let you shop there anymore. It may be worth missing a deal here and there because they don't let you use a certain coupon than to miss them all because they've banned you from the store.

Teach the Cashier about Coupons

If the cashier gives you a hard time about using coupons or tells you what a waste of time they are, then nicely explain to her how much you just saved by using the coupons. Encourage her to use them as well, and maybe even share a coupon you have so she can also grab the deal. If you explain it to her, she may understand it more and realize she shouldn't give you a hard time and that what you're doing is perfectly okay. If the cashier is a coupon user, she is more apt to be friendlier when you are using coupons.

ESSENTIAL

Keep a copy of the store ad in your shopping cart while shopping. Be prepared to pull it out if there are any questions about your transaction. It's possible the cashier doesn't know what's on sale, and if you have the ad there to show her, you'll spend less time at the checkout. But be sure that ad is for your particular store, as sales can vary from location to location.

The Store Employees Think You're Stealing

There is nothing worse than an anti-coupon user ringing up your order. He will make you feel like you are doing something wrong and may even tell you that you are stealing from the store by using so many coupons. As long as coupons are issued, then the manufacturer wants you to use them. And as long as the store's policy is to accept coupons, then you can use them. Just make sure that you are using them properly.

Stop Giving Them Your Business

If you continue to have problems and no one will do anything about it, including corporate, then perhaps it's time to find another store to shop at. Even if you have to spend a little more somewhere else, no deal is worth it if you are given a hard time every time you shop. If you know that you are using coupons properly, and no one at the company will help you to use them hassle-free, then they obviously don't want your business and you shouldn't give it to them. Another store will be more than happy to have you as a customer.

CHAPTER 10

Loyalty Programs

Every store wants your business, but they have competition and need to give people a reason to shop at their store. As a result, store loyalty programs were born. The idea behind these programs is to offer discounts that you hopefully can't pass up. These stores believe if they give you lots of incentives to shop at their store, you will. The hope is that the loyalty programs will get you in the door, and then you'll do all your shopping there. In many areas these stores are a dime a dozen; therefore you can take advantage of all the store loyalty programs, and still shop around!

Store Incentives

The stores know you have lots of options; therefore, they like to give incentives so you'll shop at their store and hopefully come back each week. Depending on the store and what they sell, the incentives may vary. Every time you walk into a store you should be looking around for the ways they offer to save even more money than the everyday sales. These are what the stores call loyalty programs or store incentives. These incentives could be store coupons, hot sales, or some other form of reward that is specific to their store. Nowadays it's very hard to find a store that does not offer you incentives, which is great since saving money should be your number one goal.

Using Competitors' Coupons

Some stores will even honor some of their competitors' incentives. The store coupons pretty much represent a loss that the company takes, as most manufacturers don't reimburse them for store coupons. It's a loss they take to get your business. Other stores will sometimes take their competitors' coupons in the hope that even if you receive the other stores' coupons, you'll still come to their store to shop. Of course, they want you to spend all your money in their store, so they are willing to lose a little bit to gain your business. Check with your local stores to see if they take competitors' coupons or honor any of their competitors' loyalty programs. It doesn't hurt to ask.

Drugstore Programs

Drugstores are known for great programs that offer savings on products they know you need to buy. They want to make it convenient for you so that when you're picking up your prescriptions, you'll do the rest of your shopping while you are there. Some people don't realize the wonderful deals that you can get at the drugstores on health and beauty products, paper products, over-the-counter medicines, and even everyday food staple items.

Perhaps you never thought about picking up bread or milk while getting your prescriptions. You probably assumed that even if the drugstore did carry them that they would be much more expensive than at the grocery store. Well, you might be surprised, because when the drugstores put those items on sale, they are sometimes cheaper than at the grocery stores. Of course, this will vary depending on your area, but it's worth a look next time you're there.

ESSENTIAL

CVS, Walgreens, and Rite Aid are the three biggest national drug-stores. They each have their own rewards program, and they all differ slightly, but what it comes down to is they reward you for making purchases in their store in the form of a coupon. You are required to make a qualifying purchase in order to receive the coupon, but the best part is, you can use coupons on those purchases to maximize your savings.

CVS Extra Care Program

CVS offers you Extra Care Bucks when you purchase qualifying items, as well as on everyday purchases, beauty products, and prescriptions. With the cost of health care, it's nice to get a little something back for prescriptions that you need! But one of the greatest incentives at CVS is the 2 percent cash back for your quarterly spending. This includes all products whether they were on sale or not. You'll receive the 2 percent cash back four times a year, and it's issued the first day of the quarter in the form of an Extra Care Buck. Extra Care Bucks are store coupons you can use on your next purchase, excluding prescriptions, tobacco, and a few other items. These Extra Care Bucks are like free money just for shopping at their store.

Earn Extra Care Bucks on Purchases Each Week

CVS also offers Extra Care Bucks every week on different products. Essentially, they give you an instant rebate back on certain purchases. The products are listed in their weekly ad, and they are always on sale, too. And let's not forget, you can use coupons on these purchases and still receive the same Extra Care Bucks rewards. And the best part is, if you roll your Extra Care Bucks from week to week, you can score items for free or close to it! Here is an example: One week toothpaste is on sale for $2.99, and you'll receive $1.99 Extra Care Bucks with this purchase. You also have a coupon for $1.00 off the toothpaste. You pay $1.99 after the coupon and receive $1.99 Extra Care Bucks. Then the next week shampoo is on sale for $2.99, you'll receive $2.00 Extra Care Bucks with that purchase and you have a $1.00 coupon for that shampoo. When you use the $1.99 Extra Care Bucks from the previous week combined with the $1.00 shampoo coupon, you will receive the shampoo for free since it's on sale for $2.99. You will also receive another $2.00 Extra Care Bucks to use next time you shop. You can then hold that for the next week or use it to pick up something you need that may or may not be on sale, like milk. But if you keep it for the next week, you can roll it into another transaction like the toothpaste and shampoo transactions. This is how people get things for free at CVS.

FACT

If you scan your CVS Extra Care card at the coupon printing center when you get to the store, you will not receive any coupons on your receipt when you make your purchases. You can only receive the coupons one way or the other. However, when you scan your card, be sure to scan it up to three times because you may get more coupons. The key is to keep scanning it until the machine tells you that there are no more coupons available.

Earn Extra Care Bucks for Your Prescriptions

CVS also has a program in which you'll receive Extra Care Bucks for your pharmacy purchases. For every two prescriptions you fill at CVS, no matter how you pay for them, you'll receive a $1.00 Extra Care Buck. These rewards are issued at the beginning of the quarter for the previous quarter. CVS has other programs in their pharmacy, including one for diabetes. Check with your local store for more information and to see if you qualify.

CVS Store Coupons

CVS offers their customers store coupons that you can receive several ways; the easiest one to find is on your receipt when you make a purchase. They print out almost every time you shop and since they are store coupons, you can combine them with manufacturer coupons and sales to save even more. If you'd like to check to see what coupons are available before you shop, scan your card at the coupon printing center and maybe you'll get lucky and receive a coupon for something that you are purchasing already. You may also receive a coupon for either a free product or a certain dollar amount off your entire order. Those are especially great since the total purchase required is before coupons. If you register your card online, you will occasionally receive CVS store coupons in your e-mail in-box.

Rite Aid Savings Program

Rite Aid has a few different savings programs to help customers save on their everyday products including rebates, +UP rewards, and store coupons. Their program is similar to CVS's; you'll earn rewards for making qualifying purchases during the week, and a reward after spending a certain amount of money in the store. They also offer discounts on their store-brand products, which is really nice since you don't normally find coupons for store-brand products. To receive these savings, you are required to sign up for a wellness+ Rewards Card, which you will then present to the cashier each time you shop, to track savings and receive your rewards. If you forget your card, they can look it up with your phone number as long as you register it online. You can sign up online or in the store to receive your card, and it will fit on your keychain with all the other rewards cards, just in case you didn't have enough already!

QUESTION

Will the shopping passes at Rite Aid work with sale prices?
If the Rite Aid store-brand product is on sale and you give the cashier your wellness+ card, you'll receive the lower price of the two amounts as your final discount. If the 10 percent off is greater than the sale price, you'll receive that discount. If it's not, you'll receive the sale price. This is the same for the 10 percent and 20 percent shopping pass you can earn for all your items. You'll always receive the greater discount and you'll know that you will save at least 10 percent to 20 percent depending on the shopping pass.

Once you receive your wellness+ card, you'll be eligible for savings on products just for having the card. These items will be noted in the sale ad for those who have a wellness+ card. You will also receive 10 percent off Rite

Aid brand-name products every day. If you purchase enough products, that can add up to a nice savings!

Earn Points for Every Dollar You Spend

At the same time that you are saving with the wellness+ card, you're also accumulating points that then turn into rewards. Each time you shop at Rite Aid and have your wellness+ card scanned, you'll receive points for your purchases. The more points you receive, the higher your member level will be, and the greater your reward. For every 125 points, you'll get a one-time 10 percent shopping pass. This coupon is good on regular-priced items and some sale items. You can also use coupons along with this shopping pass to save even more! So that would be the perfect time to purchase that item that you need that never goes on sale. When you reach 500 points and Silver status, you'll receive another 10 percent shopping pass, but this one is good for the rest of the calendar year. It will work just like the other shopping pass, and it is for some sale items and regular-priced items. If you continue to spend more during that calendar year and reach Gold level with 1,000 points, you'll then receive a 20 percent shopping pass that will also be valid through the end of the calendar year. It's a nice incentive for you to continue to shop at their store, and it's a great way to save on those items that either never go on sale or for which you can never find coupons.

Single Check Rebate Program at Rite Aid

Rite Aid also has a rebate program in which you'll receive cash back in the form of a rebate check at the end of the month for making qualifying purchases. These items are noted in the weekly ad, but they also have a special ad in the store with all the Single Check Rebate items for the entire month. You can find that ad in the store with the weekly ads. When you purchase the qualifying items, you can use coupons with them as well and when combining the two, you will sometimes receive the items for free—or even better, make money on them. For example, toothbrushes might be on sale for $2.99 and you'll receive a $2.99 Single Check Rebate back, making the item free after the rebate. You might also have a coupon for $1.00 off the toothbrushes, which means you'll only pay $1.99 at the store and then receive a Single Check Rebate for $2.99 with a final profit of $1.00.

It's very easy to submit the Single Check Rebates because you can do it online. All you need is the receipt and some information from it. First, sign up online at *www.RiteAid.com*. Look for "Single Check Rebates." Once you sign up and log in, you can view the offers for that month, enter receipts, and then at the end of the month, request your check. Do not request your check before the month is over or you won't be able to submit any more receipts for the remainder of the month. You have about thirty days after the month ends to submit your receipts and request your check. If you don't manually request your check, it will be automatically sent after the extended time period is up. You will then receive a check that you can cash, deposit, or use at Rite Aid toward your next purchase. You can check the status of your rebate anytime online.

Rite Aid Store Coupons

Rite Aid has several types of store coupons, which can be used with manufacturer coupons and on-sale items, to save you even more. You can find store coupons in the weekly ad. They might say "manufacturer coupon" on them, but as long as the bar code begins with "RA," they are store coupons. You would not be able to use them anywhere else like you would manufacturer coupons.

ALERT

You must actually watch the Rite Aid Video Values videos in order to receive the coupons. How will they know? If you click into another window or open another program, the video will automatically stop and you'll have to go back to the beginning and start over. When the video is over, you need to enter a code to verify that you are sitting there watching the video. If you don't enter the code in the time allowed, you'll need to start over again.

Another place you can find Rite Aid store coupons is online at *www .RiteAid.com*. You'll find a section of the website called Video Values. There are short videos for all sorts of products, including items they will have on sale that month. Once you watch a video, you'll be able to print out a coupon for that item. You'll know beforehand exactly what the coupon is for, so you can decide if you want it or not. What's great about these coupons is they change monthly and while you have to watch the videos before the end of the month, you don't have to print or use the coupons until the end of the following month.

Walgreens Register Rewards

Walgreens's customer loyalty program is different from the other drugstores, but that doesn't mean it's harder to follow. The biggest difference is you don't have a card to scan. Anyone can receive the sale prices and participate in the program. They offer two things to their customers as incentives to shop at their store: the Register Rewards program and store coupons. Both of them work with sales and with manufacturer coupons to maximize your savings. Taking advantage of these programs will score you free items and even allow you to make money on some purchases, as well.

The Register Rewards program is similar to the other drugstore programs; you'll receive a coupon for money off your next purchase for making qualifying purchases that are listed in the weekly ad. You can use coupons, which will help you get items for free and even make money on purchases too! For example, shampoo might be on sale for $3.99 and you'll receive a $3.99 Register Rewards coupon to use on your next purchase. You might have a $1.00 coupon for the shampoo, which means that you'll only spend $2.99, so you will make $1.00 on that purchase. You can use the Register Rewards coupon from your purchase on almost anything. There are some restrictions and they are noted on the coupon.

Register Rewards coupons can be used on sale items, and you can use other coupons along with them, but you have to be careful. The system reads the Register Rewards coupons as manufacturer coupons, and since you can only use one manufacturer coupon per item, you cannot use the Register Rewards coupon if you are using a manufacturer coupon. As long as you have more items than manufacturer coupons, you can use the Register Rewards coupon in the same transaction. If you know this ahead of time, plan on grabbing a small item as a "filler" like a pack of gum or pencil. Otherwise you won't be able to use the Register Reward along with all your coupons.

You can use a Register Rewards coupon that you just received to purchase another of the same item, but you will not receive another coupon the second time. However, you will reduce the price of the item by the Register Rewards coupon, and possibly make it free. If you use the Register Rewards coupon to purchase a different item that also produces a Register Rewards coupon, you will receive that one since it's a different item, unless it's part of the same reward.

Walgreens also has store coupons that change weekly and monthly and can be combined with manufacturer coupons. You can find them in several places. Each week in the sales ad, there will be coupons that you need to clip in order to receive the sale price or discount at the time of your purchase. You can combine these coupons with manufacturer coupons. Usually there are limits noted on the coupon for how many items you can purchase at that price or discount. They also have a coupon booklet each month with coupons that you can use all month long. You can find it in the store next to the weekly ads. Some of the items that have coupons in this booklet may go on sale throughout the month to help you save even more. They are store coupons as well, and they don't normally have limits on them, but it's always best to read the entire coupon for any exclusions. You can also find these coupons online at *www.walgreens.com* and print them out.

ESSENTIAL

Walgreens is testing a new program in some areas, in which you receive points when you shop and then you turn those points into coupons. This system replaces the Register Rewards program. It's a test program that may or may not be rolled out nationally. If it does, then the Register Rewards program will change.

It's best to keep your eye out in Walgreens for more coupons, since there is occasionally a store coupon booklet somewhere in the aisles or at the pharmacy. If you follow any blogs that cover Walgreens's deals, they will alert you to a new coupon booklet when it's discovered.

Grocery Store Programs

Some areas have a different grocery store on every corner, which can make deciding where to shop that much harder. As there is so much competition, the stores will do whatever they can to get your business. This means they will try to offer deals that you may not be able to get down the street at their competitor's store. Thankfully, the grocery store programs are pretty similar to one another, which makes your life a little bit easier.

Double and Triple Coupons

Along with the different store prices and regional coupon values, stores in different regions also have different policies on how they will accept coupons; for example, if they will double or triple a coupon. If you have the $.50 coupon that is good off one item and your store doubles coupons, you'll actually receive $1.00 off the one item. If your store triples coupons, then that $.50 coupon now turns into $1.50 off the item. Triple coupons are more rare than double coupons and are almost always limited to a few per transaction. Some stores may have specials during which they offer triple coupons, but not on a regular basis.

Store Coupons

Grocery stores offer store coupons that can be combined with manufacturer coupons and sales. You can find these coupons in their weekly ads and sometimes in the stores themselves. It's also great to register your grocery card with your home address and then you may get some coupons sent right to your house. You can register your card by either giving them your home address, when you apply for it, or by going online afterward and filling in your account information. Some stores will reward their loyal customers with great savings for either a particular item or a dollar amount off your entire purchase. Coupons like this are sometimes accepted at a competitor's store, so if you do receive them, check with the other stores to see if they will honor them. It doesn't hurt to ask!

Loss Leaders

Loss leaders are those items that the stores use to get you into the stores. These items are offered at rock-bottom prices that you won't want to pass up. The stores figure that if they lower the price enough on some items, you'll come to their store that week and do your entire shopping. In other words, you'll pay full price for everything else you need. But if you are a smart shopper, you will plan on buying those items only and anything else that's on sale and then move on. No one says you have to purchase everything at one store.

How can you find the loss leaders easily? They are usually the items on the front page of the sales ad. The store wants to get your attention with these items and they won't if they are buried on page four. By scanning the front page of each ad, you can easily locate the loss leaders for that week at each store. To get the most bang for your buck, only purchase those items and use coupons if you can.

Other Store Programs

Each store will tailor incentives to their customers. And with regional differences, some stores may have a special offer for their customers that other stores don't. For instance, some may accept expired coupons for a short period of time after they expire. This would be done at the store's or manager's discretion but it's not unheard of. Other stores may have weeks in which they have dollar sales or buy-one-get-one-free sales on canned goods. That's obviously a great time to stock up. But with a sale like that, you have to be sure to watch the sale price and the regular price as sometimes the discount isn't as great as it seems.

Lots of stores are now also offering you a discount on gas according to how much you spend. What's great about this is it doesn't require you to change your spending habits; instead it just rewards you for spending. Gas prices are near an all-time high right now, so any savings on that is helpful. It almost makes it worth driving to the grocery store.

ALERT

The gas programs will unfortunately mean longer lines at the gas pump. If you constantly find a line at the pump, save up your points until it's worth it to wait your turn. If you are saving $.50 off a gallon, it may be worth that little bit of a wait to get your savings.

How this works is the store gives you so many points for your spending and then coverts them into gas savings by the gallon. They also run specials in which if you buy certain products, you'll receive a bonus in gas savings. This can be a good time to consider stocking up on products if the price point is good. Keeping a grocery notebook will help you figure that out too.

Get Paid to Use Reusable Bags

Reusable bags have become more and more popular. Between the costs for the grocery stores and the lack of room in the landfills, the need to reduce the use of plastic bags has become a big concern. More and more stores are offering incentives, often in the form of money back, to those who bring their own bags. They don't care what bags you use. They can be from their store, from another store, or whatever you have. But if you use them, they will give you a discount off your order for each bag you use. Even if you have to purchase the bags up front, they pay for themselves and then some in a very short amount of time. It's free money for helping out the environment.

CHAPTER 11

Saving on Fresh Produce, Meats, and Organics

Some people think that those who use coupons buy only unhealthy processed foods. They draw this conclusion when looking quickly at coupons because a lot of them are for this type of food. However, you can use coupons and save money on other items besides nonperishable processed foods. Will you find coupons for them all? Probably not. However, if you shop properly and save on everything else, you have more money to spend on those items that you don't have coupons for. But there are other ways to save on fresh produce, meats, and organics; it just takes some planning and possibly some rearranging.

Shop Meat Markdowns

Every cut of meat has a limit on the number of days it can sit in the grocery store before they can no longer sell it. If they just threw away all that meat, they'd be wasting a lot of money on meat that can still be used. So instead of tossing it all, they mark it down to offer incentives for people to purchase the meat. The meat is still perfectly fine to purchase and eat. It can even still be kept in the refrigerator for a few more days. But the stores can no longer keep it in their coolers.

FACT

Shopping markdowns is a great way of getting organic food that might not otherwise go on sale. With organic food prices being higher than nonorganic foods, there's a good chance that they will not sell out before the food is no longer fresh enough for the store to sell. If you shop the markdowns, you'll receive a nice savings on something you otherwise might not have purchased.

If you take advantage of meat markdowns, you can grab meat at a fantastic price, a price you may not even get when it's on sale. If you plan it right, you can possibly purchase all your meat and poultry this way and never pay full price for meat.

Become Friends with Your Butcher

Having your grocery store butcher as your friend can come in handy. And not because he can give you free meat, because he can't. But he may be able to give you some inside information on when the meat is generally marked down. The store may do this daily or only a few times a week. But if you know when to expect it, you can try to shop those days and get the pick of the litter when it comes to marked-down meats.

If you shop regularly at one store, or even two stores, say hello to the people working in the meat department so you become a familiar face. It may seem silly at first but if they see you smile at them, they may be more apt to be friendly. Then when you see some marked-down meat, ask them if this is something they do at a particular time of the day, or a certain day of the week. Ask about their routine for marking down meat and if they can tell you when they do it so you can stop by and see what they are trying to get rid of. They may be more than happy to share this information, because after all, they want to sell the meat rather than taking a total loss.

Plan to Stock Up with Meat Markdowns

If you can't find out about the markdown routine or you are just too shy to ask, then be sure to always be on the lookout for something marked down, and purchase it before someone else does. You can always allocate a portion of your monthly budget just for meat markdowns to stock up your freezer. And as long as it's in your budget, grab it. If you don't find many markdowns one month, carry the unused money from your budget over to the next month, and then you'll have more room for stocking up. Meat can cost a lot of money each month, but if you stock up with the markdowns, you can cut that cost in half, if not more!

You don't have to use much of your budget for stocking up on meat. You can start with as little as 5 percent of your monthly grocery budget. There may be months that 5 percent gets you less than others depending on what you find, but any little bit that you can stock up will be money saved. For example, if your monthly grocery budget is $800, then 5 percent of that will be $40. Take that $40 and put it aside to only stock up on meat that is marked down. It may not seem like much, but $40 can go a long way when purchasing discounted meat. Each time you shop, scan the meat department for the markdowns and see what items would work best that will fit your budget.

Precook and Freeze

Of course if you get the fresh food at a good price, you'll still want to make sure you use it before it goes bad; otherwise it wasn't such a great price. This may require a little bit of time and effort on your part, but if it's saving you money in the long run, it's worth it. Besides, you'll be saving yourself time later in the week or month by being a little prepared. You can also recruit your family to help and, at the same time, spend quality time together and teach the little ones a few things!

Precook Meat to Freeze and Save Time

If you stock up on some markdown meat, then you'll have to either cook it or freeze it within a few days before it's no longer any good. But you don't need to spend a lot of time doing this. Just about anything can be precooked and frozen and it will be as fresh as it was once it's thawed out. You don't need to make the complete meal; just cook the meat. If you normally use it ground up, then cook it and put it in freezer bags according to how much you will use with your recipe. Be sure to write the date and contents of the package on the freezer bag so you know what it is.

Prepare Foods from Bulk Packaging

If you would prefer to make some burgers out of the ground beef, chicken, or turkey that you purchased at a good price in bulk, you can form the patties and then freeze them individually. You may want to flash-freeze them first by putting them on a cookie sheet in a single layer in the freezer until they are almost completely frozen. Then you can stack them in the freezer bag and they won't stick together. This is great if you only want to use a few at a time; you won't have to thaw out the entire package.

If you find a good deal on chicken pieces in bulk, split the package up in the size that you'll use for cooking. Add any seasonings or marinades before you freeze them; then when you thaw out the package, it will be ready to cook. This is also a great way of using up dressings, marinades, and sauces that are close to expiring.

Preparing Ahead of Time

If you find a great deal on meat or poultry, you can always prepare an entire meal ahead of time and then freeze it to eat at a later date. This is perfect for the person who doesn't have time to come home and cook a complete meal, but also doesn't want to eat takeout or processed foods for dinner each night. If you prepare ahead of time, you can avoid spending the extra money and get a fresh meal as well.

Most foods can be frozen, especially after they have been cooked! You can prepare your meals ahead of time in two ways. You can double up when you are making a meal and then freeze half for another time, or you could spend a day cooking and making meals that can be frozen for later in the week. Remember, you're doing this with meat or poultry that you purchased at a discount because it could no longer be sold at the store, so you want to cook it or freeze it before it goes bad.

Freeze Leftovers So They Won't Go to Waste

How many times did you have food leftover from a meal that sat in the refrigerator all week long and no one ate it? Now you have to throw it in the trash because it's no longer good. Even if you saved money on the purchase, it's now wasted money. If you immediately freeze the leftovers, then you won't be wasting them. If someone wants the leftovers later in the week, you can pop them in the oven or microwave for quick reheating. It will only take a few extra steps to freeze them, and then you won't waste your money.

Have Leftovers for Lunch and Save Every Day

Frozen leftovers are also great to take to work or school for lunch because they will probably thaw out before you are ready to eat them. Then you have a fresh meal instead of going out to eat or having fast food. If you invest in some containers that can go from the freezer to the microwave, you'll save in the long run. For example, if you went out for lunch one day, you'd spend at least $10. If you purchase a container that you can take your lunch in, you would spend no more than $5 on it. If you use that every day and take something from home to eat instead of spending the $10, you'll save $50 on lunch and only spend $5 on the container the first week. Imagine the savings in just one month!

ESSENTIAL

If you are short on time in the morning, and making a lunch isn't easy to squeeze in before work, grab a frozen leftover meal, toss it in a bag, and head out the door. By the time you have lunch, it should be thawed out and ready to eat. You may have to heat it up in the microwave for a little while, but it's a great way to use your leftovers and have a healthy lunch.

Now of course you are paying for the food that you are taking with you to lunch—it's not free. But if it's a leftover from dinner that you probably would have tossed in the garbage, then yes, it is like free food.

Flash-Freezing and Buying Frozen

You don't need to purchase fresh to get fresh foods. Lots of items that are frozen have been frozen fresh and when they thaw, they will still be fresh. When vegetables are out of season, they can be extremely expensive, but the price of frozen vegetables stays the same all year long, and they go on sale in regular intervals. Some items are just as good frozen and are easier on the budget.

However, when fruits and vegetables are in season, you may be able to score a better deal on the fresh ones than on frozen. When this happens, you want to stock up as much as your budget allows. You will probably be purchasing more than you'll use before it goes bad, so you'll need to do a little planning and prepping to make sure it doesn't go to waste. If you like to cook with some vegetables, you can chop them up and flash-freeze them for use later. Then you'll have fresh vegetables to use when you want them and not pay full price.

How to Flash-Freeze

Flash-freezing is when you freeze fresh items at a very low temperature to preserve all the liquid inside. If you have a regular freezer, you don't have the ability to lower the temperature enough to do a true flash-freeze, but you can do something along the same lines that will work just as well. Flash-freezing is helpful when you want to freeze food that you don't want to stick together once frozen. By not sticking together, you can take just a little out at a time to use.

Flash-freezing is helpful when you find fresh fruits and vegetables at a great price and you want to stock up and take advantage of the great price. You use what you can while it's fresh and then flash-freeze the rest for later use. Before you flash-freeze, you may want to prepare your fruits and vegetables so you can easily use them at a later date. The best way to do this would be to chop them up to prepare for freezing.

Once the vegetables are chopped and ready to be frozen, you'll want to get a cookie sheet or something else that will allow the pieces to lay flat. First you lay them out in a single layer, being sure not to let the pieces touch so that they don't freeze stuck together. Next you'll want to put the cookie sheet in the freezer until the items are completely frozen. Once they are frozen you can transfer them to a bag and store it in the freezer. Then when you want to use them, you can take out as much as you want.

ESSENTIAL

It may be worth it to invest in some reusable freezer containers. Make sure that they stack easily and can go from freezer to microwave for easy use. Find containers that you can write on so you will know what's inside and the date it was put in—this way you'll be more likely to use the food rather than toss it. As long as you plan on using the containers over and over, they will pay for themselves in no time.

Buy Frozen Vegetables for Cooking

If you cook with fresh vegetables, have you ever considered buying frozen vegetables to save money? If you save the fresh vegetables for only when you are eating them raw, you can probably cut down your grocery bill a substantial amount by purchasing frozen vegetables to use while cooking. And guess what? There are coupons for lots of frozen vegetables and they go on sale so you can save even more!

If you like to bake with fresh fruits, you might also want to try frozen fruits. They are frozen fresh, work just as well in recipes, and cost much less than fresh fruits. Frozen fruits are also perfect for smoothies and to add to yogurt and ice cream for a special treat!

Splitting the Purchase

You may have noticed that the meat department likes to price the bulk packages of meats and poultry better than the smaller packages. They do this to get you to purchase more. They figure if they give it to you for a good price, then you'll want to buy it no matter how big the package is. It's a savings, right?

Unfortunately it may not always fit your budget, especially during weeks when just about every cut of meat is priced great in bulk packages. It may be priced the best you've seen it in a while. You even have room in your freezer for it . . . if only you had the room in your budget. This would be the perfect time to get a friend to split the packages and split the cost. It may sound silly but if you purchase bulk packages of ground beef, chicken breasts, pork chops, and rib eye steaks and split them with a friend, you could possibly save a lot of money and stock your freezer at the same time.

For example, ground beef may be priced $4.99/lb. in the 1-pound packages but the 5-pound package is on sale for $2.99/lb. That's a very nice savings, but you don't have an extra $15 in your grocery budget that week to purchase the five-pound package. If you found a friend to pay half the cost and split half the meat you can get 2½ pounds at $2.99/lb. and spend only $7.48 instead of $12.48 (if purchased at $4.99/lb.) for a savings of $5! It's like getting a pound of hamburger for free.

Buy a Meat Bundle or a Cow with a Friend

The meat department may offer bundles of a mix of different cuts of meat at great prices, but there may be more than you can afford to purchase, or even use. However, if it's a great price it may be hard to pass up. This is another great opportunity to find a friend or a group of friends who may want to go in on the purchase so you can fill up your freezers. It may be the only way you can even fit certain cuts of meat into your budget. Depending on where you live, you may even be able to purchase an entire cow and split it with friends.

Purchase a Deep Freezer

If you decided to stock up on meats on a regular basis, you may want to consider purchasing a deep freezer to be sure that your meats will last. A deep freezer will keep them at a lower temperature, especially since it's opened less than a regular freezer. The purchase may set you back a bit, but if you plan and save some money for it, in the long run the money you'll save on meat will pay for the freezer over and over again.

You won't want to just run out and purchase the first freezer you see. Shop around to find out what the best price is. Ask around if anyone you know may be getting rid of one or knows of someone who has one he no longer uses. It doesn't have to be a brand-new freezer, as long as it works. Check the local newspaper and even Craigslist to see if anyone is selling one. Or better yet, place a want ad describing exactly what you are looking for and what you are willing to pay for it. It might be easier than you think to score one at a great price.

FACT

Until you fill your freezer, you'll want to fill up bottles of water and put them in the freezer to fill the space. The more you have in there, the more efficiently it will run. It actually works harder to cool an empty freezer than to cool a freezer full of frozen foods. It will also keep it from cooling off when you open up the door.

Using Your Savings on Organics

Organic foods are much more expensive than nonorganic. And while you will find coupons for some organic foods, you won't find coupons for organic fruits, vegetables, or meats. If you really want to feed your family organic foods, it could put a huge dent in your budget. Some items may cost as much as twice the price of nonorganic foods. This makes it extremely difficult to fit them into a tight budget.

Adjust your budget to find the money to use toward organic foods. Use coupons on nonfood items whenever possible so you can save money to use on organic foods. Almost all paper products and health and beauty items can be purchased with coupons. Take the savings you receive from those purchases and apply it toward your organic purchases. You won't be cutting your budget by doing it this way; you'll instead shift the savings from one to afford the other.

For example, one week you need to purchase shampoo, deodorant, and toilet paper. Scan the ads to see who is having a sale on the three items you want to purchase. If you're not brand loyal, it won't be hard to find one store with all three on sale. Next you'll want to find some coupons to use along with the sales to maximize your savings. Let's say the shampoo is on sale from $3.99 to $2.50, the deodorant is on sale from $3.79 to $1.99, and the toilet paper is on sale from $11.99 to $9.99. Already just with sales you're going to save $5.29. Then you find a coupon for $1.00 off the shampoo, $.50 off the deodorant, and $.50 off the toilet paper for an additional $2.00 savings. By purchasing all three of these items on sale and with coupons, you've saved $7.29. Now you can use that $7.29 to purchase some organic foods.

Use Overage and Incentives to Pay for Organic Foods

If you are fortunate enough to score a deal in which you'll receive overage on an item, use that overage toward purchasing organic foods. Or if you earn a coupon for your next shopping trip by purchasing certain products, use that coupon to purchase organic items. For example, you may find a deal in which if you spend $20 on certain health and beauty or paper products in the grocery store, you'll receive a coupon at the checkout for $5 off your next purchase. You may have to stock up on a few items to reach the $20 purchase requirement, but as long as they are products you will use and they are on sale, make the purchase and then use the $5 on an organic purchase. Of course you'll want to be sure that the items you do buy are on sale so you get the most bang for your buck.

Only Purchase Things on Sale

Another way to fit organic items into your budget is to only purchase them when they are on sale. The sale price may never match that of the nonorganic foods, but at least you'll be saving some money off the regular price. When you find something that is at a really good price, stock up and freeze it. And follow the sales cycles so you know when you are truly getting a good deal on organic products.

Ask someone in the produce and meat departments if they ever have to mark down organic foods to sell them. It's possible they don't because their stock may be limited and get depleted. But if they do mark down the organic products, you want to be there when they do so you can get first dibs at some organic foods at great prices.

CHAPTER 12

Get It for Free

If you use your coupons correctly and at the right time, you can score some free items. It's possible to get free stuff all the time, and not just useless gimmick items but items that you will use. It does take some time and planning, but it's very doable. Sometimes you don't even need to do much work to get them; they may be delivered right to your door. Is this legal? It most certainly is. Can anyone do it? You sure can. It's all about knowing the right time and combination of coupons to use. After you learn how, you won't believe that you actually used to pay for these things, when all along you could have been getting them for free!

Travel, Sample, and Small-Sized Purchases

You don't always have to buy in bulk to get the best deal; as a matter of fact, you don't even have to purchase a full-sized product to get a good buy! Sometimes with the right coupons and sales, the smallest-sized items are the best deal, especially when they end up being free. A perfect example of this is travel or trial-sized items. You may not have even thought of purchasing these items, thinking they were a complete waste of time, when in fact you can usually get them for free with coupons.

Have you ever noticed on a coupon where it says "Not Valid on Trial Size?" The manufacturer puts that there so you can't use the coupon on the trial size and get it for free. Most trial-sized items are about $1.00. If you have a coupon for $1.00 off a product that does not have this disclaimer on it, then you can use it on the smallest-sized item and get it for free. If you have a few of these coupons, then you can purchase a few of them and probably get as much as you would in a full-sized product, or close to it.

Next time you're shopping, take a look in the section where your store keeps the trial-sized items. They are usually kept in the same place and sometimes in bins. Scan the section and see what products they have there that you use or would use if you got them for free. Make a list if you have to so you'll remember. Then when you're going through your coupons, keep an eye out to see if you have any coupons for these items. If you do, you'll want to make sure they can be used on trial sizes. If the disclaimer isn't on the coupon, you can use it.

FACT

It can be confusing trying to figure out the difference between what some stores will call a trial-sized item and what they call a travel size. Ultimately they are the same thing; just a smaller size of the original product that can be used when traveling (because they meet the travel requirements) or as a sampling of a product.

Some of these items may be priced at $.99 each or $1.00. You may find that a few of them will be more than that, but generally not many. If your coupon is for $1.00 off the item and it's priced at $.99, you will still get it for free. However, just be prepared that the register is going to beep because the coupon is for more than the item. That is okay. The cashier will do one of two things. Put the coupon through for $1.00 and give you the $.01 overage or adjust the coupon to $.99 and give you the item for free without the $.01 overage. Either way is fine. Of course if they give you the overage, then it's a penny saved on another item.

Problems Using Coupons with Trial/Travel-Sized Items

You may run into problems using coupons on trial-sized items, even if the coupon doesn't exclude trial-sized items. Because the register will beep, the cashier may be hesitant to use the coupon especially if the picture on the coupon is for the full-sized product. If this happens, calmly explain to the cashier that the coupon does not have a size restriction and it does not state on the coupon that it's not valid on the trial size. Therefore using it on this size product is perfectly acceptable.

The store may have this written in their coupon policy, so perhaps it's best to keep a copy of that policy with you at all times. Then you can pull it out to show the cashier or the manager if needed. They may not know the rules. The policy may also state whether they will give you the overage or not. If they don't want to give you the overage, that's fine, as long as they let you use the coupon and get the item for free.

What Can You Do with the Trial-Sized Items?

Once you find you can get the trial-sized items of your favorite products for free, you may wonder what you are going to do with all these small items. They aren't the easiest size to store since they are so small, so they can become a nuisance. But don't let that stop you from getting them. There are so many uses for these small items and since they are free, it's worth it to do something with them.

If it's a product you use often and you happen to have a full-sized bottle handy that is either empty or close to empty, then pour the contents into that bottle and toss the smaller bottles. Just make sure you recycle the smaller bottles or use them for something else. For example, small bottles are fun for little ones to play with in the bathtub. They can pour water in and out of them and will be amused for quite some time.

The trial-sized items are perfect for traveling since they are usually less than the 3-ounce requirement to carry onto a plane. It's also less you have to take back from a trip since you may just use the entire thing while you're there. If you are traveling with your family and plan to do laundry while on vacation, the trial-sized detergents are great to take along and use. Otherwise you'll probably spend an arm and a leg purchasing it at the hotel!

Trial sizes are also great to toss into a diaper bag, your purse, and even the glove compartment of the car. Have you ever been out on a hot day and need some refreshing? A trial-sized deodorant or powder is perfect to take with you for a quick fix-me-up! If you have small children, it's great to have something with you in case the public bathroom doesn't have toilet paper, soap, or even hand towels. Taking along a sample of toilet paper, a small bar of soap, or some wet wipes/baby wipes is perfect for this exact use!

If you have a guest bathroom in your house, trial-sized products are perfect to put together in a nice basket for your guests to use. They may forget something, so rather than having to ask for it, you can have it all prepared for them. Plus the basket will make a nice decoration on your bathroom counter and your guests will be impressed with your hospitality. They don't have to know how you obtained them all. Know some friends who are moving into their first home? Put together the same type of basket so they have all the essentials they need while getting settled into their home. Now your free finds have doubled as a gift as well.

ESSENTIAL

Trial-sized products are perfect to make into care packages for the troops. They can always use them and what fun for them to receive something from home from either someone they know or better yet, someone they don't know. Check the website Packages From Home (*www.packagesfromhome.org*) for a list of items needed and where to send them.

How Much Money Can You Really Save with Trial Sizes?

Because the size of the item is small, you may not be able to visualize the savings that can be made with using your coupon on the trial size to get it for free, rather than just getting the full-sized product for $1.00 less. But when you figure it out, then you'll see how the savings can add up. If you make small changes here and there, they eventually equal a big savings. For example, you may have a $1.00 coupon off toothpaste that is on sale for $3.00. If you use your coupon, you'll get it for only $2.00. But instead, if you use the $1.00 coupon on a trial size, you'll get it for free. If you have three coupons, and get three of the 3-ounce trial-sized toothpastes all for free, then you have 9 ounces of toothpaste for free.

Using Rebates to Get Items for Free

You can also score full-sized items for free with rebates. How many times have you seen a rebate in the newspaper and just thought it was too much trouble to go through for something free? It's really not that much of a hassle, especially if it's a product that you use all the time or could easily use in place of another item. All it costs is a postage stamp, if even that! All you need to do is purchase the product, fill out a short form, and send the company a few items to prove you purchased the item. Sometimes rebates are for the full amount other times it's just for a portion of the cost. But for a few minutes of time, it's worth doing to get cash back.

Why do companies offer rebates? Manufacturers know that one way to get you to try their products is to give them to you for free. If they offer you a full refund on your purchase, then there's a good chance you'll choose theirs over a competitor's. How do they actually make money this way? Their hope is that you'll like the product so much that next time you'll purchase it without a rebate. Of course there is no guarantee but if you don't try it, there's no way of knowing if you'll like it. It's a risk they are willing to take to sell a product. They also realize that not everyone who purchases the item is actually going to fill out the rebate form and request their money back.

Submitting Rebates Online

Sometimes you don't even have to mail anything to receive your rebate back. A few stores let you submit your rebates online, making it even easier to get your money back! It takes even less time to complete the form, and you don't have to spend money on postage.

To submit a rebate online, you'll be required to open an account online at the company's website. If you don't want to use your personal e-mail address, set one up just for rebates or purchases like this. You'll need to give them your mailing address so they know where to send your check. Once you're ready to submit the rebate, you'll need information from your receipt and possibly some information from the product you purchase, but that's it! You will even be able to track your rebate online so you know when it's coming.

Staples and Rite Aid are two stores that let you submit rebates online and it's quick and easy. Once you have your account set up, you'll be ready for next time. Be sure to read each website to find out how to submit your rebate as they may be slightly different from store to store.

ALERT

Rebates are often limited to one per address or per family. Normally you can't use a post office address for a rebate either. Be sure to check the fine print. If you purchase an item in one state and have the rebate sent to someone else in another state trying to cheat the system, you will be caught.

Use Coupons and Make Money on Your Purchases

When purchasing a product for a rebate, you can use a coupon to lower your purchase price. If you do this, then there is a possibility that you'll make money on your purchase. Read the rebate carefully to see if it says that you'll receive the purchase price less any discounts including coupons. If it doesn't, then you'll receive the entire cost of the item before the coupon.

Here is an example of making money with a rebate: You purchase shampoo for $3.99, for which you can submit a $3.99 rebate. You have a $1.00 coupon that you use when making your purchase, which brings your total cost to $2.99. You then submit the rebate for $3.99 and receive a check back for $3.99. You've now made $1.00 on your purchase since you only paid $2.99. Pretty easy money, especially if you were able to submit the rebate online and you didn't even have to pay for postage.

How Much Money Can You Make Submitting Rebates?

If you start submitting rebates regularly, you'll begin to see exactly how much of a difference it makes. To keep track of your rebates, use an Excel spreadsheet or if you don't have access to that, just a notebook will be fine. Be sure to include in the list the date you sent the rebate, what the item was for, what the purchase price was, what you paid for the item, what the rebate is for, and if you are making money on the item. Keep a running total of how much you've saved and how much you've made with these rebates. It's best to also note the date you submitted the rebate and when you receive it, as well.

Rebates can take anywhere from four to twelve weeks to arrive, but if you submit them weekly or monthly, eventually you'll begin to receive checks on a regular basis. It'll almost be like receiving a paycheck. If you submit two rebates a month that are valued at about $3.00 each, that comes to $72 a year. If you made $1.00 on just one of those rebates each month by using a coupon, your total now comes to $84. Imagine how much it would be if you submitted more than two rebates a month or used more coupons! It's entirely possible to make a couple hundred dollars a year submitting rebates for products you would have spent money on anyway.

If you really want to see if it's worth your time, track the amount of time you spend submitting the rebates to see how much you're making an hour. You may be surprised at how much it's worth sending in rebates!

Getting Items for Free with Store Incentives

Rebates aren't the only way to get full-sized items free. If you use store incentives, you will also score free items. Like rebates, you'll have to put the money out up front, but in the end you receive your total purchase price back. Do keep in mind, you will have to pay taxes on the items.

The stores you can score free items with using their store incentives are CVS, Walgreens, and Rite Aid. They each have programs in which you'll earn money back in their store rewards, which result in the item costing you nothing after the incentive. CVS calls them Extra Care Bucks, Rite Aid calls them +Up Rewards, and Walgreens calls them Register Rewards, but they work pretty much the same way. It's not cash like a rebate check, but it works like cash and you can use it to purchase something else at the store. When added up, you'll save just as much as, if not more than, rebates. For more on drugstore incentive programs, see Chapter 10.

QUESTION

Do I need to use the store rewards immediately?
No, you don't have to use the store rewards immediately. They are actually for your next store purchase, so you can use them at a later date. However, they do expire, so be sure to check the expiration date so you don't miss out on this great deal. Especially if it means you can get something for free.

How to Save with Coupons and Store Incentives

If you combine your store rewards with coupons, you can save even more! Before you make your original purchase, figure out how to get the most for your money. You can do this by purchasing items that you have a coupon for, are on sale, and offer a reward on your next purchase. For example, you have two coupons: one for $1.00 off shampoo and one for $1.00 off toilet paper. The shampoo is on sale for $3.99, and you'll receive a $3.99 reward off your next purchase. The toilet paper is on sale for $4.99. You are going to make two purchases using the reward from the first transaction on the second transaction and spend $2.99 and save $5.99.

First, purchase the shampoo for $3.99 and use the $1.00 coupon. By doing this, you'll pay $2.99 plus tax for the shampoo and then get a $3.99 reward you can use on your next purchase. Next purchase the toilet paper that is on sale for $4.99. You will use the $1.00 coupon for the toilet paper and the $3.99 reward from the previous purchase. When you do this, you will owe the cashier nothing and ultimately get the toilet paper for free. Now, had you walked into the store and purchased the shampoo and the toilet without coupons or using the store rewards, you would have spent almost $9.00 on both of them. But instead, what would have cost you $8.98 only cost you $2.99, which means you saved $5.99. Not bad for just a little bit of planning.

If you made a similar transaction every week, you would save over $300 a year! However, if you shop at all three drugstores, by using their rewards systems you can easily save three times that a year, which would be almost $1,000. Imagine cutting your budget by $1,000. You could use this savings toward a vacation, to purchase a big-ticket item, or even make an extra payment on your mortgage, which in turn will save you a lot in interest.

ALERT

Make sure you have a filler item to eat up the overage you may receive when using store rewards because the store will not give you cash back. This is a great time to grab something you need that isn't on sale, like bread or milk. Perfect for those items that you never receive a discount on.

Buying Products You Don't Need

Once you start following the store incentives and using their rewards, you'll notice there are lots of these deals each week, and sometimes for items you don't use. Should you buy those items? Yes, you should. Why? Because if you have a coupon, and you are going to receive an overage, you can then apply it to another item that you do need. Even if it's $1.00, it's worth your time because it all adds up.

You may have a store coupon that you can use on a certain transaction total. If you do, then an extra item will help bring your total up so you can save that extra money. For example, you have a coupon for $5 off a $25 purchase, but the items you want to purchase don't total up to $25. You may be able to purchase an item you'll ultimately get for free, to bring up the transaction total. You'll spend the $25 needed to save the $5 and have rewards to use on your next purchase of items you need that are not on sale or that you don't have coupons for.

If you begin making purchases for items you don't need, you will soon have a stockpile of items you have no use for taking up space in your house. There are several things you can do with them including share them with your friends, families, or neighbors. They will be very appreciative for the freebie and you'll feel good about helping someone else. You can also donate them to several places. Check with your local church, food bank, women's shelter, and even schools. Lots of those places will take donations of just about anything. So before you pass up something because you won't use it, think of who can use it.

Samples, Trials, and Product Reviews

There are lots of other ways you can receive items for free. Sometimes you can get these items sent right to your house! Wouldn't that be nice? There are a few ways this can happen, and the easiest way is by requesting free samples. Free is free, no matter what size it is, and sometimes the free sample will even come with a coupon. By requesting free samples, you know they will be for products that you'll use since you chose them yourself.

When requesting a free sample, you will need to give them your name, mailing address, phone number, and e-mail address. They may ask you for a little more information, including your birthdate. The reason they need this is to make sure you are of age to request a free sample. They may ask you a few questions about your previous use of the product or a similar product, or even your shopping habits. Sometimes these questions are optional and you can skip right over them; other times you'll have to answer them to get the free sample. It's also possible you will not qualify for the free sample. This doesn't happen too often, but don't be surprised if it does.

Lots of people don't like giving out their e-mail address for fear of getting spam. These companies that are requesting your e-mail address should have a privacy policy somewhere on the website telling you what their exact policy or intention is with your e-mail address. You won't be able to send for the free sample without giving them your information. You don't need to give them your personal or work e-mail. You can set up an e-mail address to use just for offers like this. Then you won't be handing out anything personal. However, you will have to give them your mailing address so they know where to send your free sample. There's not really a way around this. Use your instincts. If it's not a company you know, then don't give them the information. If you sign up for company e-mails at the same time as you request the sample and you decide you don't want to receive it anymore, look along the bottom of the e-mail for an opt-out link to remove yourself from their mailing list.

Finding Free Samples Online

There are lots of places you can find free samples online, and one of the most common places is on the company's website. Check the websites of the companies whose products you use and see if they are offering a free sample. If you don't see one, check back the next month and each time after that. If you know they are releasing a new product, there is an even greater chance they will offer a free sample. Look along the top or the bottom of the website for a tab or label that says "Free Sample" or "Special Offers." If they have something to offer, you should find it there.

You can also sign up for their e-mail newsletter and if they do offer a free sample, you may be one of the first to find out about it. Just like coupons, the free samples are limited to a first-come, first-served basis, so you'll want to act fast. The sooner you know about it, the better chance you'll have of receiving it. Free samples often come with nice value coupons, so it's good to grab them when you can.

FACT

You can get free e-mail addresses from Gmail, Hotmail, and Yahoo!, which you can use for signing up for free samples. There is no limit to the number of e-mail addresses one person can have as long as you remember them all and what you used them for. Keep a list of your e-mail addresses (and passwords) so you can find them when you need to.

You can also do a Google search for either "Free Samples" or "Free Samples of X Product" to see what's out there. Lots of blogs, like *www .KouponKaren.com*, will post free samples as they find them. Generally, you can find a location on the blogs for free samples or free stuff. This can be a huge timesaver as you can scan their lists to see what products you'd like to send for. The only caveat you must keep in mind is that old free samples are kept in the archives, so it's possible that the item may no longer be available when you send for it. Check the date the free sample was posted to know if you are looking at an old post or not. However, you can still check the website as the free sample may have come back for another round.

StartSampling.com is a website that you can visit from time to time to request free samples. You'll have to join the website and log in each time you visit it. Then you'll see a list of available samples that you can request. If you go back into your account after you receive and use your free sample, you can submit some information about it and receive points. You can then exchange those points for prizes. It's nothing big, but a little bit of an incentive to let them know what you thought about the product.

Join Communities That Send You Free Products

There are websites that offer a variety of free samples and one of the more popular ones is *www.vocalpoint.com*. Vocalpoint is a website where people gather to talk about products and share their experiences. The site also offers free products to its members. It's free to join and once you do, you'll receive access to the website, an e-mail newsletter, and free samples of products in the mail from time to time. You don't even have to request them!

Each shipment will either contain one free product, or a coupon for a free product along with high-value coupons you can use on future purchases and share with friends and family. You can then visit the website after you've used the product and share your thoughts on it along with reading the opinions of others. It's a great way to share what you like or don't like about a product and the companies will see it. They want to see the good and the bad about their products. And you get a free product to try!

KraftFirstTaste.com is another online community that you can join that will also offer you free samples from time to time. However, these are always full-sized samples! They actually send you a free-product coupon; then you can pick up the product at your convenience. When it's a perishable product, it's the only way to do it. Once you sign up with Kraft First Taste, you'll receive e-mail newsletters that will sometimes contain a notice that there is a free sample in your account. You will then have to sign in to your account to request the free item.

Once you receive your free product, you can give them your feedback on the website and also read other people's thoughts as well. It's very similar to Vocalpoint in this way. The biggest difference between the two websites is that these will all be Kraft products, whereas Vocalpoint will be a variety of different products.

ALERT

If you receive an e-mail or see an ad saying you can test and keep a free product, chances are it's not real. Read the fine print. If it says something along the lines of "upon completion of program requirements," it's not really a free sample. You will have to sign up for other offers or purchase some items in order to receive your free product.

Take Surveys and Receive Free Products

There are several survey sites that are real and they want to get your opinion on products they produce or sell. They will also pay you in exchange for your opinions, thoughts, and comments on their survey site. And from time to time, they will send you products to sample and then take a survey on. This is a great way to try something out and give the company feedback, especially if they are trying to develop a new product or change one slightly. They need to know how it will actually work in the field, and who better to test it than those who will eventually buy it?

You'll need to do some research to find the companies that are actually real and those that are not. The biggest red flag when researching is if you find a company that wants you to pay to join or to get a list of websites—then it's a scam. You should never pay anyone to take surveys or to give you access to those that will pay you. All this information can be found online at several websites including *www.KouponKaren.com*. You'll find reviews of real survey sites that pay you for your opinions along with those that offer you free items to test, keep, and then report back on. Some of the valid survey sites that will pay you for your opinion are MySurvey.com, Opinion Outpost.com, ValuedOpinions.com, and Toluna.com. They are all free to join and will pay you and may even offer you products to try and review.

CHAPTER 13

Stockpiling 101

There are many benefits to having a stockpile of items you use all the time. The biggest benefit is that you almost never have to pay full price! If you are stockpiling when things are on sale and when you can use a coupon, you'll always have the items on hand that you use the most. You can avoid the last-minute decisions to eat out, which costs so much more than cooking at home, and you'll be able to accommodate last-minute guests since you have plenty of food in the house! And if you happen to have bad weather, you'll be all set for food. Stockpiling does save you money, if you do it slowly and correctly.

Starting Your Stockpile

Before you begin a stockpile, you need to know what a stockpile is. A stockpile is a supply of items that you use often and that you purchase and replenish when found at a great price. When you begin a stockpile, you need to start slow; don't try to get everything in one shopping trip. It won't happen that quickly. To have a successful stockpile, you need to allow yourself time. It could take months to build up a good stockpile.

QUESTION

Can I stockpile items that I can't find coupons for?
You can stockpile items that you don't have coupons for, but only purchase those items when they are on sale and at the best price possible. You can follow this by tracking sales cycles. Remember, the purpose of a stockpile is to help save money. Stockpiling items that are not on sale isn't going to save you money; it will just tie up money that you could be using more effectively elsewhere.

The idea of a stockpile is to save money and time by having everything on hand that you need. If you purchase everything in one shopping trip, you're not saving any money at all! That's just filling up your house with stuff. Your stockpile should not be a bunch of products you pay full price for just to have them on hand. It should consist of items you saved money on by purchasing at a reduced price or even got for free.

Here are some steps to get you started with your stockpile:

1. **Figure out and set a stockpile budget.** This is the amount of money you want to spend to build and maintain your stockpile. You can begin with as little as $10 a week if that is what your budget allows. With sales and coupons, $10 can go *very* far. Once you have your budget set, stick to it. It you don't use it each week, you can add the balance to the following week or put it aside for bigger dollar–valued items.
2. **Make a list of the things you use the most or run out of the quickest.** Those are items to stockpile first. You are stockpiling more than just food. Do not forget about health and beauty items, cleaning products, and paper products too. This list may change from month to month or even

season to season, so pay attention to that when making your list. It may be something you want to revisit every month until you have a master list.

3. **Each week when you get your sales ads, look for items on your list that may be on sale that week.** But watch out for items that are listed in the ad but not really at a low price. Some items may be priced differently at times. Just because it's in the ad doesn't mean it's at the best price it can be. After several weeks of paying attention to the prices, you will be able to identify what's a good price versus a great price.

4. **Next, see if you have coupons for those items.** You can use an online coupon database like the one found on *www.KouponKaren.com* to find coupons that may be available for the items you wish to purchase. If you have a coupon, you'll lower the price even more. Now you want to sort through the items on the list and only buy the items that you have coupons for and that are also on sale that week. Even if it is just one or two items each week, figure out how many you can purchase with your stockpile budget to last until they are on sale again.

5. **Repeat this each week until you have a good stockpile going.** Then just replenish as needed.

Free Stuff for Your Stockpile

There will be weeks when you can get items for free with the right sale and the right coupons. If that's the case, go crazy and stockpile. Just make sure to leave some on the shelf for the next person. There is nothing more frustrating than going to the store and finding there are no more items left. Sometimes you cannot avoid it, but try to think of the next person shopping after you.

ALERT

In order to purchase more than one item, you'll need more coupons. Pay attention to how much you are spending to get these extra coupons. If you are purchasing multiple newspapers for just one coupon, then really the item isn't free. You need to factor in to your budget what you are spending to acquire the newspapers. Something that is free may not really be free at all.

The drugstores have store incentives: Extra Care Bucks at CVS, Register Rewards at Walgreens, and +Up Rewards at Rite Aid. If you roll them from week to week, you'll be able to score free items all the time like toothpaste, toothbrushes, shampoo, deodorant, and more. These items are usually priced better at the drugstores than at the grocery stores, even when on sale. The cycles on these products are pretty close together, so you'll find it easy to stock those sorts of items at the beginning of your stockpile.

For example, between all three drugstores, toothpaste might be on sale every two to three weeks, and you can score it for free with coupons and store incentives. If you grab a tube from each store, you will build up your stockpile of toothpaste pretty quickly.

Know When to Stop Stockpiling

There are some items that you will always be able to get for free with coupons and store incentives. It may be hard to resist the temptation to purchase them every time you shop, but at some point you just have to. When you get to the point at which you have more than you need, only purchase these items with the thought of donating them if you are ultimately getting them for free. Even though the option is there for everyone to get them for free, not everyone has the means or time to shop every week, even for free items. It's just a nice way of paying it forward from your stockpile.

For example, you may only go through one or two tubes of toothpaste a month, depending on how many people are in your family. If you pick up one tube of toothpaste at each drugstore every time it's on sale, eventually you'll have enough of a stockpile that you won't need to buy any more, even if it's free. You need to make the decision to skip that sale, or get it and give it to someone else to use.

Best Time to Buy

Remember, timing is everything and that goes for stockpiling as well. Items that you add to your stockpile should be purchased when they are at their best rock-bottom prices and hopefully close to free. Every item is different, and the rock-bottom price for some items may even be $5.00. If it's something that normally costs you up to 75 percent more, $5.00 is a good price.

For example, a package of diapers is regularly priced at $11.99. But with sales, coupons, and store incentives, the cheapest you can find them may be $4.00. So, when you catch them for $4.00 each, grab as many as you can until they are on sale again. As always, be sure to leave some for the next person. If you use your grocery price list to track items when they are at their cheapest, you'll know when it's a good price. And follow the sales cycles to plan for when it will be on sale again.

Because you are on a budget and you're only allowing yourself a certain dollar amount each week to shop, it's okay to pass on a deal—even if it's not going to cost you much. If you continually go over your stockpile budget, then eventually it will get in the way of your regular budget. As hard as it may be, try to stick to your stockpile budget and know that you will find that deal again. It will also teach you to try and spread your stockpile budget as thin as you possibly can each week by asking yourself if you really need to buy four deodorants just because they are $1.00 each. You can use that $1.00 to stockpile another item because chances are, the deodorant will be that cheap again before you run out.

Running Out of Stockpile Items

It's possible that you may run out of an item before it goes on deep discount again. If that's the case, you'll still want to try and purchase it at the best price you can. If you know a good sale will be coming soon, don't stockpile too much so you can catch it at the best price possible. Keep an eye on how much you need and try to at least purchase enough on sale to hold you over long enough so that you won't have to pay full price for it.

This is especially going to happen when you first begin your stockpile. Unless you've been following sales cycles for a long time, it will be hard to gauge just how much you need to purchase before an item goes on sale again. It's going to be trial and error for a while, and there is always the chance that the sales cycle will change. If you can't avoid it and you have to pay full price for something you need, don't drive yourself crazy over it. But learn from that and maybe change your system a little bit. Are you stockpiling too much of one item you don't use as often as another? If you are, then your stockpiling budget is being tied up with something that it should not be tied up with and you may need to make a few adjustments.

If you have teenagers in your house, especially growing boys, it may be almost impossible to keep a stockpile of some pantry items no matter how much you buy! The best solution is get a lock on your pantry door; then no one can get in there without you knowing! Or you may need to put more of your stockpiling budget toward those items to avoid having to pay full price too often.

When Your Friends and Family Think You're a Store

Once word gets out that you have a great stockpile of items, you'll have lots of visitors to admire your collection and no doubt ask you for things. You'll become the person in the neighborhood whom everyone runs to when they are out of something. This can cause a problem because you've spent a lot of time to plan out your shopping trips and maintain your stockpile. If this happens more often then you'd like, just kindly offer to show them how you did it so they can do it too. Make them think you're doing it to help them, rather than to keep them away from your things. However, when you are rotating your stockpile, keep these people in mind when you find things close to their expiration date. You can toss things their way rather than in the garbage! Saving money can be addictive. Be sure to teach everyone you know how to do it so they don't take everything from your stockpile!

Maintaining Your Stock

Finding a place to store your stockpile, and keeping it neat and in order, can be a big challenge for some. Not everyone has a warehouse in their basement or attic they can use to store their stockpile. Some may have little to no room at all. But if you are creative, you can find places to store your items.

Here are a few ideas:

- Put shelves under the sinks to make better use of the space. This will work in the kitchen and the bathroom. Small plastic drawers work great for the small stuff and then put the tall stuff on top of the drawers.

- Find a corner in the garage to hang shelves and store big items. Packages of toilet paper and paper towels can go in the eaves of the garage as well.
- Hang small shelves over the back of the door and on the inside of closet doors for small items. Shoe holder pockets work great too, especially inside kitchen food storage closets.
- Try to find some inexpensive plastic rolling totes to put in corners of rooms where no one will notice them. Then use the top as a table for a light or phone. You can even put a tablecloth over it and no one will know what's inside.
- Use the tops of closets for bigger items or fill shoeboxes with smaller items and line them on the top shelf or on the floor of bedroom closets.
- Under-bed storage bins are perfect for stockpiling—even in the kids' rooms! This will also help avoid junk from collecting under their beds!

See how creative you can be with finding spaces. Every little nook and cranny can be used for your stockpile—and if it's neat, no one will even know it's there!

Don't Forget the Expiration Date

The most important thing to do with your stockpile is to rotate your stock each time you add to it. It's just like they do in the stores. The reason for this? So things don't expire before you get to use them. Almost everything has an expiration date, even toothpaste. Even before it enters your house, you should be thinking about whether or not you'll use it before it expires.

Some items have a long shelf life, and others don't. Salad dressings are the perfect example of this. You can get them pretty cheap at times, but they don't last forever. It doesn't matter how good of a deal you got when purchasing it. If you throw it out before you get to use it, it wasn't a deal at all.

If you continue to toss items from your stockpile because they are no longer good, you are wasting money. You could have used that money to stockpile something else. It may just be because you bought too much of one item. Pay very close attention to how much you buy and how fast you can use it. Otherwise you're not going to save money. Remember, most sales happen in cycles, so you'll be able to get more at a good price again.

Organization Is the Key

You want the items you've had the longest in your stockpile toward the front and anything new goes right to the back. The item in front should always be the next item to expire. Otherwise if you always put the newest items in front, the oldest items won't get used before they expire. Other members in your family may not think to check the date before they take something from the stockpile. If you always put the new items in the back, you'll know that the oldest items will be used first, even when you aren't the one taking them off the shelf.

Having a stockpile is supposed to save you money and, in the long run, save you time as well. Don't work against yourself by making more work. Make it as easy as possible from the moment you get home from the store. If you take the time then to put everything in the proper place, then you won't have to worry about organizing it in between shopping trips.

Too Much of a Good Thing?

A really good deal is very hard to pass up. However, do you really need seventy-five shampoos for your household of four? How about the fifty packages of dental floss that no one ever uses? And then there are the 100 packages of toilet paper that are lined up along your garage walls. Seriously, do you need that much toilet paper? You may use it eventually, but at some point you have to stop buying it or you will never use it all. Of course it won't expire, but enough is enough!

Try to be reasonable about how much of an item you stockpile. A good working stockpile should have enough to hold you over until the next time the item goes on sale. It *will* go on sale again and you *will* buy it again. But if you still have twenty-five pieces of an item sitting in your stockpile, then you don't need to buy more. There is such a thing as too much of a good thing.

Adjusting Your Budget

If you find you have no more room in your house for your stockpile items, either because you've simply run out of room or you're buying faster than you can use it, then it's probably time to adjust your stockpile budget. At some point you will be at the point of completing your stockpile and now you just have to maintain it. This means you may not need to purchase items every week for your stockpile. If you haven't run out, then you don't need it.

If this is the case, then you can do one of two things. You could cut your stockpile budget by 25 percent or even 50 percent each week or you could only stockpile every other week instead of every week. Then that money you have put aside for your stockpile could be used elsewhere. You could save it up and treat your family to a night out for dinner, a movie, or some sort of special treat. Or you could simply put it in the bank and let it build up for something bigger. If your stockpile budget was $10.00 a week and you decided to cut it down by 50 percent a week and bank the rest, in one year you'll have an extra $260 in your savings account. If you have a car payment, you could make an extra payment for the year, which in turn will save you a lot on interest.

Donate Your Stockpile

You may find yourself in a situation in which if you purchase an item, you not only get it for free, but you also make money on it, or get cash back! If that is the case, you can use the cash back to reduce the price of something else. But now you have an item you will never use that is going to sit in your house and take up space that you could be using for something else.

Why not give it to someone who can use it? If you're not sure what to do with it, check your local food bank or soup kitchen to see if they take items other than food items. Your local church may also take donations for people in the area who are in need, as well as senior centers. If you still can't find anything, ask your friends and family. Someone you know may even be able to use it.

ALERT

Before you donate anything, be sure to check the expiration date. You may not realize that some things like toothpaste have expiration dates, but they do. If the item is expired whoever you donate these items to won't be able to use them any more than you can and you'll be wasting their time. It only takes a minute to check the dates as you pack items up for donation.

Sometimes you end up with more of an item than you can ever use, on purpose! Lots of people say they get a rush when they score a great deal, which is why they continue to purchase items. This can lead to having more than you need, all the time. At this point, you should look at your stockpile and consider helping others. Donating some of your stockpile is a win/win for both you and the people receiving it. You'll feel great about helping someone—especially at no cost or almost no cost to you—and it can be a tax writeoff, too.

CHAPTER 14

Saving Money Online

Shopping online can be a huge timesaver, and a sanity-saver too. You don't have to deal with traffic, grouchy customers, or unhappy employees, especially when trying to use a coupon or get something for the sale price. Paying full price for items is something you should avoid doing at all times, including when you are shopping online. There is absolutely no reason why you can't find a deal on everything you purchase, especially if you plan ahead. There is a plethora of websites that can help you save money almost anywhere you shop online. Once you find these websites and learn how they work, you will never have to pay full price again!

Online Coupon Codes

Using a paper coupon while shopping online isn't always going to work. While some paper coupons will have a code for online shopping, others won't. But that doesn't mean you can't use a coupon while shopping online. It just means you have to find the right coupons. What you're looking for is a coupon code, and it usually consists of a string of numbers and letters. There will be a box on the checkout page where you'll enter the coupon code, and then you will have to apply it to your purchase to receive the savings.

Stores issue coupon codes for online purchases in several places. Sometimes they will be on the front page of the store website urging you to use them, which is always nice! Coupon codes will have an expiration date and since they're being used online, it will be enforced. But the good thing about coupon codes is sometimes they can be stacked with sales to help you save even more.

Finding Online Coupon Codes

There are several websites that exist only for listing coupon codes and you can find these by doing a search on Google for the store name and then "coupon code." You should make a habit of doing this every time you purchase something online. Check a few different websites to see what your options are. You may find a 10 percent coupon code on one site but then a 20 percent coupon code on another. Some websites let readers submit the coupons, which means there is a possibility that the coupon code may not work or may be expired. But it's worth a try to see what the best discount is that you can get.

FACT

When you sign up for e-mail newsletters, there may be an option to receive mailings at your home. You want to opt in to these offers because if you receive a coupon in the mail that is good in-store, there may also be a coupon code that can be used online. That will not only save you on gas, but also time.

Some of these codes may be stackable, which means you can use more than one on the same purchase. That's always nice, but rare; however check just to be sure. If the store didn't want you to stack them, they wouldn't make them stackable. And even if the item you are purchasing is on sale, that doesn't mean that the coupon code won't work too.

Sign Up for Store E-mails

If you like shopping at a particular store, you want to be sure and sign up for their e-mail newsletter. By doing this, you'll not only be informed of any sales they may be having but you may also receive a coupon code directly to your in-box. They may have special sales just for their loyal customers, which means you may only find these coupons in your e-mail and they are only intended for you. That means you cannot share it, post it on a website, or try and use it more than once. It's nice that these companies recognize their loyal customers and reward them with special deals.

In order to sign up for the e-mail newsletter, you'll need to give them some personal information including your name, address, date of birth, and e-mail address. The date of birth is to verify that you are at least thirteen years of age. You must provide this in order to sign up. You'll also need to provide them with your e-mail address so they can send you e-mails. You don't have to use your personal or work e-mail address. You can have an e-mail set up for receiving newsletters, but be sure to check it from time to time so you don't miss out on the sale or the coupon code. You will be able to unsubscribe from these e-mails at any time by following the link that will be at the bottom of the e-mail they send or there will be a spot in your account information where you can opt out of e-mails.

Take Surveys and Receive Savings

You have probably noticed that lots of stores now are including an option to take a survey online about your in-store purchase experience. They are using this to measure how well their stores are doing to serve you. In exchange for your time, they offer you either an entry into a drawing for cash or savings on your next purchase. While it's great to win some cash, if they are only offering you an additional discount, it still may be worth it to take the short survey to receive your savings.

While most of these coupons can only be used in-store, it's possible that some of them may be eligible for online savings as well. If you are required to print out a coupon to receive the savings, be sure to read the fine print to see if you can use it online too. You will only have a few days to take the survey, but you will have longer than that to use the coupon.

Cash-Back Shopping Sites

Did you know that there are websites that give you cash back when you shop online at all your favorite stores? There are and if you aren't using them, you're losing money. Here's how it works: You shop at your favorite stores through their websites and they give you cash back on your purchases. It will either be a percentage of your purchase or a flat dollar amount. You'll know before you shop what to expect. There are exceptions, so it's best to read each site before you shop. These websites are free to join, and some of them will give you a bonus after you make your first qualifying purchase. That should be reason enough to join!

Two of the biggest cash-back shopping websites are *www.ShopAtHome.com* and *www.Ebates.com*. Both of these sites offer you cash back with no strings attached. Before you shop, you'll need to open an account. They will require some information from you like your name, mailing address, and e-mail address. Once your account is set, you'll be able to begin shopping and earning cash-back rebates. Just search their list of stores to see what the savings will be.

ALERT

Make sure you are signed in to your account with the cash-back shopping website before you shop. You'll need to click through to the store you want to shop at or you will not get your cash back. If they can't trace your purchase through their site, they will not give you the cash back.

How Does It Work?

In order to receive your cash back, you must shop through their websites. Once you've signed up, it's simple. When you want to shop, you sign in to your account and look for the store you want to make a purchase at. Check the details to see if there are any exclusions before you make your purchase. There will be a "shop now" button or something along those lines. Click that and you'll then be taken to the store to make your purchase. When you click through, it will create a ticket, which is what the cash-back shopping site will use to track your purchase. Everything is being tracked within your account, which you'll be able to see whenever you'd like.

You can also find coupon codes on the cash-back shopping site. You can use these while making your purchase to save even more. When you search for the store you want to shop at, if there are any coupon codes that you can use and still receive the cash back, they will list them on the store page. If you use a coupon code that's not listed on the website, you may not receive the cash back, so be sure to only use those listed on the store page. When you combine both of these offers, you'll save even more.

QUESTION

When will I receive my money from a cash-back shopping site?
After you make your purchase, the store will report your spending to the cash-back shopping site and then they will credit your account. Once your account reaches the minimum needed to receive your money, you can request your payment or they will send it automatically. Check your account details to be sure. It's that easy!

For example, you have a coupon code to save 20 percent off your purchase at The Gap and the cash-back shopping site offers you 4 percent cash back on your purchase. You add $100 worth of products to your shopping cart and enter the coupon code for the 20 percent off, bringing your total down to $80. You complete your purchase and then receive 4 percent cash back, which equals $3.20. Now you've saved $23.20 on your purchase. If you shop once a month online and save on average of $3.00 to $4.00 just with the cash back, you'll save an additional $36 to $48 a year just by shopping through a cash-back shopping site. Imagine if you did all your online shopping through a cash-back shopping site. You could fill your gas tank several times and not even use it to go shopping!

You may be wondering how websites can give you this additional savings. They make a commission on your purchase, which they in turn share with you as cash back. They may be offering you 4 percent cash back, but they are making 10 percent. Instead of 10 percent, they are now making 6 percent but by offering you this money, you will probably shop through their site more often, which results in them making more money in the long run. It's better for them to give you the 4 percent because they will then make 6 percent again the next time you use their services. It's a win-win for everyone!

Receive Cash Back on Gift Cards Too!

Some stores will even allow cash back on gift card purchases. Gift cards are not only great for gift giving, but they are also great for budgeting your own money. Gift cards are also usually shipped for free so not only do you save money by getting cash back on your purchase, but you'll save money on gas since you don't have to leave your house to make the purchase. To find out if you will receive cash back on gift cards, check the store page on the cash-back website. Not every store will honor cash back on gift card purchases, and it's best to know this beforehand rather than after the fact.

If you receive cash back on gift card purchases, this probably will mean that you won't receive cash back when using a gift card to pay for your purchase at that store. This would be double dipping and they won't allow it. It's usually one or the other. If you aren't sure, it's best to contact customer service before you make your purchase to find out. But if it says on the store page that they will give you cash back on the gift card purchase, chances are, you won't get it when you make a purchase with a gift card.

Shipping Offers

Finding the time to shop for a deal is hard for busy people. Between working and taking care of their home and family, often the time needed to do the research and run to the store doesn't always fit into the day or even the week. This usually results in paying full price because it's easy to grab the first thing you see or, if it's a gift, giving cash.

Being able to shop online from your home allows you to do a little bargain shopping and possibly save money on gas. Yes, shipping costs are usually involved with online shipping, but if you take the time you would spend driving to the store to instead find a shipping deal, you may end up not just saving money because you purchased something on sale, but saving on the shipping costs too.

Shipping can be very expensive, and sometimes the amount you need to spend in order to receive free shipping is more than you want to spend. One way around this is to find a friend to make a purchase with, and then split the shipping. But that's not always possible. If your budget allows, you could purchase something else that you may need to purchase in the next few months anyway, like a present, to meet the minimum spending amount. Or you could look for a way to get free shipping or at least discounted shipping. Otherwise it may not even be worth making the purchase because you may spend less on gas driving to the store.

Free Shipping

Some stores will give you free shipping with a minimum purchase. While that is nice, it may not be enough to get you to shop with them because that minimum can be pretty high sometimes. And then there are stores that will offer you free shipping for spending as little as $25. That's even better, but what about when you want to spend even less than that? A coupon code for free shipping would come in very handy at that point. You may or may not find one, but it's worth a look.

If you aren't already receiving the store newsletter, this might be a good time to sign up for it. It's possible that they may offer you free shipping when you sign up, or at another time. They offer incentives for their loyal customers and sometimes just receiving their e-mail newsletter may be loyal enough for them! A little research may pay off, so it's worth looking into.

Free Shipping Memberships

If you do a lot of shopping online, and don't always find deals on shipping, it may be worth purchasing a free shipping membership like the one that Amazon.com offers called Amazon Prime. Amazon is the perfect place to find products at great prices. They sell so many things, including groceries. They also offer free shipping if you spend as little as $25 on items shipped from Amazon.

Since their prices are so good, it's possible that your purchase won't meet the $25 minimum. If this happens often enough to you, then you may want to look into their Amazon Prime program. You pay a yearly fee and then receive free two-day shipping for the year on items shipped from Amazon. That means if you find a great deal on cereal and you want to spend less than $25, you'll receive free shipping and get it fast! If you shop on Amazon often, you'll get your money back and more in savings pretty quickly.

If you like shopping online at more than just Amazon and would like to receive free shipping pretty regularly, there is another website you may want to look into. ShopRunner.com is a website that offers you free two-day shipping at their partner stores along with free return shipping. Like Amazon Prime, you need to purchase a membership, but then you'll receive unlimited two-day shipping and also free return shipping for the entire year. Your shipping savings is tracked within your account so you can see how fast you recoup the cost of your membership. If you are a regular online shopper, it adds up pretty quickly.

ESSENTIAL

ShopRunner offers a thirty-day free trial so you can try their service before having to pay for it. If you don't like it, you can cancel hassle-free at any time. If not you will be charged $79 for the year or $8.95 per month for a year. After trying it for a month, you'll know if a paid membership is worth it for you.

ShopRunner is easy to use. Just shop at one of their partner stores and then you sign in to your ShopRunner account right in your shopping cart. Once you're signed in, the shipping costs will disappear and you will not be charged anything for two-day shipping. Some of their partner stores are Toys "R" Us, Babies "R" Us, Drugstore.com, Lord & Taylor, eBags, Pet Smart, Timberland, Auto Zone, Radio Shack, Birthday Express, Newegg, and so many more. Check the website for a complete list as they add more every day.

Groupon, Living Social, and Daily Deals

There are a number of websites that offer you great deals on local places along with items for the home, food, clothes, gifts, and so much more. These sites have items discounted on average over 50 percent off the retail cost. It's a great way to get your hands on some items at a fabulous price. But on top of offering you this awesome discount, some of them even give you money when you join and when you refer your friends. If you have a big circle of friends, you can earn yourself some nice referral cash, and your friends will love you because you have shown them some great websites for bargains.

How does this work? Each day they have new deals listed in cites all over the United States. Some of the deals are specific to that location, and others are online deals or for places that are national. When you join the sites, you sign up to get e-mails for your area, but you can also receive e-mails for other areas as well. So if you work or visit another part of the state often, you can receive e-mails for that area as well so you'll know what they offer each day. You can also check the website every day to see what's being offered anywhere in the United States.

If you find a deal you like, you purchase a voucher to use later either in person or online. It's pretty comparable to a gift certificate that is valid at a certain location or for a certain item. Usually about twenty-four to forty-eight hours after your purchase, your voucher will be available in your account. You can then print out the voucher or if it's for an online purchase, you'll just need the voucher number to complete your purchase.

ALERT

Be sure to read the fine print before purchasing your voucher. Shipping may or may not be included in the voucher. If it is not, check to see what the cost will be to have your item shipped. Sometimes a deal isn't as good when you add in the cost of shipping. It's good to check this before you purchase your voucher so there are no surprises afterward.

Finding the Daily Deal Websites

You've probably seen advertisements on TV for a few of these sites including Groupon and Living Social. They are two of the popular sites along with

Eversave that feature lots of great deals every single day. But they aren't the only ones. As of right now you'll find daily deals at the following websites:

- *www.groupon.com*
- *www.livingsocial.com*
- *www.eversave.com*
- *www.saveology.com*
- *www.mamasource.com*
- *www.8moms.com*
- *www.plumdistrict.com*
- *www.bitsybug.com*

There are more sites popping every day, so make sure you search around to find the best deal.

QUESTION

Can I return items I purchase from the daily deal sites?
Sometimes you can return and sometimes you can't. Each website has its own return shipping rules. It may depend on the item you are purchasing—whether it's a final sale or not. Before you make a purchase, check the website's return policy so you aren't surprised afterward. Then you can make the decision if you want to purchase the item or not.

Give the Voucher as a Gift

Need a gift? Consider giving one of these vouchers as a gift; then the recipient can make the purchase herself. There are so many options for items on these sites every day that you are bound to find a gift for someone you know. If you don't want to give them the actual voucher, you can purchase the voucher, save the 50 percent or more, then make the purchase yourself, wrap it up, and they will have no idea how good of a deal you just found!

Because you can purchase vouchers from all over the United States, you can look in other cities and purchase those vouchers as well for gifts.

Let's say you want to purchase a gift for friends who live in another state. Just head on over to the page that has the deals listed for their area and if you find a restaurant that you know is local to them, you can purchase the voucher and then send it to them as a gift. And guess what? You can even e-mail it since they usually come in a PDF file. How easy is that?

You will also find deals on these sites for gift delivery items like flowers, candy, and cookies. Those things can get very expensive especially when you add in the delivery service. But if you purchase the voucher at a savings of at least 50 percent, then spending that extra on the delivery service is well worth it, especially if this is something that you would be sending anyway. Why not save on it? You can save on just about anything you need to buy, including flowers delivered to Mom for Mother's Day.

Designer Markdowns

Have you ever wished that designer items actually fit into your budget? Do you have a friend who always seems to have designer items but yet doesn't seem to have the money to purchase these items? You may have thought that they spend way beyond their means, but perhaps they don't.

There are websites that have designer-brand items at markdown prices every day that you can be shopping at, without breaking the bank. They are the real thing, and not defective items. The stores sell them off in low quantities and the websites purchase them and pass on the savings to you. Some items are marked down as much as 90 percent off the retail price.

There are a ton of these websites right now and more popping up every day. A few of them are Rue La La, Modnique, Totsy, Zulily, HauteLook, One Kings Lane, and The Foundry. If you want to hear about these deals, your best bet is to sign up to receive their daily e-mails. Then each day you'll receive a list of the designer sales they currently have along with how long they will last. Of course the quantities are limited, so they may sell out before the sale is over, but if you receive the e-mails, then you have a better chance of catching the items you want before they are gone.

You can also refer your friends to these designer deals websites and earn referral credits to use on purchases for yourself. This is an even better way of getting things even cheaper.

What You Can Find on Designer Closeout Websites

You never know what you may find on these designer closeout websites, which is why it's best to check as often as you can. One day there may be items for your home that you've drooled over before, and now can afford. Another day you may find the clothes you walk by in the stores and don't even dare try on since you normally can't afford them, even with a sale. And the next day you may find some gourmet food that you've always wanted to try, but could never fit into your budget.

You could redecorate your home by shopping at these designer closeout websites and even replace your entire wardrobe. Of course this won't happen overnight, but if you were planning on making these purchases already, you will probably spend the same amount of money you would have spent, only on designer items rather than no-name brand items.

ESSENTIAL

If you are the type of person who likes to plan ahead, there may be a list of future sales on the websites to give you an idea of what you can expect. They may list in detail what will be on sale or they may just give you a description of the brand that will be on sale. You can use these previews as a tool for when to check the website or your e-mail. Because quantities are limited, things sometimes go very fast!

Tips to Save Even More

The prices on these websites are already great, but getting an even better price is always something to aim for. There are a few ways that you can score big on these already marked-down items. However, you may be taking a chance on losing out on something you really want. Be sure that it's worth the risk of missing out on the good deal. If not, then grab it while you still can save big.

These sites hold their sales for a certain amount of days, which is always displayed on the website, or until stock runs out. You may not know how much they have in stock, but you also don't know if anyone else is interested in the products either. So it's a gamble but, if you wait until the last day of the sale, they may mark them down even more. The idea is they want to sell these products and not have to store them any longer than they have to because it costs them money to keep items in stock. This is why it's important to sign up for the e-mails because if they mark any items down even more, they will let their e-mail subscribers know.

It's possible that the website also does a big markdown on a certain day of the week, like on Sundays. It may not matter when the sale ends, but one day a week may be designated for even deeper discounts. Read the website to find out all the details of their sales. If you can't find anything about a discount day or last-minute sales, send an e-mail to customer service and inquire about it. This way if you find something you want, but you don't need to have, take a gamble and see if it gets marked down even more. Or don't look at the sales until they are at their deepest markdown and only purchase items then! That will be one way to be sure you'll grab the best deal you can get.

Expect to have to pay shipping when making your purchase. Figure out ahead of time what their shipping costs are and then factor that into the price you are paying. Do they charge shipping according to items, weight, or a flat fee? Do they have a day that things will ship for free? These are all things you also want to research beforehand so you know when the best time is to make your purchase to save the most on shipping. Some sites may offer a flat rate of shipping all day long once you make your purchase. That's a good time to either grab a few things you want or find a friend and do some shopping together and split the cost of shipping.

CHAPTER 15

Social Media and Coupons

Social media has become a haven for just about everything. It's not just for having a short conversation between friends or sharing pictures of your family's latest adventures; it's also a great way to keep up with the companies that you like the most and sometimes even score good deals from them. It may seem a bit odd to follow these companies on several social media platforms, and one may work better than the other for you, but you may get savings from them on both Facebook and Twitter. They may not share these deals anywhere else, so if you really want to find the best deals, it's best to follow them on both platforms.

Finding Coupons on Facebook

Facebook is a great place to find printable coupons. You can either look on the wall of the company on Facebook or find it in your News Feed. Just about every company is on there now, and they understand that you are on Facebook every day. They realize that to get your attention, they have to be where you are. Unfortunately, not everyone is on Facebook and if you're not, you're missing out. If you're afraid of putting personal information on Facebook, you don't have to. If you want to be part of it just to connect with companies, then you can do just that.

Sign Up for a Facebook Account

In order to access any coupons on Facebook, you will need to have a Facebook account. It's free and easy to join. Head on over to *www.facebook .com* and sign up. You'll need to give them your name, e-mail address, and date of birth. Once you sign up, you can then add more information to your profile and set your privacy settings.

FACT

If you only want a Facebook account to follow companies and businesses that you like, all you have to do is set the privacy settings to only allow people that you become friends with to see any of your personal information. You don't have to "friend" anyone on Facebook; you can just use it to get coupons and savings from companies. "Liking" a company's fan page on Facebook won't give them access to your personal information as long as your privacy settings are set correctly.

Connecting with Companies on Facebook

If you do a search on Facebook for a company, you may notice that some of the pages look official and some of them don't. This can be very confusing. Your best bet would be to go to the company website and find the link to their Facebook page from there. Then there is no confusion.

The first time you go to their page on Facebook, you'll need to "like" it in order to access all of the information. To "like" a Facebook page, just click the "LIKE" button on the top of the page next to the company name. You only need to do this once. Now you have access to everything on their Facebook page. The updates will also show up in your news feed. If at any point you decide you don't want to follow their page anymore, just go to the company page and on the left-hand column toward the bottom you'll see an "unlike" link. Click that and you won't receive their updates anymore.

Printing Coupons on Facebook

If there are coupons on a company's Facebook page, there should be a tab on the left-hand side that says either "coupons" or "special offers." If you don't see either of those, click all the options to see if one of them may be a coupon.

Once you find the coupon, you may have to give them a little bit of information before you can access it. You may be required to give them your name and e-mail address and to verify your date of birth before you can print the coupon. Then you'll be brought to the coupon page. You should be able to print the coupon twice, like other printable coupons. If you would like more than one, just print again until it tells you that you've printed the maximum allowed.

ALERT

Sometimes you may have to install an app to get to the coupon. If this happens, it's because of the program they use to print the coupon. Once you install the app and print your coupon, you can remove it. If you aren't comfortable doing this, that's fine. Saving $.50 or even a $1.00 isn't worth doing something you are not comfortable with.

Once you are following the company on Facebook, if they have a new coupon, they will post it on their wall and then you'll see it in your news feed.

Some companies would rather send you a coupon in the mail than have you print it from their Facebook page. If these coupons are available, check the coupon or special offers tab on the left-hand side of their Facebook page. If they are sending you the coupon in the mail, you will need to give them your mailing address. If you don't feel comfortable doing this, that is fine, but it may be the only way you can get the coupon.

Check the Company Website for Facebook Coupons

If you are not on Facebook all the time or you don't want to have to search for coupons that are offered on Facebook, you may still be able to find them when they are available. If you check the company website, they may announce a coupon that's available on their page or even that there is one coming up. They may also put the information in their e-mail newsletter.

Follow Blogs on Facebook for Coupon Updates

The coupon blogs also have Facebook pages that you can "like" and follow along for great deals including coupons. Most of their posts are fed to their Facebook page, or they post them manually to make it more personal. Find some coupon blogs on Facebook and "like" their pages so you'll be notified of coupons throughout the day. There are lots of them on Facebook and you can usually find the link to their Facebook page on their blogs. KouponKaren.com has a Facebook page and if you follow it, you will be informed of printable coupons almost immediately. The sooner you find the coupon, the better chance you have of printing it before it reaches its print limit.

Coupon Codes on Twitter

Twitter has become increasingly popular over the past year. Twitter is a little harder to follow than Facebook because if you follow a lot of people, your Twitter feed moves along pretty quickly. The characters are also limited to 140 per tweet. It's not always easy to get a lot of information in 140 characters, but those that do it all the time find ways.

Some companies will post links to their printable coupons that can be found on their websites or on Facebook. Companies that have online stores will also post coupon codes on Twitter.

Sign Up for a Twitter Account

Twitter accounts are free and anyone can have one. Just go to *www .twitter.com* to sign up. You'll need to pick a Twitter handle, which is what is seen when you tweet. It can be anything, but it's public, so don't use your last name if you don't want people to know it. You'll want to fill in your profile and check all your account settings. If you choose, you can upload a picture and even design the background on your Twitter page.

Do I have to tweet in order to have a Twitter account?
You can have a Twitter account even if you don't want to tweet. If you just want to be able to follow other people or companies, that is perfectly fine. Once you open a Twitter account and choose a Twitter handle, you can then search for companies or people and follow them. Then you will just see their tweets each time you log in to your account.

Following Companies on Twitter

If you do a search on Twitter for the company name, you may come up with a few different Twitter handles that match the name. You might have to sort through these to see which one is really the company. If you can't figure it out, head over to the company website to see if they have a direct link to their Twitter page.

Once you locate the proper Twitter handle for the company you are looking for, you'll want to follow them by clicking the "follow" button. After you are following them, their updates will show up in your timeline.

Finding Coupons and Coupon Codes

It may be difficult to find a company's tweets if you follow a lot of people. There are a few other ways to find them. The easiest way is to just go to their Twitter feed. If you click on the company's Twitter handle, you'll be brought to their page where you'll find an option to see their tweets. Click "tweets" and a list will appear. It will have their most recent tweet on top and then the rest in order as they were tweeted. You can scan the tweets looking for coupon codes or printable coupons. It might take a while if they have a lot of tweets, but at least the list only shows their tweets.

Another option would be to do a general search for the coupon code you are looking for in the search box on the top of the Twitter page. For example, if you want to find some Old Navy coupon codes, you can type in "Old Navy coupon codes" in the search box. The results below will include any tweets that contain the words "Old Navy coupon codes." Some may be links to sites that post the coupon codes, some may be other coupons, and some may list the coupon code. If you don't find anything, do a variation on the search; maybe leave out "coupon" and just search for "Old Navy code."

Using a Hashtag on Twitter

If you want to start some conversations on a certain topic on Twitter, you can do so by using a hashtag before the word you want your topic to be about. For example, if you want to get a conversation going about how cute your kids are, you would send a tweet and include #mycutekids somewhere in the tweet. Then if people want to talk to you about this subject, they will also include the hashtag #mycutekids in their tweets. If you want to see what everyone is saying about that topic, you would do a search for #mycutekids and any tweets that include that hashtag will show.

Companies and people include hashtags in their tweets when they want the topic to be found. Bloggers also include a hashtag in their tweets if they are talking about something that people may search for, including coupons and coupon codes. If you do a general search for #couponcodes, then you will see a huge list of tweets that are about coupon codes. If you want to be more specific, you can try to look for #oldnavycouponcodes and there may be some listed under that hashtag.

ESSENTIAL

When you are searching for something on Twitter with a hashtag, try a few different searches to see if you can come up with what you are looking for. Once you find one you like, you can save the search. This will give you easy access to the search the next time you are looking for it.

Follow Local and National Stores

You may notice when you walk into your local food store, they are advertising that they are on Facebook or Twitter. So many of them are trying to find ways to connect with people, which means they need to go where you are.

And that just happens to be Facebook and Twitter. The national chain stores can also be found on Twitter and Facebook. It's really a great way to connect and share what's going on at their stores. It's also a great way for you to find out about deals and steals at their stores too.

Find Sales on Facebook and Twitter

The food stores want to make sure you know exactly what kinds of deals you can find each week. Even though they have an ad that is circulated to many, they realize that you may not see that and they still want you to know what's on sale each week. If you follow them on Facebook and Twitter, they may not only post their ad each week for you to see, but they may also tell you about some of the hot items that are on sale that week. If they point them out to you, you are more likely to notice them and shop at their store.

You can find these deals either on your Facebook and Twitter news feeds or on the companies' pages. You'll need to make sure you "like" them on Facebook and "follow" them on Twitter in order to see them. They may also have a hashtag that will make it easier for you to follow them and locate the deals.

Follow Your Favorite Stores for Coupons and Special Sales

Companies really like to reward their loyal customers. It's great customer service and another way to get you to shop in their store. They may offer their e-mail subscribers a coupon that only they can use. They may also post a coupon on their Facebook page that only their followers can use.

If they have an online store, they may offer a coupon code that is only visible to their Facebook fans. Again, anyone can become a fan of their page, but you will only get the coupon code if you are. Following their page may also be the only way you find out about it, so you want to be sure that you are following them all the time.

CHAPTER 16

Couponing Game Plans

No matter how much time you have, the most important thing you need to do is set a spending budget. You can break down that budget by week or month. Once you have your budget in place, then figure out how much time you have each week to plan out your shopping trip. This may also vary from week to week, which is fine. You can learn how to adjust your planning to the time you have available. Also factor in the time you spend at the stores. This is all part of the couponing game; it's not just about finding the coupons, but also about using them the best way you can, to help you save the most you can.

If You Have Thirty Minutes a Week to Coupon

If you don't have a lot of time each week to coupon, then it will be harder to save a lot. However, as you learn how to fit it into your schedule and learn the ropes, it gets easier and eventually you'll save more money. But you do need to allow yourself time to build up the savings. Even in just a short amount of time each week, you can save money.

Always Think Ahead

If your time for planning is limited, you need to set your mind in the mode of always thinking "How can I save on my next purchase?" even if it's while you're in the car or in the shower. If you know you need to purchase something, even clothes, think beforehand if there is a way to save on that purchase. Perhaps you might have received a coupon in the mail or an e-mail with a savings code you can use to purchase it online instead of in the store. It's possible you have the means of saving right in front of you so you don't have to spend any time looking for the deal.

Whenever you have the opportunity to get a coupon, grab it. It will take less than a second to grab that coupon and immediately file it away. If you're walking down the aisles of the grocery store and see a tear pad with a coupon for a product you use but don't need now, grab one coupon as you walk by and file it immediately in your coupon binder. There is no way of knowing if this coupon will be there the next time you make the purchase.

Make Use of All Downtime and Multitask

If you are the type of person who can multitask, then making use of your downtime can be very helpful when trying to save money and use coupons. Use the time while chatting on the phone or watching TV to cut coupons from the Sunday paper. If you can, spend lunchtime surfing the blogs for deals and printing coupons while you eat.

While waiting in the doctor's office or at a kid's sporting event, make your shopping list. If you finish up somewhere early and are near a store you have a plan already to shop at, pop in and do some shopping, even if it's just half of what you need if time allows. Because you're limited on time, you won't be able to catch every great deal. You'll need to look at it as whatever you can save is better than no savings at all.

Stay Organized

Figure out a filing system for all sorts of deals, not just coupons for the grocery store and drugstores, but also for everything else you need to purchase. You should save on every purchase you possibly can. How many times have you left the house to go clothes shopping knowing that you received a coupon for the store earlier in the week, but you can't find it? It happens all the time and when you don't have that extra time to spend searching all over the house, then you lose the savings. Figure out a system that works for you when you first receive the coupon and then you'll be able to grab it as you walk out the door.

Set up a folder or an envelope for coupons you receive in the mail for department stores or big box stores. As you open the mail, if you receive any coupons or discounts, file them immediately so you know exactly where they are when you need them. Keep them in a place where you can easily grab them while walking out the door to go shopping. Then you won't spend extra time to find them and won't take the chance of leaving them behind and losing out on the savings.

ESSENTIAL

If you tend to shop online more often, you'll want to set up a folder in your e-mail to keep all the discounts and coupons you receive. Then, when you are ready to shop, you can look quickly through the folder to find anything you may have. As you add new ones to the folder, take a quick look at the older ones and see if you can delete any that have expired.

Choose One Grocery Store and Only Shop the Sales

If you only have thirty minutes to spend couponing each week, then you will need to choose one grocery store to shop at each week. Only buy stuff on sale since cutting coupons isn't really something you have time for. If you grab a coupon here and there and are able to print some out, then that's great, but don't plan on using coupons on a regular basis. Instead use that time to scan the ads and find the store that has the most deals, and do your shopping there.

Try to plan your meals around what you can find on sale each week to save the most. There isn't room for stockpiling in your schedule, so you are shopping on a week-to-week basis. Over time as you get better at using your time wisely, you may be able to grab a few things and stockpile a little bit, but that is not your focus right now.

If You Have One Hour a Week to Coupon

Having an hour a week to coupon isn't much better than having thirty minutes a week, but it can make a big difference. You should still multitask as often as you can with thinking of how to save money while doing other things. Grab coupons as you see them and file them right away. The extra thirty minutes you can use to actually gather coupons and sort them. But you're still going to keep it to a minimum because let's face it, your time is still very limited. But you can still save money.

Get One Sunday Paper a Week

If there are lots of coupons in the Sunday newspaper, you could purchase an extra paper to get more coupons. But when time is limited, you don't need the extra coupons because you aren't stocking up on much of anything. You are just buying what's on sale each week and that's it. So you only need one newspaper; any more would be a waste of money.

QUESTION

What types of coupons should I use if my time is limited?
The only coupons you are going to use for now are the ones in the Sunday insert. The reason for this is they are the easiest ones to get your hands on and you can clip and sort them anywhere. You don't need a computer to find them, and you don't need a printer to print them. It will take the least amount of time to get them in your hands.

Scan the Grocery Store Ads Quickly

If you like to find the deals in the actual ads, and not online, then grab the ads for the stores you like to shop at or are the most convenient to get to, and quickly scan them to see what's on sale. As you do this, keep in the back of your mind what you may have a coupon for. Make a list as you scan the ads and find the one grocery store that has the best deals for you, because you don't have time to go to more than one.

You should still be planning meals around what's on sale. This should be something you do naturally no matter how much time you have to spend couponing. There is a little time for stocking up, if you have room in your budget. But only if you find something that's at a really good price. Making a stockpile isn't something you have time for with only one hour a week, but as you get better at making good use of your time, you can always try to start a stockpile. It definitely will save you in the end.

Grab Some Things at One Drugstore

If you have a little time left in your hour, check the drugstore ads. They have health and beauty items along with paper goods and some grocery items at great prices, when they are on sale. The drugstore ads will also tell you if there is a coupon in the Sunday insert, which is a nice timesaver. It may be worth making a quick trip to one drugstore to grab a few things, but only one, as there isn't time for more. Find the store that has the best deals for what you need; remember, you're still only buying what you need and are not stockpiling!

ALERT

The reason you aren't stockpiling is because of the lack of time. If you have a short amount of time each week, then you want to use that time to concentrate on getting what you need each week only. If you happen to be able to carve some extra time out, and you find a good deal, then you may be able to grab a few extra items to stockpile, but generally you probably won't have the time.

If you earn store rewards at the drugstore, you can keep them for the following week or use them immediately to get something you need that may or may not be on sale. Of course, if you purchase something that's on sale, you'll get more value, but if it's something you need, then look at it as a savings that you may not have received otherwise. If you don't need anything, keep the reward for next week to help save even more on what is on sale then.

Price Match

Some stores will price match other stores' weekly sales, so if you are short on time and don't have the option to go store to store, this could come in handy in helping save money. While you are going through the grocery store ads, if you find that there are actually two stores that have some items you'd like to buy, then your best outcome would be to price match from one store at the other. If you aren't sure if your store price matches, give them a quick call. If you can, purchase all you need at one store.

The items have to be the exact same things for the stores to price match. Be sure to bring the ad with you, just in case they don't have it in the store. You will also be able to use your coupons on those items. When you first arrive at the store, ask them if you can go through a regular cashier to get the prices matched or if you have to go to the service desk for it to be done. This way you don't waste time in line only to find out you are in the wrong place.

If You Have Five or More Hours a Week to Coupon

If you have five or more hours a week to coupon, then you should be able to get some great savings and almost immediately start slashing your family's grocery budget by almost half of what you have been spending. You have plenty of time to search for coupons both online and off and keep them organized in a way that will work best for you.

There is also no reason that you can't shop at a few stores each week to grab all the savings that you can. You'll have plenty of time to menu plan and purchase the items you need to make those menu items, at the best price possible. Of course you need to learn how to do this first, and you won't learn it all overnight, but as you go along, save what you can until you become a pro.

Follow the Blogs

The coupon blogs can save you time by listing the weekly sales and where to find the coupons. Of course you need the time to scan the websites to find the ones that have your stores listed. But once you do, be sure to either bookmark them or add them to an online reader. As you see the deals that they find, write them on your list. If there is a printable coupon to help save on an item, print it immediately because it may not be there when you are ready to shop.

QUESTION

What can I get from the coupon blogs?
Each week the coupon bloggers get the store ads and type up some of the best deals of that week. Then they search for any coupons that can be used along with the sale, to help you save even more. They tell you exactly where to find the coupon and how to use it to save the most. If there are any store incentives offered for purchases, they will tell you about those and even how to plan your shopping trip to include those incentives, again to help you save the most that you can.

If you are looking for something specific, don't be afraid to e-mail the bloggers and ask if they've found any deals on that item. Most of the time, they will be more than happy to help. You can also follow the blogs on Facebook and can easily ask questions, and not only will the bloggers help, but the other readers will too.

Get Extra Newspapers and Look for Coupons Online

If there are some good coupons in the Sunday paper, then you definitely want to grab a few extra copies. Since you have plenty of time to stock up, using coupons is the best way to do it. Just keep in mind that the newspapers cost you money, so if you aren't going to use the coupons in them, then you are wasting money.

You can find out ahead of time what coupons to expect by finding a preview of that weekend's coupons online. The coupon blogs, including *www.KouponKaren.com*, post a preview each week. One thing to keep in mind is that coupons are regional and you may not find all the coupons listed or if you do, they may be a different value. But it still gives you an idea of what to expect. You can also purchase one paper, check what coupons are there, then purchase more if you want more coupons. Just make sure you check the paper before leaving the store to make sure the coupons are actually in there.

Stockpile Each Week

Set a stockpile budget and use it each week. You should be grabbing an extra newspaper to get more coupons and have time to shop around, so it's a great opportunity to start a stockpile and maintain it. Be sure you are purchasing the items that you use most and at the best price you can find them. You should also always use coupons on items you stockpile; otherwise the sale price must be very good in order to justify a purchase. To get the most out of your stockpile budget, you should be buying items at rock-bottom prices.

Shop a Few Different Stores Each Week

Since you have more time in your week to shop for deals, you're better off shopping at a few stores including the drugstores. Pick two or three grocery stores that have a lot of items on sale that you want to purchase. You can still price match if needed to avoid making a trip to one store for just a few items. But purchase as much as the budget will allow, and aim for all those items to be on sale, unless there is something you really need.

Be sure to check the markdown items, especially the meat, with the idea that you can purchase them and freeze them for later use. There may be some fruits and vegetables that you can incorporate into your meals that are marked down because they need to be used immediately. And some of those items can also be precooked and frozen.

Include at least two of the drugstores in your shopping trip plans each week. Remember, they sometimes have milk, bread, and cereal on sale, at even better prices than the grocery stores! Keep this in mind while scanning the ads, because you could avoid going to another store if you can grab these items while you're at the drugstore. You can also use their store rewards to purchase other items you need and maybe even score a few items for the stockpile for free. Sometimes drugstores are overlooked because people think they are priced too high. This isn't the case for sale items, so look each week to find out what you can get.

Creative Ways to Lower Your Budget

There are so many other creative ways to save money and lower your budget, not just on grocery items, but on everything you purchase. You should be constantly looking for sales and deals. Plan ahead when you need to spend money so you have plenty of time to find a deal, even for holiday shopping.

Shop Thrift Stores and Consignment Shops

Think about the things you don't have to purchase new, and find places where you can look for a deal. Shop thrift stores for household items, toys, books, and even clothes. The kids go through clothes so fast when they are small that it's silly to pay full price for them. If you are just going to buy more again in a few months, then the thrift store is perfect for that. If you want more designer-brand items and your thrift store doesn't have them, then check for a consignment store. They tend to have more brand-name items because people make money on the items that they consign. You can find new brand-name clothes with the tags on many times at consignment stores.

ALERT

Check to see if your local thrift store or consignment store has dollar days. If they do, plan to stop in and grab what you can then. These sales may be at the end of the season, but perhaps you can purchase a few items for next season, if you know what size you need.

Have a Clothing Swap with Friends

If you have a circle of friends who have kids, have a clothing swap to get new items for your kids as they grow and pass on the ones that don't fit. What you want to do is as you find clothes that don't fit your kids, put them in a bin or a bag. Have your friends do the same thing. Once the bins are full or the new season is approaching, you can do two things. You can all gather for an afternoon or evening and go through the bins to see what you can use. It's a nice way to spend some social time with friends and walk away with a new wardrobe for the kids. If time is an issue, then you can swap the bins and everyone takes one at time. While you have the bin, you take out anything you can use, leaving the rest for someone else to use. This may take several weeks to complete, but once you receive your bin back, you can donate anything that's left.

ESSENTIAL

Since these are coming from your friends, you know that they have been gently loved and cared for. You should always wash the clothes before you put them in the bin and anything with noticeable stains should be either donated or discarded. But by doing this you'll have money for when you need to purchase a special outfit for your children.

Share Meals and Split the Cooking

Sharing meals with friends is a great way to stock the freezer with pre-made meals for nights that you don't have time to cook. Let's face it, most families with young kids are running around from the minute school gets out until bedtime. Between after-school activities, homework, and running any errands, there isn't always time to cook a complete meal. Stopping at a fast-food restaurant is not only a waste of money, but high in calories for your family. A home-cooked meal is always going to trump fast food.

Find a friend or a few friends who want to do a meal swap. What happens is you double the recipe for one meal you make during the week, and make an extra meal. Wrap it up ready for the freezer and hand it off to a friend. They will do the same thing for you. Now you have a complete, cooked meal that you can have one night made by a friend. Of course you could do this yourself and just freeze the other half. But when you swap with a friend, you'll get items you may not normally cook.

Find a few friends and cook up meals on the weekend and swap them out to fill your freezer. You'll be happy on the nights you don't have to cook. If you find weeks you don't have time to even make a double batch of something, that's fine—just do it when you can or when you have extra stock.

Make Your Own Cleaning Products

No matter how good of a sale you get, unless you get it for free, it's possible to be even cheaper when made yourself. There are lots of recipes online for making household cleaning products that are not only cost-efficient, but sometimes more friendly for the environment as well. You can make laundry detergent, shampoo, soap, and even baby wipes. You will need to purchase some items to make all of them, but chances are you're going to purchase in bulk and only use a little at a time. Split the cost of the initial purchase with a friend and save even more.

FACT

There are lots of products you can make on your own that work just as well as those you can purchase in the stores. You'll also find other ideas on how to use products you may already have on hand. For instance, baking soda, which you can purchase for less than $.50 when on sale, can be used as a scouring powder and whitener at half the cost of store-bought cleansers.

Sell Your Old Items to Purchase New Items

Once you are done with something, if it's still in very good used condition, then why not sell it and earn money to purchase a replacement item? You can do this with clothes by bringing them to consignment stores. Consignment stores sell items and then split the price paid with you. It may be 50 percent of the selling price or less. But anything is good since you only have to drop off the clothes and they do the rest of the work. There may be a yearly fee to actually become a consignor, and you will need to sign some kind of contract or agreement. But if you have a lot of items to sell, then it's probably very worth your time to do it.

Another great place to sell items you no longer want or need is on *www
.ebay.com*. You can find just about anything on eBay, which means you can also sell just about anything as well. There are fees associated with listing the items—eBay has to make some money too. But if you figure it out before you price the items, you'll know whether it's worth your time. With eBay you

need to then ship the items to the purchaser and you need to account for the cost of the shipping and packing materials.

ALERT

Be very careful when meeting with someone in person that you are selling items or giving them away to. Always meet in a public place and never give your home address out. You never know, so you should always be safe. It's great to get things at a bargain, but only if you are safe doing so.

Find Free Stuff on Craigslist or Freecycle

Getting something for free is always nice, but it's not something you can count on. It's a great way to make room in your budget for other things. If you need something, it's great to ask around with friends and family to see if they just happen to have it lying around, unused. But they won't always have everything you need. If you have access to the Internet, there are a few options online where you might be able to score some free items and even request what you need. People are always looking for ways to clean out their junk and keep the landfills empty. No better way of doing that then to give things away.

Craigslist is a great place to look for free stuff. They have a section in each state for anything that is free. You'll find it under the "for sale" section. It's best to check the site often as free stuff may go very fast. If you decide you want to get rid of some items, you can also list them there.

Freecycle is another great way to get items for free. Freecycle is an e-mail list that allows you to offer people in your area items you no longer need that you'd like to keep out of the local dumps. Anyone can ask to join the e-mail list and you can list most products. Just visit *www.freecycle.org* to find an e-mail list in your area. If you join the e-mail list, you should join with the idea of also giving items away, not just getting them. The e-mail list works because people give and take, so if you want something, you should always try to offer up something you don't need anymore at the same time. It's a good way to also clean your clutter.

RECIPES

After you have spent countless hours preparing your shopping trip and using your coupons to purchase the products you need at the best price, it only makes sense to have budget-friendly recipes to help use those products. Following are some simple and scrumptious recipes, all costing less than $2.00 a serving. Because feeding your family well for less money is a reward you (and your budget!) will feel great about.

CHAPTER 17

Budget Breakfasts

Silky Scrambled Eggs

By cooking your scrambled eggs in a double boiler instead of in a hot pan, you ensure that they cook more slowly, softly, and evenly, yielding a better end product.

INGREDIENTS | SERVES 8

3 tablespoons butter
14 eggs
½ cup skim milk
¼ cup sour cream
½ teaspoon salt
⅛ teaspoon pepper

1. Place a large saucepan with 1½" of water over medium heat and bring to a simmer. Carefully place slightly smaller saucepan in the water and add butter; let melt. In large bowl, combine eggs, milk, sour cream, salt, and pepper and beat well with an eggbeater or wire whisk.

2. Pour egg mixture into melted butter in top saucepan. Cook, stirring occasionally, for about 30–40 minutes or until eggs are set and creamy. Serve immediately. You can also cook the eggs in a skillet directly over medium heat, stirring frequently, for about 5–7 minutes.

Hearty Slow Cooker Oatmeal

Steel-cut oats are the only kind that will not cook to mush in the slow cooker. Toast the oats and the nuts until fragrant before you place them in the slow cooker.

INGREDIENTS | SERVES 6

1½ cups steel-cut oatmeal
2 tablespoons butter
1 cup chopped walnuts
6 cups water
½ cup brown sugar
1 teaspoon salt
½ teaspoon cinnamon
⅛ teaspoon nutmeg

1. Place oatmeal in large skillet over medium-high heat. Toast, stirring constantly, for 8–9 minutes or until oatmeal is fragrant and begins to brown around the edges. Remove to a 3½-quart slow cooker.

2. In same pan, melt butter and add chopped walnuts. Toast over medium heat, stirring constantly, until nuts are toasted. Combine with all remaining ingredients except spices in 3- or 4-quart slow cooker. Cover and cook on low for 7–9 hours, until oatmeal is tender. Stir in spices, cover, and let stand for 10 minutes. Serve topped with a bit of butter, maple syrup, brown sugar, and more chopped nuts.

Scrambled Eggs Benedict with Easy Hollandaise

This is a quicker, easier version of the classic breakfast staple. There is no chance of the sauce breaking in this version, and substituting ham for Canadian bacon will save money.

INGREDIENTS | SERVES 8

4 English muffins
2 tablespoons butter, softened
¼ cup mayonnaise
⅓ cup sour cream
2 tablespoons heavy cream
2 tablespoons lemon juice
2 tablespoons butter, melted
10 eggs
⅓ cup milk
½ teaspoon salt
⅛ teaspoon white pepper
2 tablespoons butter
1 cup chopped ham
1 cup shredded Swiss cheese

1. Preheat the broiler. Split English muffins and spread each with a bit of the butter. Place on broiler pan and broil until golden brown; set aside. In blender or food processor, combine mayonnaise, sour cream, heavy cream, lemon juice, and melted butter. Blend or process until smooth. Set aside.

2. In large bowl, combine eggs, milk, salt, and pepper and beat until frothy. In large saucepan, melt 2 tablespoons butter; add egg mixture and cook over medium heat, stirring frequently, until eggs are creamy but not quite set. Stir in ham and continue cooking until eggs are set.

3. Top each toasted English muffin with some of the cheese, a spoonful of the egg and ham mixture, and a spoonful of the sauce. Broil for 2–3 minutes or until heated through; serve immediately.

Egg Safety

Did you know that it's not considered safe by the USDA to eat poached or fried eggs done "softly set" or "over easy"? Eggs must be fully cooked to be safe. In other words, the yolk must be set and firm. You can use pasteurized eggs and still eat them softly set, but they are very expensive. This recipe solves that problem by making Eggs Benedict with scrambled eggs.

Crispy Cinnamon French Toast

French toast is easy to make and it's an inexpensive way to stretch bread. You can use any bread you'd like in this recipe.

INGREDIENTS | SERVES 4

2 eggs, beaten
⅓ cup milk
2 tablespoons sugar
½ teaspoon cinnamon
8 slices white bread
2 cups finely crushed leftover cereal flakes
¼ cup butter

1. In shallow bowl, combine eggs, milk, sugar, and cinnamon and beat until smooth. Dip each slice of bread into the egg mixture, letting stand for 1 minute, turn over, and then dip into crushed cereal to coat.

2. In large skillet over medium-high heat, melt butter. When it's melted and foamy, add the coated bread pieces, two to three at a time. Cook on first side for 3–5 minutes until golden brown. Carefully turn and cook on second side for 2–4 minutes until golden brown and crisp. Serve immediately.

Cereal Flake Breakfast Treats

This inventive recipe makes use of the leftover cereal pieces that accumulate at the bottom of the boxes, turning them into a tasty and healthy treat!

INGREDIENTS | YIELDS 24 COOKIES

⅓ cup butter, softened
¼ cup applesauce
½ cup brown sugar
¼ cup sugar
1 egg
¾ cup all-purpose flour
¼ cup whole-wheat flour
2 tablespoons wheat germ
½ teaspoon baking soda
2 cups leftover cereal flakes
¾ cup raisins

1. Preheat oven to 325°F. In large bowl, combine butter, applesauce, brown sugar, sugar, and egg and beat well. Add flour, whole-wheat flour, wheat germ, and baking soda and mix until a dough forms. Stir in cereal flakes (and any crumbs) along with raisins.

2. Drop by tablespoons onto ungreased cookie sheets. Bake for 15–20 minutes or until cookies are set and light golden brown. Cool completely on wire racks. Store covered at room temperature.

Healthy Cottage Cheese and Oatmeal Pancakes

You can make these pancakes without a blender, but they won't be as fluffy. In that case, beat the egg whites separately and fold into the batter just before cooking.

INGREDIENTS | SERVES 4

⅓ cup quick-cooking oatmeal

4 eggs

1 cup small-curd cottage cheese

2 tablespoons orange juice

¾ cup all-purpose flour

1 teaspoon baking soda

3 tablespoons sugar

¼ teaspoon salt

2 tablespoons butter or margarine

1. In a blender or food processor, grind oatmeal until fine; remove. Add eggs, cottage cheese, and orange juice to blender and blend until mixed. Add oatmeal, flour, baking soda, sugar, and salt and blend just until smooth.

2. Heat a large skillet over medium heat until a drop of water sizzles on it. Add butter and melt; spread evenly. Pour batter by ¼ cup portions onto skillet, four at a time. Cook until edges look dry and bubbles form on surface and begin to break, about 3–4 minutes. Carefully turn with a spatula and cook for 2 minutes on second side. Serve immediately.

Homemade Granola

This whole-grain granola makes use of several great protein sources and natural sweeteners to provide a delicious and nutritious breakfast pick-me-up.

INGREDIENTS | YIELDS 12 CUPS

½ cup orange juice

½ cup brown sugar

¼ cup honey

¼ cup vegetable oil

2 teaspoons cinnamon

6 cups rolled oatmeal

2 cups quick-cooking oatmeal

1 cup chopped walnuts

2 cups sunflower seeds

1 cup raisins

1. Preheat oven to 250°F. In small bowl, combine orange juice, brown sugar, honey, oil, and cinnamon and mix well. In large roasting pan, combine both kinds of oatmeal, walnuts, and sunflower seeds and mix well.

2. Drizzle orange juice mixture over the oat mixture and stir to mix and coat all dry ingredients; spread into even layer. Bake for 60 minutes, stirring every 15 minutes, until granola is crisp and light golden brown. Stir in raisins, then cool completely. Store in airtight container.

Hearty Rolled-Oat Pancakes

The combination of quick and rolled oatmeal creates a lovely texture in these filling pancakes. You can adjust the sweetness of this recipe to your liking.

INGREDIENTS | SERVES 6

2 cups buttermilk
1½ cups quick-cooking oatmeal
½ cup rolled oatmeal
¼ cup brown sugar
½ cup all-purpose flour
¼ cup whole-wheat flour
1 teaspoon baking powder
1 teaspoon baking soda
½ teaspoon salt
2 eggs, beaten
¼ cup vegetable oil
2–4 tablespoons butter

1. In large mixing bowl, combine buttermilk, both kinds of oatmeal, and brown sugar. Mix well and let stand for 10 minutes. Add flour, whole-wheat flour, baking powder, baking soda, and salt and mix well. Then blend in eggs and vegetable oil until just mixed.

2. In large skillet or electric skillet, melt 2 tablespoons butter over medium heat. Stir batter; you may need to add more buttermilk. Pour batter onto skillet in ¼ cup portions. Cook until bubbles form and start to break on pancakes; carefully flip and cook for 2–3 minutes on second side. Repeat with remaining batter, adding more butter to skillet if necessary. Serve immediately.

Berry-Oatmeal Muffins

The frozen raspberries are a novel breakfast surprise, and they add both a sweet and tart kick to these hearty muffins.

INGREDIENTS | YIELDS 12 MUFFINS

1 cup all-purpose flour
½ cup whole-wheat flour
½ cup brown sugar
¼ cup ground oatmeal
1 teaspoon cinnamon
2 teaspoons baking powder
½ teaspoon salt
1 cup leftover cooked oatmeal
1 egg
¼ cup butter, melted
3 tablespoons vegetable oil
1 cup frozen raspberries

1. Preheat oven to 400°F. Line 12 muffin cups with paper liners; set aside. In large bowl, combine all-purpose flour, whole-wheat flour, brown sugar, ground oatmeal, cinnamon, baking powder, and salt and mix well.

2. In small bowl, combine oatmeal, egg, butter, and vegetable oil and mix well. Add to dry ingredients and stir just until combined. Fold in raspberries. Spoon batter into prepared muffin cups.

3. Bake muffins for 18–23 minutes or until they are set and golden brown. Let stand for 5 minutes, then remove from muffin cups and cool on wire rack. Serve warm.

Breakfast Pitas

These sandwiches taste like those at your local drive-through, but better. Plus, they're about half the price. If you don't like to eat bell peppers in the morning, leave them out.

INGREDIENTS | SERVES 6

2 tablespoons butter

1 green bell pepper, chopped

2 cups frozen hash brown potatoes

6 eggs

¼ cup milk

½ teaspoon salt

⅛ teaspoon pepper

1 cup shredded Swiss cheese

3 pita pockets, halved

Other Breakfast Sandwiches

For an easy and inexpensive breakfast on the run, you can make a sandwich out of any cooked egg mixture. Scramble up an egg or two, add some cheese and chopped tomatoes, and wrap it in a corn or flour tortilla. English muffins make great breakfast sandwiches, filled with a fried egg and a bit of crumbled cooked sausage.

1. In large skillet, melt butter over medium heat. Add bell pepper; cook and stir until crisp-tender, about 3 minutes. Add potatoes; cook, stirring occasionally, until potatoes are tender and beginning to brown.

2. In medium bowl, combine eggs, milk, salt, and pepper and beat well. Pour into skillet with vegetables. Cook, stirring occasionally, until eggs are scrambled and set. Sprinkle cheese on top, remove from heat, cover, and let stand for 3 minutes. Divide egg mixture among pita breads and serve immediately.

Doughnut Holes

These doughnut holes have a more refined flavor than the ones you can get at your local coffee shop. The combination of chocolate, cinnamon, and orange is a lovely flavor that your family will rave about.

INGREDIENTS | YIELDS 30 DOUGHNUT HOLES

1¾ cups all-purpose flour
¼ cup whole-wheat flour
¼ cup sugar
2 teaspoons baking powder
1 teaspoon baking soda
½ teaspoon salt
½ teaspoon cinnamon
¼ cup butter, melted
¼ cup milk
½ cup orange juice
1 egg
3 cups peanut oil
½ cup powdered sugar
1 teaspoon cinnamon
½ cup chocolate chips

Used Cooking Oil

If you carefully cool and strain oil used for deep-frying, it can be reused up to three times. But consider what was cooked in the oil before. You don't want to use oil that was used to fry fish to cook doughnuts or apple fritters. Be sure to refrigerate the oil after it has been cooled and strained.

1. In large bowl, combine all-purpose flour, whole-wheat flour, sugar, baking powder, baking soda, salt, and ½ teaspoon cinnamon and mix well. Add melted butter, milk, orange juice, and egg and combine until well blended.

2. In large heavy saucepan, heat peanut oil over medium heat to 375°F. In small bowl, combine powdered sugar and 1 teaspoon cinnamon and mix well; set aside. Rinse a spoon in cold water and scoop up a spoonful of dough. Push three chocolate chips into the center of the dough and smooth over the dough to cover. Drop into the hot oil; fry for 3–4 minutes or until doughnut balls are golden brown. Repeat with remaining dough and chocolate chips.

3. As the doughnut balls are fried, carefully remove from oil with slotted spoon; drop into powdered sugar mixture and roll to coat. Then place on wire rack to cool.

Breakfast Pizza

If you like, you could add any cooked vegetables such as mushrooms, asparagus, or red bell peppers to these cute pizzas.

INGREDIENTS | SERVES 4

4 pita bread pockets

1 (3-ounce) package cream cheese, softened

2 tablespoons butter or margarine

4 eggs, beaten

2 tablespoons milk

¼ teaspoon salt

2 Healthy Chicken Sausage Patties (Chapter 20), chopped

1 cup shredded Cheddar cheese

1. Preheat oven to 400°F. Place pita bread on a cookie sheet and spread each with ¼ of the cream cheese; set aside.

2. Heat butter in small skillet over medium heat. In small bowl, combine eggs with milk and salt and beat well. Pour into skillet. Cook and stir until eggs are set but still moist, about 5 minutes. Divide among pitas.

3. Top with chopped Healthy Chicken Sausage Patties and cheese. Bake for 10–15 minutes or until pizzas are hot and cheese melts and begins to bubble. Let cool for 5 minutes and serve.

Fruit and Yogurt Smoothie

With this much fruit, you're actually getting a lot of your daily fruit requirement in one delicious smoothie. For a splurge, top each smoothie with some fresh raspberries.

INGREDIENTS | SERVES 6

2 cups frozen strawberries

1 cup frozen raspberries

1 cup vanilla frozen yogurt

1 cup plain yogurt

1 cup orange juice

In blender or food processor, combine all ingredients. Blend or process until mixture is smooth. Serve immediately.

Frozen Fruit

Frozen fruit is sold as two types: loose pack and solid pack. For these drinks, you'll want to purchase loose pack fruits without sugar. Loose packs are easier to measure and are of higher quality. Do not thaw before using in baking recipes.

Graham Cracker Streusel Muffins

This is a simple recipe with a big taste payoff! You can save the last few graham crackers in each package by freezing them, and then grind them when you're ready to use them here.

INGREDIENTS | YIELDS 24 MUFFINS

1 (18-ounce) package spice cake mix
1½ cups finely crushed graham cracker crumbs, divided
3 eggs
¼ cup oil
¾ cup water
¼ cup butter, softened
½ cup brown sugar
½ cup chopped walnuts

Freezing Muffins

Muffins freeze beautifully, so when you make a batch, freeze some for breakfast on the run. Freeze muffins individually on a cookie sheet, then wrap each in freezer wrap and package into freezer bags. Label and freeze for up to 3 months. To thaw, unwrap muffins and let stand at room temperature for 30–40 minutes.

1. Preheat oven to 350°F. In large bowl, combine cake mix, ½ cup graham cracker crumbs, eggs, oil, and water. Mix until blended, then beat on medium speed for 2 minutes. In small bowl, combine remaining graham-cracker crumbs, butter, brown sugar, and walnuts and mix until crumbly.

2. Line 24 muffin cups with paper liners. Divide cake mix into prepared muffin cups; sprinkle each with some of the walnut mixture. Bake for 18–23 minutes or until muffins are set when touched with finger. Let cool in pans for 5 minutes, then remove to wire racks to cool completely.

CHAPTER 18

Affordable Appetizers

Fiesta Salsa

Salsa is one of the easiest recipes to make, although it can be very expensive to buy. If you have fresh tomatoes from your garden, all the better!

INGREDIENTS | YIELDS 3 CUPS;
SERVING SIZE ¼ CUP

3 red tomatoes, chopped
1 green bell pepper, chopped
1 jalapeño pepper, minced
½ cup chopped red onion
1 clove garlic, minced
2 tablespoons lemon juice
½ teaspoon salt
⅛ teaspoon cayenne pepper
1 tablespoon olive oil

Combine all ingredients in medium bowl and mix gently. Cover and refrigerate up to 8 hours before serving.

Freezing Salsa

Salsa will freeze and defrost well, but the consistency will be different. Because tomatoes and pepper are so high in water content, they will be a little mushier (like cooked sauce) when frozen and defrosted. But this texture will still be acceptable to most people.

Strained Yogurt Vegetable Dip

*Yogurt cheese is a marvelous substitute for cream cheese, both healthier and cheaper!
You'll have to give yourself an extra day to make this recipe, however.*

INGREDIENTS | SERVES 10

2 cups plain yogurt

1 tablespoon olive oil

4 cloves garlic, minced

½ cup shredded carrots

½ cup pesto

Freezing Whey

Whey is full of vitamins and minerals and is a great addition to almost any soup (except clear soups). To freeze it, place it in ice cube trays and freeze until solid. Remove the cubes from the trays, package into freezer bags, label, and freeze up to 3 months. To use, just drop the cubes into the soup and heat.

1. The day before, place the yogurt into a strainer or colander that has been lined with a double layer of cheesecloth or a paper coffee filter. Place the strainer over a bowl, cover the whole thing with plastic wrap, cover with a small plate and weight with a 1-pound can, and let stand in the refrigerator for 24 hours.

2. The next day, remove the cheese from the strainer and freeze the whey to use in other recipes.

3. In microwave-safe medium bowl, combine olive oil, garlic, and carrots. Microwave on high for 1 minute, remove and stir, then microwave on high for 30-second intervals until vegetables are tender. Drain well and let cool for 20 minutes. Stir into yogurt cheese along with pesto. Cover and chill for at least 2 hours before serving.

Guacamole

The lima beans in this recipe are not completely traditional, but they act as a thickener that really stretches the amount of product you can get out of your avocados.

INGREDIENTS | SERVES 8–10

1 cup dried lima beans
½ cup chopped onion
3 tablespoons lemon juice
½ teaspoon salt
1 tablespoon butter, melted
¼ teaspoon cayenne pepper
3 ripe avocados
1 tomato, chopped

How to Store Guacamole

When storing guacamole, be sure to press waxed paper or plastic wrap directly on the surface (don't use aluminum foil). When avocados are cut, enzymes in the cells react with air and turn brown. Keep air away from guacamole, and it won't turn brown! Lemon juice or other acid also helps delay this chemical reaction.

1. The day before you want to serve the dip, sort the lima beans, discarding any foreign objects. Rinse thoroughly and drain well. Combine in heavy saucepan with cold water to cover and chopped onion. Cover, bring to a boil, reduce heat, and simmer for 1 hour until very tender. Refrigerate cooked beans overnight in the cooking liquid.

2. When you want to serve the dip, combine lemon juice, salt, butter, and cayenne pepper in a food processor. If necessary, drain the bean mixture; add the cooled bean and onion mixture to the lemon juice mixture and process until smooth. Then peel and slice the avocados; add to processor and process again until smooth. Stir in the chopped tomato. Serve immediately, or cover and refrigerate up to 8 hours before serving.

Poached Cod Egg Rolls

Cod is a dense fish, and when you cook it in juice, it begins to taste like lobster. Think of these bite-sized appetizers as an imitation-lobster dish, at a fraction of the price!

INGREDIENTS | **YIELDS 12 EGG ROLLS**

1 cup apple juice

½ pound cod fillets

2 tablespoons butter

2 cloves garlic, minced

½ cup finely chopped onion

½ cup finely chopped carrot

1 tablespoon lemon juice

¼ teaspoon Old Bay Seasoning

12 (6-inch) egg roll wrappers

1 egg, beaten

2 tablespoons water

2 cups peanut oil

Old Bay Seasoning

Old Bay Seasoning is the classic blend of spices used for cooking seafood. You can make your own mix; it's cheaper and it's fun. Combine 1 tablespoon celery salt, ½ teaspoon paprika, ⅛ teaspoon dry mustard, ⅛ teaspoon each white and cayenne peppers, and ⅛ teaspoon allspice.

1. In heavy saucepan, bring apple juice to a simmer. Add fish, cover, and simmer for 3–5 minutes or until fish flakes when tested with fork. Remove fish from apple juice and place in medium bowl; discard apple juice, wipe out pan, and add butter, garlic, onion, and carrot. Cook and stir over medium heat for 4–5 minutes, then pour over fish in bowl; sprinkle with lemon juice and Old Bay Seasoning. Using a fork, flake fish and blend ingredients together; set aside.

2. Open egg roll wrappers; dampen a dish towel and lay over the wrappers. In a small bowl, combine egg and water; beat until combined. Working with the wrappers one at a time, lay out wrappers with the point toward you. Place about ¼ cup of the filling in the center. Roll up once, fold in ends, and roll to close. Use egg mixture to seal edges. Repeat with remaining wrappers and filling.

3. Heat peanut oil in large heavy saucepan until it reaches 375°F. Fry egg rolls, two to three at a time, until golden brown, turning once, about 4–6 minutes. Drain on paper towels, cut in half, and serve.

Spinach Pesto

Frozen chopped spinach not only reduces the cost of pesto, but it adds nutrients and fiber. The lemon juice keeps it a nice bright green color.

INGREDIENTS | SERVES 16

1 (10-ounce) package frozen spinach, thawed

½ cup fresh basil leaves

1 teaspoon dried basil leaves

2 tablespoons lemon juice

½ cup chopped walnuts

1 teaspoon salt

⅛ teaspoon white pepper

⅓ cup grated Parmesan cheese

½ cup virgin olive oil

1. Drain thawed spinach in a colander, pressing with your fingers to remove excess water. Combine in blender or food processor with basil, dried basil, lemon juice, walnuts, salt, pepper, and cheese. Process until finely chopped.

2. While processor is running, slowly add olive oil until a smooth thick sauce forms. Serve immediately or cover and refrigerate up to 3 days. Freeze up to 3 months.

Tropical Fruit Salsa

This delicious salsa can be served with corn or tortilla chips, or used as a sauce on grilled fish or chicken.

INGREDIENTS | SERVES 12; SERVING SIZE ½ CUP

1 (15-ounce) can pineapple tidbits

1 (16-ounce) can sliced peaches

1 cucumber

¼ cup peach preserves

1 jalapeño pepper, minced

½ cup finely chopped red onion

½ teaspoon salt

⅛ teaspoon cayenne pepper

2 tablespoons lemon juice

1. Drain pineapple, reserving ¼ cup juice. Drain peaches, reserving 2 tablespoons juice. Chop peaches and combine with pineapple in medium bowl.

2. Peel cucumber, cut in half, remove seeds, and chop. Add to bowl with pineapple. In a small bowl, combine reserved juices, preserves, jalapeño, red onion, salt, pepper, and lemon juice and mix well. Pour over pineapple mixture and toss gently. Serve immediately or cover and refrigerate up to 2 days.

Roasted Potato Skins

Making mashed potatoes from scratch is most cost-effective. What to do with the leftover skins? Make this fabulous appetizer, of course! To splurge, double the bacon.

INGREDIENTS | **SERVES 6–8**

12 potato skin halves

3 slices bacon

¼ cup butter

3 cloves garlic, minced

1 teaspoon salt

¼ teaspoon cayenne pepper

1 cup finely grated Cheddar cheese

1. Preheat oven to 400°F. Cut the potato skin halves in half again to make 24 slices; set aside. In a heavy skillet, cook bacon until crisp, remove from skillet, and drain on paper towels. Crumble and set aside. To the drippings remaining in skillet, add butter and garlic. Cook over medium heat until garlic is tender, about 3 minutes.

2. Remove skillet from heat and let stand for 10–15 minutes to cool slightly. Then dip each potato skin slice into the butter mixture and place on ungreased baking sheets. Sprinkle skins with salt and pepper.

3. Bake the potato skins for 10 minutes or until they start turning golden and crisp. Remove from oven and sprinkle with cheese and reserved crumbled bacon. Return to oven and bake for 5–8 minutes longer until potato skins are crisp and cheese is melted. Serve immediately.

Freeze-Ahead Cheese Puffs

Leftover bread, cream cheese, Cheddar cheese, and onion can be used in this wonderful freeze-ahead appetizer recipe.

INGREDIENTS | YIELDS 32 PUFFS

1 (3-ounce) package cream cheese, softened

1 tablespoon grated onion

½ cup mayonnaise

2 tablespoons chopped cilantro

¼ cup grated Cheddar cheese

8 slices bread

About Your Freezer

If you have a garden or make a lot of foods to freeze, think about investing in a chest freezer. You can find them at scratch-and-dent sales and sometimes at garage sales. Have an electrician check it out to make sure it's safe to use, then keep a freezer thermometer in it.

1. In medium bowl, combine cream cheese with onion; beat well. Add mayonnaise gradually, stirring to mix well. Stir in cilantro and cheese.

2. Cut bread into 4 triangles each. Spread bread with cheese mixture. Place on baking sheet and freeze until solid; remove and pack into hard-sided freezer containers. Freeze up to 3 months. To bake immediately, bake at 350°F for 12–15 minutes. To bake from frozen, bake for 16–20 minutes.

Parmesan Potato Chips

Homemade potato chips are so fun to make, and they taste so much better than packaged chips. The pregrated Parmesan cheese has a texture that is perfect for dusting over these golden chips.

INGREDIENTS | SERVES 8

2 russet potatoes, peeled or unpeeled

4 cups peanut oil

⅓ cup finely grated shelf-stable Parmesan cheese

1 teaspoon salt

1. Slice potato into paper-thin slices, using a vegetable peeler, the slicing blade on a box grater, or a mandoline. As you work, place the potato slices into a bowl of ice water.

2. In a large deep and heavy pot, heat peanut oil over high heat until it reaches 375°F. Remove a handful of potato slices from the ice water and dry thoroughly on kitchen towels. Carefully drop potato slices into the hot oil. Cook and stir to separate. Fry until golden brown.

3. Remove with a large strainer and place in a single layer on fresh paper towels to cool. Immediately sprinkle with some cheese and salt and toss. Repeat with remaining chips, cheese, and salt. Cool completely, then store in airtight container up to 1 week.

Hummus

The peanut butter in this recipe is a stand-in for tahini paste, which is made from expensive sesame seeds. The taste will be slightly different, but no less delicious!

INGREDIENTS | SERVES 8

¾ cup dried garbanzo beans (chickpeas)
1 onion, chopped
6 cloves garlic
2¼ cups water
3 tablespoons lemon juice
3 tablespoons olive oil
3 tablespoons peanut butter
1 teaspoon salt
¼ teaspoon white pepper

1. Sort through the garbanzo beans and rinse well. Cover with cold water and let stand overnight. The next day, drain the beans, rinse well, and place in saucepan with onion, whole garlic cloves, and water. Bring to a boil, reduce heat, cover, and simmer for 1½ to 2 hours until beans are tender.

2. Drain beans. Place beans, onion, and garlic in food processor along with lemon juice, half of the olive oil, peanut butter, salt, and pepper. Process until smooth. Place in serving dish and drizzle with remaining olive oil. Serve with tortilla or pita chips.

Crackly Crostini

Crostini can be stored for up to a week. It's the ideal type of cracker to use with salsas, hummus, or any other dip.

INGREDIENTS | YIELDS 48 CROSTINI

1 loaf French bread
3 tablespoons olive oil
3 tablespoons butter
3 cloves garlic, minced
½ teaspoon salt
⅛ teaspoon pepper

1. Preheat oven to 325°F. Slice the bread into ¼" slices and set on a baking sheet.

2. In small saucepan, combine olive oil, butter, and garlic. Cook and stir over medium heat until garlic is fragrant, then remove from heat. Using a pastry brush, brush the olive oil mixture on both sides of the bread. Season with salt and pepper.

3. Bake for 10 minutes, then turn all the bread slices and bake for 10–15 minutes longer until bread is light golden brown and very crisp. Store covered at room temperature.

CHAPTER 19

Saving on Soup, Salad, and Sandwiches

Light and Fresh Gazpacho

Gazpacho is the perfect answer to a garden bursting with ripe tomatoes. It's the ultimate summertime or early-fall dish, since it's best when the vegetables are at their peak.

INGREDIENTS | SERVES 8–10

4 ripe tomatoes, chopped
½ cup orange juice
2 teaspoons sugar
2 cucumbers
1 (46-ounce) can tomato juice
2 green bell peppers, chopped
1 red onion, chopped
1 teaspoon salt
⅛ teaspoon white pepper
½ teaspoon Tabasco sauce
1 teaspoon dried tarragon leaves
1 cup water
¼ cup chopped fresh parsley (optional)

1. In large bowl, mix tomatoes, orange juice, and sugar. Peel cucumbers, cut in half, remove seeds, and chop. Add to tomato mixture along with tomato juice, bell peppers, and red onion.

2. Add salt, pepper, Tabasco sauce, tarragon, and water and stir gently but thoroughly. Cover and chill soup for at least 2 hours before serving. Top with parsley.

Tomato Bisque with Basil

You can replace the heavy cream in this recipe with milk for a dish that's almost as rich, and more cost-effective.

INGREDIENTS | SERVES 6

1 tablespoon olive oil
2 tablespoons butter
1 onion, finely chopped
5 cloves garlic, minced
2 (10.75-ounce) cans condensed tomato soup
1 (8-ounce) can tomato sauce
3 cups water
½ teaspoon dried basil leaves
½ cup heavy cream
½ cup milk

1. In large pot, combine olive oil and butter over medium heat. Cook onion and garlic, stirring frequently, until tender, about 5–6 minutes. Add soup, sauce, water, and basil. Bring to a simmer and simmer for 10 minutes.

2. Add cream and milk and stir well. Heat soup through but do not boil. Serve immediately with optional croutons and a sprinkle of Parmesan cheese.

Classic Beef Stew

This easy and wholesome stew bakes in the oven, so you can go about your day without worrying about it. You'll love the way your house smells after you cook this dish!

INGREDIENTS | SERVES 6

1 pound ground beef

1 tablespoon olive oil

2 onions, chopped

4 carrots, sliced

3 cloves garlic, minced

1 (10.75-ounce) can cream of mushroom soup

2 cups water

3 russet potatoes, sliced

2 cups frozen peas

½ teaspoon dried tarragon leaves

½ teaspoon salt

⅛ teaspoon pepper

1. Brown ground beef in large skillet. Remove meat from skillet with slotted spoon and place in 3-quart baking dish. Drain all but 1 tablespoon of drippings from skillet. Add olive oil, then cook onion and carrots in drippings for 3–4 minutes until glazed. Add to beef in baking dish.

2. Add garlic, soup, and water to the skillet and bring to a simmer, scraping any brown bits from the bottom of the skillet. Then pour into baking dish along with remaining ingredients and stir well. Cover tightly with foil and bake at 325°F for 1½ to 2 hours or until vegetables are tender and soup is bubbling.

Soup Science

Soup is one of the most forgiving recipes in all of food science. You can add almost anything to it, and leave everything out but the liquid. It's a great way to use leftover vegetables and meats. Just remember, if the ingredients are already cooked, add them at the very end; you just want to reheat them, not overcook them.

Vichyssoise

This classic soup, which sounds so expensive, is just potato and leek soup, blended until smooth and chilled. Because leeks are expensive, onions are a good substitute.

INGREDIENTS | SERVES 6

2 tablespoons butter

2 onions, finely sliced

3 potatoes, peeled and diced

2 cups chicken stock

2 cups water

2 cups whole milk

½ teaspoon salt

⅛ teaspoon white pepper

½ cup heavy cream

2 tablespoons minced fresh parsley

Blending Hot Liquids

Hot liquids expand in the blender, so whether you're blending a soup or a sauce, don't fill the blender all the way to the top. Filling it halfway and blending in batches is the safest way. Remember to cover the lid with a folded kitchen towel; hold on to the towel to keep the lid down.

1. In large pot, melt butter over medium heat. Add onions; cook and stir until translucent. Add potatoes, stock, and water and bring to a simmer. Cover and cook until potatoes are tender, about 10–15 minutes.

2. Purée the soup either by using an immersion blender or a standard blender, or forcing the soup through a sieve. Return to pot. Add milk, salt, pepper, and cream and heat through. Soup can be served hot with a sprinkling of parsley, or chilled and served cold with some optional diced fresh chives.

Hearty Split Pea Soup

Combining several cans of condensed soup and adding some fresh vegetables is a great way to add flavor and nutrition to canned soup. Look for soups when they're on sale, and stock up.

INGREDIENTS | SERVES 6

2 tablespoons olive oil

1 onion, chopped

1 cup lentils

5 cups water

2 chicken bouillon cubes

1 (11-ounce) can condensed split pea soup

1 (11-ounce) can condensed cream of potato soup

1 (5-ounce) can evaporated milk

1. In large pot, combine oil and onion over medium heat; cook and stir until onion is tender and starts to brown around the edges, about 10 minutes. Stir in lentils and add water and bouillon cubes. Bring to a boil, cover, reduce heat, and simmer for 20 minutes.

2. Add condensed soups to pot and stir well. Bring back to a simmer; cook for 10 minutes. Then stir in evaporated milk and heat through but do not boil. Serve immediately.

Chicken Bouillon Cubes

Some brands of bouillon cubes are better than others. Buy the best brand that you can afford. You can find them at the large container stores and at dollar stores. They're made from concentrated chicken stock and other flavorings. Try to avoid those with MSG added. Buy a lot, because they last for years!

Zesty Black Bean Stew

Combining legumes, such as these black beans, with grains (the corn and rice) makes a complete protein out of this healthy and simple stew. The chili powder in this recipe adds a warming kick to the dish that will taste great on a cold night.

INGREDIENTS | SERVES 4–6

1 tablespoon olive oil

1 onion, chopped

2 (15-ounce) cans black beans, drained

1 (14-ounce) can corn, undrained

1 (10.75-ounce) can condensed tomato soup

1 (14-ounce) can vegetable broth

2 cups water

¼ teaspoon pepper

1 tablespoon chili powder

½ cup brown rice

1. In large pot, heat olive oil over medium heat. Add onion; cook and stir until tender, about 6 minutes. Stir in all remaining ingredients except rice. Bring to a boil, reduce heat, cover, and simmer for 10 minutes.

2. Uncover and stir in rice. Simmer for 20–30 minutes longer until rice is tender and soup is blended.

About Canned Foods

Canned foods are totally prepared and ready to eat. They can be higher in sodium than the raw variety of the food. Look for lower-sodium types (read labels!). You can also rinse the food before use to reduce the sodium content. Beans and vegetables such as corn and peas especially benefit from rinsing.

Burgers with Onions and Garlic

By adding ingredients to the hamburger meat, you are not only infusing it with additional flavor, but you are stretching your meat to fill more burgers. It's the best of both worlds!

INGREDIENTS | SERVES 5

1 tablespoon olive oil
½ cup chopped onion
4 cloves garlic, minced
3 tablespoons dried bread crumbs
1 egg
1 tablespoon water
1 tablespoon soy sauce
½ teaspoon salt
⅛ teaspoon pepper
1 pound 80 percent lean hamburger

1. In small saucepan, heat olive oil over medium heat. Add onion and garlic; cook and stir until very tender, about 6 minutes. Remove from heat and let cool for 15 minutes. Place onion mixture in blender or food processor and add bread crumbs, egg, water, soy sauce, salt, and pepper. Blend or process until smooth and remove to large bowl.

2. Add hamburger to puréed mixture, gently mixing with hands just until combined. Cover and refrigerate at least 4 hours.

3. Preheat grill or broiler. Form hamburger mixture into 5 patties and grill or broil until meat thermometer registers 165°F, turning carefully once. Serve on toasted buns with relish, mustard, and ketchup.

Grilled Tuna Melt with Apple and Green Onion

*These open-faced sandwiches combine the classic taste of tuna
salad with fresh apple pieces for a memorable recipe.*

INGREDIENTS | SERVES 4

1 (6-ounce) can tuna, drained

2 green onions, sliced

½ cup chopped apple

¼ cup chopped celery

2 teaspoons mustard

¼ cup mayonnaise

4 slices white or whole-wheat bread

2 tablespoons butter or margarine

8 slices American cheese

What Kind of Tuna?

Canned tuna varies in cost depending on the type and form. Solid pack tuna is the most expensive. Albacore, or white tuna, is the most expensive packed tuna because the fish is larger and costs more to catch. "Light" tuna is the other type most commonly sold in the U.S. It is darker and less expensive, and actually contains *less mercury* than the larger albacore.

1. In medium bowl, combine tuna, onions, apple, celery, mustard, and mayonnaise and mix gently but thoroughly.

2. Preheat broiler. On broiler pan, place bread slices and spread with butter. Broil for 2–4 minutes or until bread is toasted. Turn bread slices over. Top each with a slice of cheese, then divide the tuna mixture and place on top. Top with another slice of cheese.

3. Broil sandwiches 6" from heat source for 3–6 minutes, watching carefully, until the cheese melts and tuna mixture is hot. Serve immediately.

Marinated Steak Pockets

Marinating round steak makes it almost as tender as filet mignon.
Make this sandwich filling ahead of time to eat lunch in a flash.

INGREDIENTS | SERVES 4

½ pound bottom round steak
3 tablespoons olive oil
3 tablespoons apple cider vinegar
1 tablespoon soy sauce
3 tablespoons ketchup
1 teaspoon salt
2 tablespoons water
1 cucumber, peeled and chopped
2 stalks celery, chopped
2 green onions, chopped
2 pita pockets

Marinating Meats

Marinating meats in an acidic mixture breaks down the meat structure, which results in a tender steak. Acidic ingredients include lemon juice, wine, and vinegar. But don't marinate the meat too long! Meats that have been marinated more than 24 hours can turn mushy, and the flavor could be compromised by the marinade ingredients.

1. Place steak in heavy-duty plastic zip-top bag. Add olive oil, vinegar, soy sauce, ketchup, salt, and water. Close bag and squish with your hands to mix marinade. Place in large bowl and chill in refrigerator for 8 hours.

2. Preheat broiler and remove steak from marinade. Pour marinade into a small saucepan and set aside. Broil steak, 6" from heat source, turning once, for 5–9 minutes or until desired doneness. Let steak stand for 10 minutes.

3. Bring marinade to a boil over high heat; boil for 1 minute. Thinly slice steak against the grain and place in medium bowl with cucumber, celery, and green onion. Pour marinade over, cover, and place in refrigerator up to 3 days.

4. When ready to eat, slice pita pockets in half and fill with drained meat mixture.

Tabbouleh Pitas

This super-healthy sandwich is extremely quick to make. It's a great on-the-go snack for the family when there's no time for a sit-down meal.

INGREDIENTS | **SERVES 4**

1 cup tabbouleh

1 (15-ounce) can great northern beans, drained

1 cup chopped tomatoes

4 pita pockets

In small bowl, combine tabbouleh, beans, and tomatoes and mix well. Cut pita breads in half and fill with tabbouleh mixture. Serve immediately.

Zesty Pasta Salad with Mushrooms and Cabbage

Add a can of tuna or chicken and this becomes a hearty main-dish salad.

INGREDIENTS | **SERVES 8**

½ cup mayonnaise

½ cup plain yogurt

½ cup zesty Italian salad dressing

1 head purple cabbage

1 green bell pepper, chopped

1 cup sliced mushrooms

2 cups frozen peas

1 (16-ounce) package penne pasta

1. Bring a large pot of salted water to a boil. Meanwhile, in large bowl, combine mayonnaise, yogurt, and salad dressing and mix well.

2. Wash cabbage and cut in half. Remove core and cut crosswise into ¼" thick pieces. Add to mayonnaise mixture in bowl. Add bell pepper and mushrooms.

3. Place frozen peas in a colander. Cook pasta in boiling water until al dente according to package directions. Drain over peas in colander and add to salad mixture. Toss gently to coat and serve immediately or cover and chill for 3–4 hours before serving.

Classic Potato Salad

This salad has a cooked dressing and two kinds of potatoes for added interest. You'll find the cider vinegar gives the dish a hint of tartness that complements the creamy potatoes and mayonnaise very well.

INGREDIENTS | SERVES 8

4 slices bacon

1 tablespoon butter

½ cup finely chopped onion

3 tablespoons all-purpose flour

1 teaspoon salt

⅛ teaspoon pepper

1 (12-ounce) can evaporated milk

⅓ cup apple cider vinegar

¼ cup sugar

2 tablespoons mustard

2 large sweet potatoes

2 pounds red potatoes

½ cup mayonnaise

½ cup whipped salad dressing

½ cup chopped green onions

4 radishes, thinly sliced

1. In large skillet, cook bacon over medium heat until crisp. Remove bacon from pan, crumble, and refrigerate. To drippings remaining in pan, add butter, then cook onion until tender, about 5 minutes.

2. Sprinkle flour, salt, and pepper into pan; cook and stir until bubbly, about 3 minutes. Then add evaporated milk; cook and stir until thickened. Stir in vinegar and sugar and bring back to a boil. Remove from heat to small bowl, stir in mustard, cover, and chill.

3. Bring a large pot of salted water to a boil. Cook sweet potatoes until tender, about 15 minutes; remove to wire rack. Then add red potatoes; cook until tender, about 10 minutes; remove to wire rack.

4. When potatoes are cool enough to handle, take dressing out of fridge and add mayonnaise and whipped salad dressing. Peel potatoes and cut into 1" pieces, adding to the dressing as you work. Stir in green onions, radishes, and reserved bacon. Cover and chill for at least 4 hours before serving.

Mixed Greens with Tarragon and Oranges

For a splurge, use pecans or cashews instead of the almonds in this fabulous salad.

INGREDIENTS | SERVES 6

¼ cup slivered almonds

3 tablespoons sugar, divided

1 tablespoon brown sugar

¼ cup sliced almonds

2 (11-ounce) cans mandarin oranges

½ cup mayonnaise

½ teaspoon dried tarragon leaves

¼ teaspoon salt

⅛ teaspoon white pepper

6 cups mixed salad greens

3 stalks celery, chopped

Melting Sugar

Melting sugar isn't difficult, but it does take some patience. It can take up to 15 minutes. The melted sugar will turn liquid and also change color to a dark golden amber. Don't raise the heat because it burns easily. Be very careful with the melted sugar—it can scald you!

1. In small skillet, combine slivered almonds, 2 tablespoons sugar, and brown sugar over low heat. Cook, stirring frequently, until sugar melts. Add the sliced almonds and stir well until the melted sugar coats almonds. Remove from heat and spoon onto parchment paper; let cool and break into small pieces.

2. Meanwhile, drain mandarin oranges, reserving ½ cup liquid. In small bowl, combine mayonnaise, 1 tablespoon sugar, reserved orange juice, tarragon, salt, and pepper and mix well. Set aside.

3. When ready to serve, combine salad greens, celery, and drained oranges in large serving bowl. Drizzle half of dressing over salad and toss to coat. Sprinkle with the cooled almonds and serve remaining dressing on the side.

Curried Waldorf Pasta Salad

Waldorf salad is a classic combination of apples, walnuts, celery, and raisins in a creamy dressing. This updated version adds curry, pasta, and chicken to turn it into a main dish.

INGREDIENTS | SERVES 8–10

1 cup vanilla yogurt

¼ cup mayonnaise

1 tablespoon curry powder

¼ cup milk

2 tablespoons honey

2 Granny Smith apples, chopped

1 (16-ounce) package penne pasta

1 cup raisins

1 (12-ounce) can dark chicken meat, drained

4 stalks celery, chopped

½ cup chopped walnuts

1. Bring a large pot of salted water to a boil. In large bowl, combine yogurt, mayonnaise, curry powder, milk, and honey and mix well.

2. Wash apples and chop (do not peel) and add to the yogurt mixture as you work. Add pasta to boiling water and cook according to package directions until al dente.

3. Meanwhile, add raisins, chicken, celery, and walnuts to yogurt mixture and stir to coat. When pasta is done, drain and add to bowl; toss to coat. Cover and chill for 3–4 hours before serving.

CHAPTER 20

Cheap Chicken, Pork, and Beef

Slow-Cooked Pot Roast

This really is an entire meal in one; all you need to do is add a salad and some bread if you'd like. Save all of the meat drippings to make a quick gravy to serve with your meal.

INGREDIENTS | SERVES 8

1 (3-pound) bottom round or chuck roast
3 tablespoons all-purpose flour
1 teaspoon salt
1 teaspoon paprika
¼ teaspoon pepper
1 tablespoon olive oil
2 tablespoons butter
2 onions, chopped
4 potatoes, cubed
4 carrots, sliced
¼ cup water
1 (10-ounce) can condensed tomato soup
2 tablespoons cornstarch
⅓ cup water

1. Trim excess fat from roast. On shallow plate, combine flour, salt, paprika, and pepper. Dredge roast in this mixture, coating both sides. Heat olive oil and butter in large saucepan over medium heat. Add roast; brown on both sides, turning once, about 5–8 minutes.

2. Meanwhile, place onions, potatoes, and carrots in a 5- or 6-quart slow cooker. Top with the browned roast. Pour ¼ cup water and tomato soup into saucepan and bring to a boil, scraping the pan to loosen drippings. Pour over roast.

3. Cover and cook on low for 8–10 hours until meat and vegetables are very tender. If necessary, you can thicken the gravy by removing the roast and covering with foil. Then combine cornstarch and ⅓ cup water in small bowl and stir into the gravy; cover and cook on high for 20–30 minutes until thickened.

Quick Beef Stir-Fry with Spinach and Ginger

This easy stir-fry recipe uses ingredients you probably already have around the house. Parmesan is not a traditional ingredient in an Asian stir-fry, but it works beautifully here.

INGREDIENTS | SERVES 6

1 pound 80 percent lean ground beef

2 cups sliced mushrooms

1 onion, chopped

4 cloves garlic, minced

1 (10-ounce) package frozen spinach, thawed

½ teaspoon ground ginger

2 tablespoons soy sauce

4 eggs

¼ cup milk

⅓ cup grated Parmesan cheese

1. In large skillet, crumble ground beef. Cook and stir over medium heat for 3 minutes. Add mushrooms, onion, and garlic; cook and stir until beef is browned and vegetables are crisp-tender. Drain well.

2. Drain spinach thoroughly and add to skillet along with ginger and soy sauce; cook and stir for 2 minutes until hot.

3. In small bowl, combine eggs, milk, and cheese and beat well. Add to skillet; stir-fry until eggs are cooked and set. Serve immediately.

Stir-Fry Tips

You don't need a wok to stir-fry; a large heavy-duty frying pan will do, preferably one without a nonstick surface. Have all the ingredients ready to cook and the sauces mixed. Heat the pan over high heat and add the ingredients in the order the recipe specifies. Keep the food moving with a sturdy spatula or wooden spoon. And be sure to serve immediately!

Potato Miniburger Casserole

This hearty casserole is for meat and potato lovers. You'll be amazed how far you can stretch these ingredients and still end up with a filling meal for the family.

INGREDIENTS | SERVES 6

1 tablespoon olive oil

1 onion, finely chopped

2 cloves garlic, minced

1 egg

¼ cup fine dry bread crumbs

½ teaspoon salt

⅛ teaspoon pepper

¼ cup ketchup

¾ pound 80 percent lean ground beef

4 cups frozen hash brown potatoes, thawed

1 (12-ounce) can evaporated milk

2 plum tomatoes, chopped

½ cup shredded sharp Cheddar cheese

¼ cup grated Parmesan cheese

1. In large skillet, heat olive oil over medium heat. Add onion and garlic; cook and stir until tender, about 5 minutes. Remove from heat. Remove ¼ cup of onion mixture to medium bowl and add egg, bread crumbs, salt, pepper, and ketchup; mix well. Add ground beef; mix until combined. Form into 8 small hamburgers.

2. Remove remaining onion mixture from skillet and place in 2-quart casserole dish; do not wipe skillet. Place hamburgers in skillet; cook, turning once, over medium heat until hamburgers are almost fully cooked, about 6–8 minutes. Remove hamburgers to paper towel to drain. Drain fat from skillet.

3. Add potatoes, milk, and plum tomatoes to skillet; bring to a simmer. Pour into casserole dish and mix with onion mixture. Add cooked hamburger patties, stirring gently. Sprinkle with cheeses. Bake for 30–40 minutes or until casserole is bubbling and cheese is melted.

Swiss-Style Steak

This traditional preparation of cube steak will take you straight back to the 1950s! Don't neglect the Worcestershire sauce in this recipe—it's a key component of the flavor in the dish.

INGREDIENTS | SERVES 6

1½ pounds cube steak

¼ cup all-purpose flour

1 teaspoon salt

⅛ teaspoon pepper

3 tablespoons olive oil

1 onion, diced

2 (14-ounce) cans diced tomatoes, undrained

1 cup grated carrot

1 (4-ounce) can mushroom pieces, undrained

1 tablespoon Worcestershire sauce

½ teaspoon dried marjoram leaves

1. Cut cube steak into 6 portions if necessary. On shallow platter, combine flour, salt, and pepper and mix well. Dredge steaks in this mixture on both sides.

2. Heat olive oil in large skillet over medium heat. Add steaks; brown on both sides, turning once, about 3–5 minutes. Remove steaks from heat. Add onion to drippings in skillet; cook and stir until crisp-tender, about 4 minutes.

3. Add tomatoes, carrots, mushrooms, Worcestershire sauce, and marjoram to skillet and bring to a simmer. Return steaks to skillet, covering with the sauce. Reduce heat to low, cover, and simmer for 60–80 minutes or until meat is very tender. Serve immediately.

Cube Steaks

Cube steaks from the supermarket have been run through a tenderizing machine. You can make your own cube steaks by buying thin cuts of bottom round and cutting into individual portions. Cover the meat with plastic wrap, and pound vigorously with a meat mallet or rolling pin. This breaks down the meat fibers, tenderizing the steak.

Homemade Chili

This chili cooks all day in the slow cooker, so you can do other things.
It's thick, hearty, and filling—all the things chili should be!

INGREDIENTS | SERVES 6

1 pound 80 percent lean ground beef

1 onion, chopped

3 cloves garlic, minced

2 (15-ounce) cans kidney beans, drained

2 (14-ounce) cans diced tomatoes, undrained

1 (6-ounce) can tomato paste

1 tablespoon chili powder

1 teaspoon cumin

1½ cups water

½ teaspoon salt

2 tablespoons cornstarch

¼ cup water

1. In large skillet, cook ground beef, onion, and garlic until beef is browned and vegetables are tender, stirring occasionally. Drain well. Combine with all remaining ingredients except cornstarch and ¼ cup water in 4- to 5-quart slow cooker.

2. Cover and cook on low for 8–10 hours. In small bowl, combine cornstarch with ¼ cup water and mix well. Stir into chili, then turn heat to high and cook for 15–20 minutes or until chili is thickened. Serve immediately.

Canned Beans

Very often canned beans go on sale; when they do, stock up! Mark the purchase date on each can with an indelible marker or grease pencil and store the cans in your pantry. Be sure to rotate the cans and use the oldest first. Discard any cans that are dented, bulging, or leaking.

Wellington-Style Steak

Marinated round steak is almost as tender as filet mignon, and the mushroom mixture (called duxelles) adds a rich meaty flavor. Save this recipe for a special occasion.

INGREDIENTS | SERVES 4

1 pound round steak

2 tablespoons olive oil

3 tablespoons lemon juice

⅛ teaspoon pepper

1 (4-ounce) can mushroom pieces, drained

4 cloves garlic, minced

½ onion, chopped

1 tablespoon butter

½ teaspoon salt

2 tablespoons heavy cream

½ teaspoon dried thyme leaves

1 (8-ounce) sheet frozen puff pastry, thawed

Duxelles

If you like the flavor of duxelles, make a large batch and freeze it in ½-cup portions. It adds wonderful richness to almost any main-dish recipe. Stir it into stew, add it to a beef casserole or stir-fries, or spread it on top of grilled or sautéed steaks to stretch the meat and add a meatier flavor.

1. The day before, cut round steak into 4 portions and trim off excess fat. Pierce steaks with fork. Place in 9" glass baking dish and drizzle with olive oil, lemon juice, and pepper. Turn steaks to coat. Cover and refrigerate for 24 hours.

2. In food processor, combine mushrooms, garlic, and onion and process until finely chopped. In medium saucepan, melt butter over low heat and add mushroom mixture. Cook for 15–20 minutes, stirring frequently, until mixture is deep golden brown and all the liquid evaporates.

3. Sprinkle mixture with salt and add cream and thyme leaves; bring to a simmer. Remove from heat and cool completely; cover and refrigerate.

4. The next day, warm a large nonstick skillet over medium heat. Drain steaks and pat dry; discard marinade. Sauté steaks for 3 minutes on one side, then turn and cook for 1–2 minutes on other side. Remove to platter and let stand for 20 minutes to cool.

5. Preheat oven to 400°F. On lightly floured surface, roll puff pastry to a 14" square. Cut into four 7" squares. Divide mushroom mixture in the center of each sheet the size of each piece of steak. Place steak on top. Bring corners to center to completely cover meat and seal edges. Place seam side down on baking sheet; cut decorative swirls into the top.

6. Bake for 20–30 minutes or until deep golden brown. Serve immediately.

Zesty Garlic Chicken Wings

These wings are perked up with the addition of orange juice and balsamic vinegar, which cuts through the sweetness of the honey. Serve them at a party and watch them go!

INGREDIENTS | SERVES 4

⅓ cup honey
2 tablespoons brown sugar
¼ cup soy sauce
8 cloves garlic, sliced
¼ cup orange juice
1 tablespoon balsamic vinegar
2 pounds chicken wings
½ teaspoon red pepper flakes

1. The day before, in small saucepan, combine honey, brown sugar, soy sauce, garlic, orange juice, and vinegar and bring to a boil. Meanwhile, arrange chicken wings in a 9" × 13" glass baking dish.

2. Pour marinade over chicken wings and turn to coat. Cover tightly and refrigerate at least 24 hours before baking.

3. When ready to eat, preheat oven to 350°F. Bake the wings, uncovered, for 30 minutes. Turn wings with tongs and bake for 30 minutes longer. Baste with marinade in bottom of pan and sprinkle with red pepper flakes. Bake for another 20–30 minutes or until chicken wings are dark golden brown and thoroughly cooked. Serve immediately.

Classic Chicken Succotash

Succotash is a fairly easy dish to prepare, and it always comes out tasting like more than the sum of its parts. This recipe will make a great informal family meal.

INGREDIENTS | SERVES 4

½ cup chopped chorizo sausage

2 boneless, skinless chicken breasts

2 tablespoons all-purpose flour

½ teaspoon ground ginger

½ teaspoon salt

⅛ teaspoon cayenne pepper

1 tablespoon olive oil

1 onion, chopped

2 cloves garlic, minced

1 (10-ounce) package frozen lima beans, thawed

1 (10-ounce) package frozen corn, thawed

1 cup chicken stock

1 tomato, chopped

1. In large saucepan, place chorizo sausage over medium heat. Cook, stirring frequently, until crisp, about 7–9 minutes. Meanwhile, cut chicken into 1" pieces and toss with flour, ginger, salt, and pepper.

2. Remove chorizo from saucepan. Add olive oil to drippings and add onion and garlic. Cook, stirring frequently, until crisp-tender, about 4 minutes.

3. Add chicken to saucepan with onions; cook and stir for 4 minutes. Then add chorizo, lima beans, corn, and chicken stock. Bring to a simmer, reduce heat, and simmer for 5 minutes, stirring occasionally, until sauce thickens.

4. Stir in tomato and simmer for 2 minutes, then stir again and serve immediately over hot cooked rice.

Spinach-Stuffed Chicken Breasts

You could use any semi-soft cheese you'd like to flavor this recipe.
Cheddar, Havarti, and Swiss are all great choices.

INGREDIENTS | SERVES 4

4 bone-in, skin-on chicken breasts
2 tablespoons olive oil
3 cloves garlic, minced
1 cup frozen chopped spinach, thawed
3 tablespoons dried bread crumbs
½ teaspoon dried thyme leaves
½ teaspoon dried basil leaves
½ teaspoon salt, divided
⅛ teaspoon pepper
½ cup shredded Muenster cheese
2 tablespoons butter

Making It Safe

You can make any stuffing for poultry ahead of time and refrigerate or freeze it. What you shouldn't do is stuff the poultry ahead of time. For safety reasons, you can heat the stuffing in the microwave before you stuff the chicken or turkey. This helps quickly bring the stuffing up to a safe temperature.

1. Carefully cut the meat away from the bone, leaving the skin attached. Save the bone for chicken stock. Using your fingers, loosen the skin from the flesh, leaving the skin attached at one side. Set aside.

2. In large saucepan, heat olive oil over medium heat. Add garlic; cook and stir for about 1 minute until fragrant. Then add the spinach; cook and stir until liquid evaporates, about 4 minutes. Remove from heat and place spinach in a small bowl; add bread crumbs, thyme, basil, half of the salt, pepper, and Muenster cheese and mix well.

3. Stuff this mixture between the chicken and the skin, spreading evenly and smoothing the skin back over the flesh.

4. Preheat oven to 450°F. Melt the butter in same saucepan. Sprinkle the remaining salt over the chicken, and place, skin side down, in the hot butter. Cook for 3 minutes without moving the chicken. Then shake the pan to loosen chicken and cook for 2–4 minutes longer until skin is brown and crisp.

5. Carefully turn chicken, then move pan to preheated oven and cook for 10–14 minutes longer until the chicken registers 170°F. Let stand for 5 minutes, then serve.

Healthy Chicken Sausage Patties

Making your own sausage patties means you can control what goes into them. You can reduce or omit the salt if you'd like.

INGREDIENTS | SERVES 8

1 Granny Smith apple, peeled
½ cup finely chopped onion
2 cloves garlic, minced
3 tablespoons butter, divided
1 teaspoon salt
½ teaspoon dried thyme leaves
⅛ teaspoon cayenne pepper
1½ pounds chicken pieces

Ground Chicken

Once chicken or other poultry is ground, it should be used within 24 hours. Mix dark and light meat together for best taste and lower cost.

1. Finely chop the apple and combine with the onion, garlic, and 2 tablespoons butter in a small saucepan. Cook over medium heat, stirring frequently, until onion is tender. Remove from heat, pour into large bowl, and let cool, about 20 minutes.

2. Add salt, thyme, and cayenne pepper to onion mixture and blend well. Remove skin and bones from chicken. In food processor, grind chicken with the pulse feature until mixture is even. Add to onion mixture and mix well with hands just until blended.

3. Form mixture into eight patties. In large nonstick skillet, melt 1 tablespoon butter. Cook chicken patties, turning once, for 8–12 minutes or until patties are deep golden brown and chicken is thoroughly cooked, 165°F. Serve immediately, or freeze for longer storage.

Linguine with Chicken and Bacon

This is an elegant yet affordable dish, perfect for company on a weekend night. It is also a fabulous way to use up any leftover chicken breasts from a weekday dinner.

INGREDIENTS | SERVES 6

4 slices bacon

2 tablespoons olive oil

1 onion, chopped

1 pound linguine pasta

3 cooked chicken breasts, sliced

½ teaspoon dried basil leaves

½ cup half-and-half cream

1 cup shredded Swiss cheese

½ cup garlic croutons, crushed

2 tablespoons grated Parmesan cheese

1. Bring a large pot of salted water to a boil. Meanwhile, in large skillet, cook bacon over medium heat until crisp. Remove bacon, crumble, and set aside. Drain drippings from skillet and discard; do not wipe out skillet.

2. Add olive oil and onion to skillet and cook over medium heat until tender, about 5 minutes. Add pasta to boiling water and cook according to package directions until al dente.

3. When onion is tender, add chicken, basil, and half-and-half to skillet and bring to a simmer. Drain pasta and add to skillet along with Swiss cheese, crushed croutons, and Parmesan cheese; toss gently and serve immediately.

Tarragon Chicken Casserole with Potato

This comforting slow-cooked recipe can bubble away in the slow cooker all day while you work. It's extremely versatile (customize with any flavorings you want), and it's hearty enough to feed a large family.

INGREDIENTS | SERVES 6

2 onions, chopped

½ cup wild rice

5 potatoes, cubed

3 carrots, sliced

4 boneless, skinless chicken thighs

1 (10-ounce) can cream of chicken soup

1 cup water

⅛ teaspoon pepper

½ teaspoon dried tarragon leaves

1. In 4- to 5-quart slow cooker, layer onions, wild rice, potatoes, and carrots. Place chicken on top. In small bowl, combine soup, water, pepper, and tarragon and mix well. Pour over chicken.

2. Cover and cook on low for 7–9 hours or until chicken is tender and thoroughly cooked, wild rice is tender, and potatoes are cooked.

3. Remove chicken from slow cooker and cut into 2" pieces. Return to slow cooker, stir, and serve.

Rice in a Slow Cooker

Most rice doesn't cook well in a slow cooker. Brown rice and wild rice are the exceptions, as is instant rice stirred in at the very end of the cooking time. Make sure that the brown or wild rice is at the bottom of the slow cooker, completely covered by the liquid used in the recipe. Stir well before serving.

Cumin-Ginger Pork Chops in Tomato Sauce

You can buy thicker boneless chops and pound them until they're about ½" thick to use in this recipe. Be careful not to overcook thin pork chops, though.

INGREDIENTS | SERVES 4

1 teaspoon cumin seeds

¼ teaspoon ground ginger

⅛ teaspoon cayenne pepper

½ teaspoon salt

2 garlic cloves

2 tablespoons olive oil, divided

4 thin boneless (4-ounce) pork chops

1 tablespoon butter

1 cup chopped plum tomatoes

1 cup chicken stock

2 tablespoons chopped flat-leaf parsley

Pork Chops

Pork chops freeze like a dream, and they can be cooked frozen. You no longer need to cook pork to well-done; a nice light pink color is what you're shooting for. Pork is much leaner than it was 20 years ago, and healthier too. The mild flavor accepts many seasonings; change any recipe by changing the herbs and spices you use.

1. In small bowl, combine cumin seeds with ginger, cayenne pepper, salt, and garlic cloves. Work with back of spoon to mash garlic and grind seeds. Then stir in 1 tablespoon olive oil and blend until smooth.

2. Rub this mixture on both sides of pork chops, coating thoroughly. Let stand for 10 minutes.

3. Heat butter and remaining 1 tablespoon olive oil in large skillet over medium heat. Add the chops and cook without moving for 3–4 minutes, until the chops can be moved without sticking. Turn the chops and cook for 2–4 minutes on second side or until pork is just slightly pink in center, then remove from pan.

4. To drippings remaining in pan, add tomatoes, stock, and parsley. Bring to a boil and boil until reduced, about 4 minutes; pour over chops, sprinkle with parsley, and serve over hot cooked rice.

Cold-Weather Bean and Sausage Chowder

This hearty soup is perfect for cold winter evenings. It stretches 1 pound of Italian sausage to serve eight people—a real bargain. You can substitute in a different variety of beans, if you'd like.

INGREDIENTS | SERVES 8

1 pound great northern beans

1 pound sweet Italian sausage

8 cups water

1 onion, chopped

4 cloves garlic, minced

3 potatoes, peeled and chopped

2 zucchinis, chopped

2 (14-ounce) cans diced tomatoes, undrained

1 (8-ounce) can tomato sauce

1 teaspoon salt

⅛ teaspoon pepper

1. Sort beans and rinse thoroughly. Drain and place in large pot; cover with water. Bring to a boil and boil for 2 minutes. Then cover pot, remove from heat, and let stand for 1 hour. Meanwhile, cook sausage in large skillet until browned; drain off all but 1 tablespoon drippings. Cook onion and garlic in drippings over medium heat until crisp-tender, about 4 minutes.

2. Drain beans and rinse well. Cut sausage into 1" pieces. Combine in 4- to 5-quart slow cooker with water, onion, garlic, and potatoes. Cover and cook on low for 8 hours. Then stir in zucchini, tomatoes, tomato sauce, salt, and pepper; cover and cook on low for 1–2 hours longer, until beans and potatoes are tender. If you'd like, you can mash some of the beans and potatoes, leaving others whole, for a thicker chowder.

Pulled Pork Sandwiches

Pork shoulder becomes velvety, tender shredded meat when cooked in the slow cooker.

INGREDIENTS | SERVES 6

1 onion, chopped
1½ pounds shoulder pork roast
⅛ teaspoon cayenne pepper
½ teaspoon paprika
¼ cup apple cider vinegar
3 tablespoons brown sugar
2 tablespoons Worcestershire sauce
½ cup chili sauce
2 cups coleslaw
6–8 hamburger buns

1. In 4- to 5-quart slow cooker, place onion and top with pork roast. Rub roast with pepper and paprika. In small bowl, combine vinegar, brown sugar, and Worcestershire sauce and mix well. Pour over pork. Cover and cook on low for 8–10 hours until very tender.

2. Remove meat from slow cooker and shred. Return to slow cooker, add chili sauce, and cook for another hour.

3. Make sandwiches with the pork mixture, slaw, and hamburger buns. Serve immediately.

Curried Slow-Cooked Pork

This inventive recipe really livens up pork chops into an exciting dish that's still easy to pull together.

INGREDIENTS | SERVES 6

1 pound pork chops
2 onions, chopped
4 cloves garlic, minced
4 stalks celery, chopped
2 cups sliced carrots
1 (4-ounce) can mushroom pieces, undrained
2 (14-ounce) cans diced tomatoes
1 tablespoon curry powder
½ teaspoon salt
½ teaspoon paprika
½ cup raisins
1 cup instant brown rice

1. Cut pork chops into 2" pieces and combine in 4- to 5-quart slow cooker with onions, garlic, celery, carrots, and mushrooms.

2. Empty half of one can of tomatoes into the slow cooker. Add curry powder, salt, and paprika to remaining tomatoes in can and stir. Add to slow cooker. Add raisins. Cover and cook on low for 7–9 hours or until pork is tender.

3. Stir in the brown rice; cover, and cook on high for 15–20 minutes or until rice is tender. Stir and serve immediately.

CHAPTER 21

Seafood for Savers

Hearty Seafood Chowder

This rich and thick chowder is accented with just enough seafood. If you want to splurge,
increase the amount of seafood; more crabmeat would be a fabulous addition.

INGREDIENTS | SERVES 8

5 cups water

3 potatoes, peeled and diced

2 carrots, sliced

2 stalks celery, sliced

½ pound fish fillets

1 cup small raw shrimp

3 tablespoons olive oil

1 onion, chopped

¼ cup all-purpose flour

1 teaspoon salt

⅛ teaspoon white pepper

2 cups milk

2 cups shredded Cheddar cheese

Seafood on Sale

Grocery stores often have seafood on sale. When that happens, buy a couple of packages and freeze them. Most seafood freezes very well. If the fish or shrimp isn't in freezer bags, repackage them into freezer-safe bags or containers, label with the purchase date, and freeze. Use within three months.

1. In large saucepan, bring water to a boil over high heat. Add potatoes and carrots. Cover and bring back to a boil; reduce heat and simmer for 8 minutes. Stir in celery and fish fillets; simmer for 3 minutes. Stir in shrimp; simmer for 2–4 minutes until shrimp turn pink and the fish flakes. Cover and set aside off the heat.

2. In medium saucepan, combine olive oil and onion over medium heat; cook and stir until tender, about 5–6 minutes. Stir in flour, salt, and pepper; cook and stir until bubbly. Add milk; cook and stir until mixture begins to thicken. Add cheese; cook and stir until melted.

3. Stir cheese sauce into fish mixture. Cook and stir over medium heat until mixture blends and soup starts to steam; do not boil. Serve immediately.

Tuna Casserole with Swiss and Romano

This casserole has a depth of flavor that you won't find in canned casserole mixes.

INGREDIENTS | SERVES 8

5 tablespoons butter, divided
1 onion, finely chopped
3 tablespoons all-purpose flour
½ teaspoon salt
1 tablespoon curry powder
1½ cups milk
3 stalks celery, chopped
1 cup shredded Swiss cheese
1 (12-ounce) package gemelli pasta
1 (12-ounce) can tuna, drained
1½ cups red grapes
1 slice bread, toasted
2 tablespoons Romano cheese

1. Preheat oven to 375°F. Spray a 2-quart casserole with nonstick cooking spray and set aside. Bring a large pot of salted water to a boil.

2. Meanwhile, in large saucepan, melt 3 tablespoons butter over medium heat. Add onion; cook and stir until tender, about 4 minutes. Add flour, salt, and curry powder; cook and stir until bubbly, about 3 minutes.

3. Stir in milk, whisking until smooth. Then add celery. Cook, stirring frequently, until sauce thickens. Stir in Swiss cheese and remove from heat.

4. Cook pasta according to package directions until al dente. Drain and add along with tuna and grapes to milk mixture. Pour into prepared casserole.

5. Melt remaining 2 tablespoons butter. Crumble the toasted bread and combine with the butter and Romano cheese. Sprinkle on top of casserole. Bake for 20–30 minutes or until casserole is bubbly and topping is browned and crisp.

Baja Fish Tacos

*These crisp and creamy tacos are full of flavor and color. For more authenticity,
serve them with cilantro and some diced red onion.*

INGREDIENTS | SERVES 4–6

½ cup sour cream
1 tablespoon lemon juice
3 green onions, chopped
1 cup frozen corn, thawed and drained
½ cup Fiesta Salsa (Chapter 18)
24 frozen fish fingers
1 tablespoon chili powder
¼ teaspoon cayenne pepper
½ teaspoon paprika
8 taco shells
1½ cups shredded lettuce
1½ cups shredded Cheddar cheese
1 cup Guacamole (Chapter 18)

1. Preheat oven to 400°F. In medium bowl, combine sour cream, lemon juice, green onion, and corn; mix well. Add Fiesta Salsa; stir and set aside.

2. Place fish fingers on cookie sheet. In small bowl, combine chili powder, cayenne pepper, and paprika; mix well. Sprinkle this mixture over the fish fingers and toss to coat. Bake fish according to package directions.

3. Heat taco shells in oven according to package directions as soon as fish is done for about 4–5 minutes or until hot.

4. Assemble tacos by starting with the sour cream mixture, adding some fish fingers, then topping with lettuce, cheese, and Guacamole. You can let diners assemble their own tacos. Serve immediately.

Fish *en Papillote*

Simply seasoned and foil-baked fish is served on cold and crisp coleslaw for a delicious lunch or dinner.

INGREDIENTS | SERVES 4

1½ pounds frozen pollock fillets, thawed

1 tablespoon olive oil

½ teaspoon salt

⅛ teaspoon pepper

½ teaspoon paprika

1 lemon, very thinly sliced

4 cups coleslaw

Preparing Fish

Fish is such a delicate meat, it must be prepared in a way that preserves the moisture. Baking in foil, or *en papillote*, is an easy way to keep the fish moist. You can also poach fish by placing it in simmering water or fish stock and cooking for 10 minutes per inch of thickness. Fish is also tasty broiled for about 8–10 minutes per inch of thickness.

1. Preheat oven to 400°F. Pat fish dry and cut into serving-sized portions. Tear four sheets of foil about 18" long. Place foil, shiny side down, on work surface. Grease a part of the foil that is the size of the fillets with olive oil.

2. Place fish on greased area of foil. Sprinkle with salt, pepper, and paprika. Place thin slices of lemon on top. Fold foil around the fish to enclose, leaving some room for heat expansion.

3. Place foil packets on a cookie sheet. Bake for 15–20 minutes or until fish flakes when tested with fork.

4. Divide slaw among plates and top with fish. Serve immediately.

Crab Pie with Corn

*Soda crackers make an excellent and super simple pie crust for this gorgeous pie.
Surimi is imitation crabmeat that looks and tastes just like the real thing.*

INGREDIENTS | SERVES 6

1½ cups crushed soda crackers
⅓ cup butter or margarine, melted
2 tablespoons olive oil
1 onion, chopped
2 tablespoons all-purpose flour
½ teaspoon salt
½ teaspoon dried basil leaves
1 cup milk
2 cups frozen corn, thawed and drained
2 eggs, beaten
1 (8-ounce) package frozen surimi, thawed and drained
1 cup shredded Swiss cheese

1. Preheat oven to 350°F. In medium bowl, combine cracker crumbs with melted butter. Mix well, then press into bottom and up sides of a 9" pie pan. Set aside.

2. In large skillet, heat olive oil over medium heat. Add onion; cook and stir until tender, about 4 minutes. Add flour, salt, and basil; cook and stir for 3 minutes. Add milk; cook and stir until thickened. Add corn and eggs; stir well. Cook for 1 minute.

3. Chop surimi into bite-sized pieces and arrange with cheese in pie crust. Carefully pour in corn mixture. Bake for 30–40 minutes or until the pie is set, puffed, and golden brown. Let stand for 5 minutes, then serve.

Cornmeal Fried Fish

Breading fish in cornmeal is a classic preparation that's especially common with catfish and other hearty fish. You'll find that cornmeal will yield an incredibly light, crispy crust that your family will devour.

INGREDIENTS | SERVES 6

⅓ cup all-purpose flour
⅓ cup cornmeal
1 teaspoon salt
⅛ teaspoon pepper
3 tablespoons butter
1 egg
¼ cup milk
2 pounds fish fillets
1 cup vegetable oil

1. In small bowl, combine flour, cornmeal, salt, and pepper and mix well. Cut butter into small pieces and add to flour mixture; cut in with two knives until mixture is finely blended. In shallow bowl, combine egg and milk and beat well.

2. Pat fish dry. Dip into egg mixture, then into cornmeal mixture, coating both sides. Let stand on a wire rack for 10 minutes.

3. Heat oil in large skillet until it reaches 375°F. Fry fish over medium heat, turning once, until golden brown, about 8–12 minutes. Drain on paper towels and serve immediately.

Southern Shrimp and Grits

This is a classic Southern comfort food, done on the cheap! You'll find some big flavors in this dish, so make sure to taste and adjust to your liking.

INGREDIENTS | SERVES 6

3 cups water

2 cups milk

1¼ cups quick-cooking grits

½ teaspoon salt

1 cup grated sharp Cheddar cheese

2 tablespoons butter

½ teaspoon hot sauce

5 slices bacon

2 onions, chopped

4 cloves garlic, minced

1 green bell pepper, chopped

1 (14-ounce) can diced tomatoes

1 (8-ounce) jar mushroom pieces

12 ounces frozen cooked small shrimp, thawed

2 tablespoons cornstarch

1. In large saucepan, combine water with milk and bring to a boil over high heat. Stir in the grits and salt. Reduce heat to medium and cook for 5–6 minutes until grits are thick. Add cheese, butter, and hot sauce. Stir, cover, and remove from heat.

2. In large saucepan, cook bacon until crisp. Remove bacon, crumble, and set aside. To drippings in skillet, add onion and garlic and cook until crisp-tender, about 4 minutes. Add bell pepper; cook and stir for 3 minutes longer. Drain tomatoes and mushrooms, reserving liquid.

3. Add drained tomatoes and mushrooms to saucepan and bring to a simmer. Add shrimp and stir. In small bowl, combine reserved tomato liquid and mushroom liquid with cornstarch and mix well. Stir into saucepan and bring to a simmer; simmer until thickened.

4. Spoon grits into a serving dish and top with shrimp mixture. Sprinkle with reserved bacon and serve immediately.

Ginger-Mustard Fish Fillets

*The complementary flavors of ginger and mustard transform this
simple fish fillet into something fit for company!*

INGREDIENTS | SERVES 6

1 lemon
1 (21-ounce) package breaded fish fillets
¼ cup mayonnaise
2 tablespoons mustard
2 tablespoons lemon juice
½ teaspoon ground ginger
½ cup grated Parmesan cheese

Seafood Fillets

Most seafood is very expensive. Breaded
fillets are the exception, because they are
made from pieces of fish that are combined
to form a fillet shape. You're still getting a
nice serving of seafood along with all its
omega-3 fatty acids and nutrition, but the
cost is much lower. You can dress up this
food with sauces, herbs, spices, and
cheeses.

1. Preheat oven to 400°F, or as package directs. Place fish fillets in a 15" × 10" jelly-roll pan. Bake for 20 minutes.

2. Meanwhile, in small bowl, combine remaining ingredients except cheese and mix well.

3. Remove fish from oven and spread each with some of the mayonnaise mixture. Sprinkle with Parmesan cheese. Return to oven and bake for 5–10 minutes longer or until fish is thoroughly cooked and topping is bubbling.

Seafood Quiche

This dish comes together in a flash, but yields a tremendous taste payoff! For an even more cost-effective dinner, you could substitute another type of seafood for the shrimp.

INGREDIENTS | SERVES 6

3 eggs

½ cup milk

⅓ cup mayonnaise

1 tablespoon mustard

1 tablespoon all-purpose flour

½ teaspoon dried dill weed

1 (4-ounce) can mushroom pieces, drained

4 ounces small frozen cooked shrimp, thawed

1 (6-ounce) can crabmeat, drained

1 cup shredded Swiss cheese

1 Basic Pie Crust (Chapter 24), unbaked

¼ cup grated Parmesan cheese

1. Preheat oven to 350°F. In medium bowl, combine eggs, milk, mayonnaise, mustard, flour, and dill weed and beat to combine.

2. Arrange mushrooms, shrimp, crab, and Swiss cheese in layers in Basic Pie Crust. Pour egg mixture over. Sprinkle top with Parmesan cheese.

3. Bake for 40–50 minutes or until quiche is puffed and golden brown. Serve immediately.

About Crabmeat

Whether you use canned or frozen crabmeat, it always has to be picked over before use. In processing, small bits of shell or pieces of cartilage get into the meat. Drain the crab, then spread it on a kitchen towel or paper towel and run your fingers through it. Pick out and discard anything that feels hard or sharp.

Tuna Mac 'n' Cheese with Salsa

This super-easy casserole can be made without the onion, or add other cooked leftover vegetables to the tuna mixture. Omit the salsa if you'd prefer.

INGREDIENTS | **SERVES 4**

1 tablespoon olive oil

1 onion, chopped

1 (5-ounce) package macaroni and cheese mix

¼ cup milk

1 egg, beaten

1 cup Fiesta Salsa (Chapter 18)

1 (6-ounce) can tuna, drained

¼ cup grated Parmesan cheese

1. Preheat oven to 350°F. Spray a 9" baking dish with nonstick cooking spray and set aside. Bring a large saucepan of water to a boil. Meanwhile, in small saucepan, combine olive oil and onion over medium heat; cook and stir until onion is tender, about 5 minutes.

2. Add macaroni from mix to boiling water and cook until tender, according to package directions. Drain and return macaroni to saucepan. Add powdered cheese from mix, milk, egg, and onion mixture to macaroni and stir over low heat until combined.

3. Pour macaroni mixture into prepared dish. In small bowl, combine Fiesta Salsa with drained tuna and mix well. Spoon over macaroni mixture and sprinkle with cheese. Bake for 15–25 minutes or until casserole is bubbling. Serve immediately.

CHAPTER 22

Money-Smart Meatless Entrées

Meaty Yet Meatless Chili

Chili is so good for you; it's full of fiber and vitamins A and C. This chili recipe is so rich and filling, you'll never even notice the missing meat.

INGREDIENTS | SERVES 6

1 (15-ounce) can black beans
2 (15-ounce) cans kidney beans
1 (15-ounce) can cannelloni beans
2 (14-ounce) cans diced tomatoes, undrained
2 onions, chopped
4 cloves garlic, minced
1 (6-ounce) can tomato paste
½ teaspoon salt
1 tablespoon chili powder
½ teaspoon dried oregano leaves
2 tablespoons cornstarch
¼ cup water

1. Combine beans, 1 can of the tomatoes, onions, and garlic in 4- to 5-quart slow cooker. Add half of remaining can of tomatoes to the slow cooker, then mix the tomato paste into the can of tomatoes to help dissolve tomato paste. Add salt, chili powder, and oregano to the can of tomatoes and stir well; add to slow cooker.

2. Cover and cook on low for 7–9 hours or until chili is bubbling. If necessary, you can thicken chili by combining cornstarch with water in a small bowl. Stir this mixture into the chili and cook on high for 30 minutes, until thickened.

Simple Cannelloni and Tomato Pasta

The bit of butter in the sauce helps mellow the tomatoes and adds just a bit of richness.

INGREDIENTS | SERVES 4

1 tablespoon butter
1 tablespoon olive oil
1 onion, chopped
1 (16-ounce) package spaghetti pasta
1 (15-ounce) can cannelloni beans
1 (14-ounce) can diced tomatoes, undrained
½ teaspoon dried Italian seasoning
⅓ cup grated Parmesan cheese

1. Bring a large pot of salted water to a boil. Meanwhile, in large saucepan, combine butter and olive oil over medium heat. Add onion; cook and stir until onion is tender, about 5 minutes.

2. Cook pasta according to package directions until al dente. Drain cannelloni beans but do not rinse. Add to saucepan along with tomatoes and bring to a simmer, stirring occasionally. Add Italian seasoning and stir.

3. Drain pasta, reserving ⅓ cup pasta cooking water. Add pasta to saucepan and toss using tongs. Add reserved pasta water as necessary to make a sauce. Sprinkle with cheese and serve immediately.

Stuffed Cabbage with Wild Rice

Using a small amount of wild rice is a nice splurge that adds great texture and flavor to this comfort-food recipe.

INGREDIENTS | SERVES 6

1 head cabbage
½ cup brown rice
½ cup wild rice
2 cups water
1 teaspoon salt
¼ cup mustard
2 eggs
1 cup shredded Swiss cheese
2 tablespoons olive oil
1 onion, chopped
3 cloves garlic, minced
1 cup chopped celery
1 (14-ounce) can diced tomatoes, undrained
1 (10.75-ounce) can tomato soup

1. Remove the outer layers of the cabbage and discard. Cut out the core and gently remove the outside eight leaves. Place leaves in a large bowl and cover with hot water; set aside. Chop remaining cabbage.

2. In large saucepan, combine brown rice and wild rice and add water. Bring to a boil, then cover, reduce heat, and simmer for 30–40 minutes or until rice is almost tender. Drain if necessary, and add salt, mustard, eggs, and cheese and mix well. Add chopped cabbage.

3. In large skillet, heat olive oil over medium heat. Add onion and garlic; cook and stir until crisp-tender, about 4 minutes. Add celery; cook and stir for 1 minute longer. Add tomatoes and tomato soup and bring to a simmer.

4. Drain cabbage leaves and place on work surface. Divide rice filling among leaves, using about ½ cup for each, and roll up. Place, seam side down, in 13" × 9" glass baking dish. Pour tomato mixture over everything. If there is leftover rice mixture, arrange around stuffed leaves.

5. Place in oven and turn heat to 350°F. Bake for 60–70 minutes or until casserole is bubbly. Serve immediately.

Rich and Creamy Vegetable Risotto

Believe it or not, you can make risotto without the fancy arborio rice. It won't be quite as thick, but as long as you stir constantly, the end product will be very similar.

INGREDIENTS | SERVES 6

2 tablespoons olive oil

3 tablespoons butter, divided

4 cups vegetable stock

1 onion, finely chopped

3 cloves garlic, minced

½ cup chopped mushrooms

1 cup frozen chopped spinach, thawed

½ teaspoon salt

2 cups long-grain rice

½ cup grated Parmesan cheese

½ cup grated Muenster cheese

Cooking Risotto

When rice is cooked slowly and manipulated by stirring, the starch cells break open and thicken the liquid. Arborio rice is usually used because it's very high in starch. But regular rice works just as well. You do have to keep an eye on the rice, and stir very frequently, both to help release the starch and to prevent the risotto from burning.

1. In large saucepan, combine olive oil and 1 tablespoon butter. In medium saucepan, bring the stock to a very slow simmer.

2. When the butter melts, add the onion, garlic, and mushrooms. Cook, stirring frequently, until tender, about 5 minutes. Then add the drained spinach and salt; cook and stir for 3–4 minutes longer. Add the rice; cook and stir for 3 minutes.

3. Add stock, ½ cup at a time, stirring frequently and cooking until the rice absorbs the broth. Continue adding stock, stirring, until the rice is tender. Add the cheese and remaining 2 tablespoons butter; cover and remove from heat. Let stand for 4 minutes, then stir and serve.

Crispy Potato Tacos

These tacos feature nicely browned potato pieces as the star attraction. The cheese, tomato, and garlic will boost your flavor through the roof!

INGREDIENTS | SERVES 4–6

3 russet potatoes

1 onion, chopped

3 cloves garlic, minced

2 tablespoons olive oil

½ teaspoon salt

⅛ teaspoon pepper

1 (12-ounce) can evaporated milk

1 (4-ounce) can chopped green chiles, undrained

6 taco shells

1 cup shredded Pepper Jack cheese

½ cup Guacamole (Chapter 18)

½ cup chopped tomato

1. Preheat oven to 400°F. Scrub potatoes and cut into 1" pieces, including some of the skin on each piece. Combine in roasting pan with onion and garlic. Drizzle with olive oil and sprinkle with salt and pepper and toss to coat. Roast for 30 minutes, then turn vegetables with a spatula and roast for 15–20 minutes longer until potatoes are tender and browned.

2. When potatoes are done, combine evaporated milk and undrained chiles in a large saucepan. Bring to a boil over high heat, then reduce heat to low and simmer for 5 minutes or until mixture begins to reduce.

3. Stir in potato mixture until coated. Heat taco shells in the oven until crisp, about 3–4 minutes. Make tacos with potato mixture, cheese, Guacamole, and chopped tomatoes.

Anytime Quiche

This inviting recipe sounds like a breakfast, but quiche can be eaten at any time, day or night. This dish is full of protein, so it will really fill your family up.

INGREDIENTS | SERVES 6

4 hard-cooked eggs

1 cup shredded Swiss cheese

1 Basic Pie Crust (Chapter 24), unbaked

4 eggs

1 cup light cream

¼ cup milk

1 tablespoon mustard

2 tablespoons all-purpose flour

½ teaspoon salt

⅛ teaspoon pepper

1 cup frozen peas, thawed

¼ cup grated Parmesan cheese

1. Preheat oven to 350°F. Peel and slice hard-cooked eggs. Layer with Swiss cheese in the bottom of the Basic Pie Crust; set aside.

2. In medium bowl, combine eggs, cream, milk, mustard, flour, salt, and pepper and mix well with wire whisk until blended.

3. Sprinkle peas over ingredients in Basic Pie Crust and pour egg mixture over. Sprinkle with Parmesan cheese. Bake for 45–55 minutes or until quiche is puffed and golden brown. Serve immediately.

Thawing Frozen Vegetables

When thawing frozen vegetables, it's best to do it gently. One of the fastest ways that preserves the color and texture of the vegetables is to open the package and place the vegetables in a colander. Run cold water over the vegetables until they thaw. Be sure to drain the vegetables well before adding them to the recipe so you don't add too much water.

Sweet and Spicy Tofu Stir-Fry

Firm tofu is sold in blocks in the dairy or vegetarian section of the supermarket. To stir-fry, it must be well-drained to remove excess water. It will then soak up any flavors you add to it, making it a wonderful ingredient for a stir-fry.

INGREDIENTS | SERVES 4

1 (14-ounce) package firm tofu

1 tablespoon chili powder

½ teaspoon salt

⅛ teaspoon pepper

⅔ cup water

2 tablespoons soy sauce

1 tablespoon brown sugar

1 tablespoon cornstarch

½ teaspoon ground ginger

2 tablespoons olive oil

1 onion, chopped

1 (16-ounce) package frozen mixed vegetables, thawed

1. Place tofu between several layers of paper towels and press gently to thoroughly drain. Remove paper towels and repeat this process. Cut the tofu into 1" cubes and sprinkle with chili powder, salt, and pepper; set aside.

2. In small bowl, combine water, soy sauce, brown sugar, cornstarch, and ginger and mix well; set aside.

3. In large skillet or wok, heat olive oil over medium-high heat. Add onion; stir-fry until crisp-tender, about 4 minutes. Thoroughly drain mixed vegetables and add to skillet; stir-fry for 2–3 minutes or until hot.

4. Stir cornstarch mixture and add to skillet along with tofu cubes. Bring to a simmer, then stir-fry for 4–5 minutes or until sauce thickens and food is thoroughly heated. Serve over hot cooked rice.

Tex-Mex Rice Timbales

Timbales are an old-fashioned recipe using leftover rice and anything else you have on hand. These molded rice cups are fun to eat.

INGREDIENTS | **SERVES 6**

2 tablespoons olive oil

1 onion, finely chopped

3 cloves garlic

1 jalapeño pepper, minced

3 cups leftover cooked rice

1 (15-ounce) can kidney beans, drained

3 tablespoons heavy cream

½ cup milk

½ teaspoon salt

⅛ teaspoon cayenne pepper

2 eggs, beaten

1 cup shredded Pepper Jack cheese

¼ cup grated Parmesan cheese

1½ cups Fiesta Salsa (Chapter 18)

Cooked Rice

If you don't have cooked rice leftover but still want to make timbales, you can stop at an Asian take-out restaurant and buy a container of hot cooked rice. This is very inexpensive and it saves you work and time. When you're cooking rice for any dish, make some extra and freeze it in 1-cup amounts for up to 3 months.

1. Preheat oven to 350°F. Grease 6 (10-ounce) custard cups and set on a cookie sheet; set aside. In large saucepan, heat olive oil over medium heat. Add onion, garlic, and jalapeño; cook and stir until crisp-tender, about 4 minutes. Add rice; stir gently to break up rice. Then add kidney beans and remove from heat.

2. In small bowl, combine cream, milk, salt, pepper, and egg and mix well. Stir into rice mixture and mix to combine. Add cheeses and mix well. Spoon mixture into custard cups and pack down with back of spoon. Cover timbales with foil and bake for 20–25 minutes or until rice mixture is set.

3. Run a knife around the timbales to loosen, then invert onto serving plate. Top each with some of the Fiesta Salsa and serve.

Fluffy Couscous Salad

Always have a box of couscous on hand to make this sinfully easy salad. Just toss in whatever fresh, frozen, or canned veggies you have on hand.

INGREDIENTS | SERVES 6

1 cup water

½ cup vegetable stock

1¼ cups couscous

1 tablespoon mustard

3 tablespoons olive oil

2 tablespoons apple cider vinegar

½ teaspoon salt

⅛ teaspoon pepper

1 (15-ounce) can black or red beans, drained

1 cup chopped celery

½ cup chopped parsley

1 cup cubed Swiss or other cheese

1. In medium saucepan, combine water and stock and bring to a boil. Stir in couscous, cover, remove from heat, and let stand for 10 minutes.

2. In large bowl, combine mustard, oil, vinegar, salt, and pepper and stir well. Fluff couscous with fork and add to bowl along with remaining ingredients. Toss gently and serve immediately, or cover and refrigerate for 4 hours.

Cheap Salads

Growing vegetables in your own garden or pots on your porch is the best way to add fresh foods inexpensively to your diet. You could also offer to buy some of your neighbor's produce if they have a garden. Many gardeners are trying to get rid of produce in the late summer and fall!

Indian Daal with Chickpeas

*This is a protein-heavy main dish with the distinctive taste of curry.
It will remind you of your favorite Indian restaurant!*

INGREDIENTS | **SERVES 6**

1 tablespoon olive oil

1 onion, chopped

3 cloves garlic, minced

1 tablespoon curry powder

1 cup lentils, rinsed

1 cup long-grain brown rice

1 (10.75-ounce) can condensed vegetable broth

2½ cups water

½ teaspoon salt

⅛ teaspoon pepper

1 (15-ounce) can chickpeas, drained

1 (14-ounce) can diced tomatoes, undrained

1. In large saucepan, heat olive oil over medium heat. Add onion, garlic, and curry powder; cook and stir for 4 minutes. Then add lentils and brown rice and stir for 1 minute longer.

2. Add vegetable broth and water and bring to a boil. Cover, reduce heat to low, and simmer for 30–35 minutes or until lentils and rice are tender.

3. Stir in salt, pepper, chickpeas, and tomatoes and bring back to a simmer. Simmer for 5 minutes until mixture is combined. Serve immediately.

CHAPTER 23

Smart Sides

Zucchini and Tomato Picadillo

Picadillo is a Latin dish that's usually made with beef, but the zucchini here makes a delicious and healthy substitution. This side would make an excellent companion to tacos, a steak, or any Mexican recipe.

INGREDIENTS | SERVES 6

2 tablespoons olive oil

1 onion, chopped

3 cloves garlic, minced

2 zucchini, sliced

1 (14-ounce) can diced tomatoes, undrained

2 cups cooked rice

¼ cup raisins

¼ cup sliced green olives

½ teaspoon salt

⅛ teaspoon pepper

1. In large saucepan, heat olive oil over medium heat. Add onion and garlic; cook and stir until crisp-tender, about 4 minutes. Add zucchini and tomatoes; bring to a simmer. Cover and simmer for 5 minutes.

2. Stir in rice, raisins, olives, salt, and pepper and bring to a simmer. Simmer, stirring frequently, until mixture is hot and well blended. Serve immediately.

Sautéed Peas and Radishes

Frozen sweet peas are a great value. Unless you're picking the peas directly from your garden, frozen peas are actually the freshest because they're processed right after picking.

INGREDIENTS | SERVES 4

2 tablespoons butter

2 radishes, thinly sliced

2 cups frozen sweet peas

¼ cup water

½ teaspoon salt

⅛ teaspoon pepper

Melt butter in saucepan over medium heat. Add radishes; cook and stir until the radish skins turn light pink. Add peas and water and bring to a simmer. Simmer for 2–3 minutes or until peas are hot. Sprinkle with salt and pepper and serve.

Homestyle Apples with Sugar and Onions

The mingling aromas and flavors here will take you back to the best holiday meals you've ever had!

INGREDIENTS | SERVES 4

2 tablespoons butter

1 tablespoon olive oil

2 onions, chopped

2 cloves garlic, minced

2 Granny Smith apples, sliced

2 tablespoons brown sugar

1 tablespoon apple cider vinegar

½ teaspoon salt

⅛ teaspoon pepper

1. In large saucepan, combine butter and olive oil over medium heat. When butter melts, add onions and garlic. Cook and stir for 5–6 minutes until soft. Add apples; cook and stir for 1 minute.

2. Sprinkle with brown sugar, vinegar, salt, and pepper. Cover saucepan and cook for 5–7 minutes, shaking pan occasionally, until apples are just tender. Stir gently and serve.

Apples for Cooking

Some apples are best for cooking and others are best for eating out of hand. For recipes like this one, you need firm, tart apples to contrast with the sweet onions. Granny Smith apples are not only inexpensive, but they are tart and crisp and keep their shape even when cooked. Don't peel the apples unless the recipe tells you to; the peel adds fiber and nutrition.

Glazed Carrots

*Buy and slice whole carrots for this recipe—they are much cheaper
than buying the presliced carrot sticks at the supermarket.*

INGREDIENTS | SERVES 6

8 carrots, peeled and sliced

2 cups water

3 tablespoons butter

2 cloves garlic, minced

3 tablespoons honey

½ teaspoon salt

⅛ teaspoon pepper

1. In large saucepan, combine carrots and water and bring to a boil. Reduce heat, cover, and simmer for 4–5 minutes or until carrots are just barely tender. Drain and place carrots in serving bowl.

2. Return pan to heat and add butter and garlic. Cook and stir over medium heat until garlic is fragrant. Return carrots to pot and add honey, salt, and pepper. Cook and stir for 2–3 minutes until carrots are glazed. Serve immediately.

Classic Roasted Vegetables

*As the vegetables roast, they'll take on a lovely browned exterior and their
flavors will become more and more complex and delicious!*

INGREDIENTS | SERVES 6

2 russet potatoes, cubed

1 onion, chopped

3 cloves garlic, minced

3 tablespoons olive oil

1 teaspoon salt

⅛ teaspoon pepper

1 (14-ounce) package whole frozen green beans

1 (10-ounce) package frozen corn

1 green bell pepper, chopped

1 cup frozen peas

1. Preheat oven to 400°F. In large roasting pan, combine potatoes, onions, and garlic and toss. Drizzle with olive oil and sprinkle with salt and pepper; toss to coat. Roast for 30 minutes, then remove from oven.

2. Add green beans along with corn to pan; turn vegetables with a large spatula. Return to oven and roast for 20 minutes longer. Remove from oven.

3. Add bell pepper and peas and turn with spatula again. Return to oven and roast for 10–20 minutes longer or until potatoes and all vegetables are hot and tender. Serve immediately.

Creamy Polenta

You can serve this polenta immediately, or chill it, slice it, and fry it to crisp perfection.
Top it with some ground beef for a deliciously filling winter meal.

INGREDIENTS | **SERVES 12**

3 cups chicken stock or water

4 cups water

2 cups yellow cornmeal

1 teaspoon salt

⅓ cup grated Parmesan cheese

2 tablespoons butter

2 tablespoons olive oil for frying

Polenta

Polenta, also known as cornmeal mush, has been nourishing populations for centuries. Its mild taste means you can flavor it a thousand different ways. And, if you serve it with beans, wheat, or legumes, you're serving foods that can be used by your body as complete proteins, making it the ideal vegetarian main dish idea.

1. In large saucepan, combine stock, water, and salt and bring to a rolling boil. Add cornmeal slowly, stirring constantly with a wire whisk. Cook, stirring constantly, over medium heat until the cornmeal thickens, about 12–17 minutes. Remove from heat and add cheese and butter, stirring until mixture is smooth.

2. You can now serve the polenta immediately, or chill it to fry the next day.

3. To chill, butter a 9" × 13" pan and spread polenta in an even layer. Cover and chill until very firm, at least 8 hours.

4. The next day, cut polenta into 3" squares. Heat olive oil in a large skillet over medium heat. Fry polenta squares until crisp and golden brown, turning once, about 2–3 minutes per side. Serve immediately.

Green Beans with Garlic and Cheese

Your kids will never again complain about eating their green beans if this is how you serve them up.

INGREDIENTS | SERVES 4

1 (14-ounce) package frozen whole green beans

3 cloves garlic, minced

2 tablespoons olive oil

¼ teaspoon salt

⅛ teaspoon pepper

⅓ cup grated Parmesan cheese

1. Preheat oven to 450°F. Place frozen beans on a cookie sheet with sides. Roast for 10 minutes, stirring once, until beans are thawed and liquid has evaporated. Remove beans from oven and reduce temperature to 400°F.

2. Sprinkle beans with garlic, olive oil, salt, and pepper and toss with tongs to coat. Sprinkle with cheese and return to oven. Roast for 10–15 minutes longer or until beans are tender and cheese has melted. Serve immediately.

Mushroom Rice Pilaf

Mushrooms add a rich earthy flavor to this simple pilaf. Use it for any recipe that calls for hot cooked rice.

INGREDIENTS | SERVES 6

2 tablespoons butter

1 onion, finely chopped

1 (4-ounce) can mushroom pieces

1½ cups long-grain white rice

2½ cups water or chicken stock

½ teaspoon salt

¼ cup chopped fresh parsley

1. In large saucepan, melt butter over medium heat. Add onion; cook and stir until crisp-tender, about 4 minutes. Meanwhile, drain mushrooms, reserving juice, and cut mushrooms into smaller pieces. Add mushrooms to saucepan.

2. Stir in rice; cook and stir for 2–3 minutes or until rice becomes opaque. Add reserved mushroom liquid, water or stock, and salt. Bring to a boil, then reduce heat, cover, and simmer for 20–25 minutes or until liquid is absorbed and rice is tender.

3. Add parsley, remove from heat, cover pan, and let stand for 5 minutes. Fluff rice with a fork and serve.

Creamy and Crispy Potato Gratin

This makes a wonderful side for a holiday dinner, but it's equally delicious alongside simple hamburgers or steaks. Best of all, it's incredibly hearty, so a little goes a long way.

INGREDIENTS | SERVES 6

2 slices white bread
4 tablespoons butter, divided
2 tablespoons grated Parmesan cheese
1 onion, chopped
2 tablespoons all-purpose flour
1 teaspoon salt
⅛ teaspoon white pepper
1¼ cups milk
2 tablespoons mustard
½ teaspoon dried dill weed
1 sweet potato
2 russet potatoes

1. Crumble bread into tiny pieces with fingers and place in small bowl. In small microwave-safe dish, melt 2 tablespoons butter. Drizzle over bread crumbs and add Parmesan cheese; toss and set aside.

2. Preheat oven to 350°F. In medium saucepan, combine 2 tablespoons butter and the onion; cook and stir until onion is tender, about 5 minutes. Sprinkle with flour, salt, and pepper; cook until bubbly, about 3 minutes. Add milk; cook and stir until thickened, about 5 minutes. Stir in mustard and dill weed.

3. Grease a 2-quart baking dish with butter. Peel potatoes and grate directly into the baking dish. Top with milk mixture, stirring gently to coat. Sprinkle top with bread crumb mixture. Bake for 40–50 minutes or until potatoes are tender and top is golden brown and crusty.

Garlic-Lemon Broccoli

Lemon and broccoli are a classic flavor combination that is sure to delight.
Don't forget to use the salt and pepper liberally.

INGREDIENTS | SERVES 4

1 tablespoon olive oil

1 tablespoon butter

3 cloves garlic, minced

1 (13-ounce) package frozen broccoli florets, thawed

½ teaspoon salt

½ teaspoon lemon zest

⅛ teaspoon pepper

2 tablespoons lemon juice

1. In large saucepan, combine olive oil and butter over medium heat. Add garlic; cook and stir until fragrant, about 2–3 minutes. Then add thawed but not drained broccoli and bring to a boil.

2. Reduce heat and cook until most of the liquid evaporates. Remove pan from heat and sprinkle with salt, lemon zest, and pepper. Drizzle lemon juice over, toss, and serve immediately.

Lemon in Vegetables

Lemon juice not only adds fabulous flavor to fresh or frozen vegetables, it also helps preserve the color and adds a bit of nutrition. Fresh lemon juice tastes so much better than bottled that it's worth the small extra cost. To squeeze a lemon, first roll it firmly on the counter with the palm of your hand, then slice and squeeze. Lemon juice freezes well too.

CHAPTER 24

Thrifty and Thrilling Desserts

Sweet and Salty Potato Chip Cookies

Ever wonder how you could use up those tiny potato chip pieces at the bottom of the bag? Here's a recipe that does just that—you'll never throw away those crushed chips again!

INGREDIENTS | YIELDS 36 COOKIES

⅔ cup finely crushed plain, salted potato chips

½ cup butter, softened

¼ cup margarine

½ cup sugar

¼ cup brown sugar

¼ cup powdered sugar

1½ teaspoons vanilla

1¾ cups all-purpose flour

½ cup semisweet chocolate chips, chopped

1. Preheat the oven to 350°F. Make sure that potato chips are crushed very fine. In large bowl, combine butter, margarine, sugar, brown sugar, and powdered sugar and beat until smooth. Add vanilla and mix well. Stir in flour, then work in potato chip crumbs and chopped chocolate chips.

2. Press dough into 1" balls and place on ungreased cookie sheets. Dip the bottom of a drinking glass in granulated sugar and press down on cookies to flatten to ¼" thickness. Bake for 8–12 minutes or until cookies are light golden brown around the edges and on the bottom. Cool on pans for 3 minutes, then remove to wire racks to cool.

Chewy Coconut Bars

If you love coconut, you'll go head-over-heels for these delectable, chewy bars. You can substitute a different variety of nut for the walnuts, if you'd like.

INGREDIENTS | YIELDS 36 BARS

2 cups graham cracker crumbs

½ cup butter, melted

½ cup flaked coconut, finely chopped

3 eggs, separated

2 cups brown sugar

1 cup flaked coconut

1 cup chopped walnuts

Powdered sugar, for rolling

1. Preheat oven to 350°F. In 9" × 13" pan, combine graham cracker crumbs, butter, and ½ cup chopped coconut and mix well. Press into pan. Bake for 10 minutes, then remove from oven.

2. In large bowl, beat egg yolks until light-colored. Add brown sugar, 1 cup coconut, and nuts and beat well. In small bowl, beat egg whites until stiff. Fold into the egg yolk mixture. Pour on top of crust and bake for 25–30 minutes or until set. Cool completely, then cut into bars and roll bars in powdered sugar to coat.

Caramel Tea Cakes

These cookies are a variation on traditional tea cakes, but with a bit of brown sugar and caramel sauce added for more flavor. For a splurge, use pecans instead of walnuts.

INGREDIENTS | YIELDS 36 COOKIES

⅓ cup margarine

½ cup butter, softened

⅓ cup brown sugar

2 tablespoons powdered sugar

2 tablespoons caramel ice cream topping

1 teaspoon vanilla extract

2½ cups all-purpose flour

¼ teaspoon salt

1 cup finely chopped walnuts

Extra powdered sugar

Storing Cookies

Most cookies are stored at room temperature. Soft cookies should be tightly covered so they don't dry out. You can add an apple slice to the container to keep the cookies soft. Crisp cookies can be stored in looser containers, like cookie jars. Line your cookie jar with a plastic food storage bag for easiest cleanup.

1. In large bowl, combine margarine, butter, brown sugar, powdered sugar, ice cream topping, and vanilla and beat until smooth. Stir in flour, salt, and walnuts and mix until a dough forms. Cover and chill dough for at least 2 hours.

2. When ready to bake, preheat oven to 400°F. Form dough into 1" balls and place 1" apart on ungreased cookie sheets. Place more powdered sugar in a shallow bowl. Bake cookies for 9–12 minutes until they are set and light golden brown on the bottom.

3. Remove cookies from cookie sheet and drop into powdered sugar. Roll to coat, then set on wire racks to cool. When cookies are cool, re-roll in powdered sugar. Store covered at room temperature.

Ultimate Brownies

These brownies are moist, rich, and delicious. You'll find that using cocoa powder here is cheaper than the baking chocolate that many homemade recipes call for.

INGREDIENTS | **YIELDS 36 BARS**

½ cup butter

½ cup margarine

1 cup brown sugar

⅔ cup cocoa

1 cup sugar

3 eggs

2 teaspoons vanilla

1½ cups all-purpose flour

½ teaspoon salt

1 teaspoon baking powder

1 cup chopped walnuts

1 (14-ounce) can sweetened condensed milk

1 cup semisweet chocolate chips

1 cup milk chocolate chips

About Cocoa

There are many varieties of cocoa powder, from the gourmet to the generic. For baking, the cheapest will work just fine. Dutch cocoa powder has been neutralized to a pH of about 7, which makes a milder flavor, but it is more expensive. Most recipes are based on regular cocoa powder.

1. Preheat oven to 325°F. Spray a 9" × 13" baking pan with nonstick cooking spray and set aside. In large microwave-safe bowl, combine butter and margarine with brown sugar and cocoa; microwave on high for 1 minute. Remove from oven and stir; return and microwave on high for 1–2 minutes longer until butter is melted.

2. Add sugar and beat well. Then add eggs and vanilla and beat until blended. Fold in flour, salt, and baking powder until mixed; add walnuts. Pour into prepared pan and bake for 25–35 minutes or until brownies are just set. Cool for 30 minutes.

3. In small microwave-safe bowl, combine condensed milk with both kinds of chocolate chips. Microwave on medium power for 2 minutes, then remove and stir. Return to microwave and cook for 30-second intervals on high until chips are melted. Stir until smooth, then pour over warm brownies. Cool completely and cut into bars.

Graham Cracker Cinnamon Cookies

These lovely little cookies aren't messy to carry, so they make a great snack packed into a lunchbox.

INGREDIENTS | YIELDS 48 COOKIES

½ cup butter, softened
½ cup margarine
1 cup sugar
1½ cups brown sugar, divided
2 eggs
1 teaspoon vanilla
2⅓ cups all-purpose flour
1 teaspoon baking powder
1 teaspoon baking soda
½ teaspoon salt
2 teaspoons cinnamon, divided
½ cup crushed graham cracker crumbs

Replace Your Spices

Dried spices (and herbs too) only retain their flavor for about a year. When you buy fresh spices, mark the purchase date on the bottle or jar with a grease pencil. After they are about six months old, smell them before using. If the spice doesn't smell intense and flavorful, chances are it won't add flavor to the recipe. Discard and buy new spices.

1. Preheat oven to 350°F. In large bowl, combine butter, margarine, sugar, and 1 cup brown sugar and beat until fluffy. Add eggs and vanilla and beat until combined. Then stir in flour, baking powder, baking soda, salt, and 1 teaspoon cinnamon.

2. On shallow plate, combine ½ cup brown sugar, graham cracker crumbs, and 1 teaspoon cinnamon and mix well. Form dough into ¾" balls and roll in graham cracker mixture to coat; gently press graham cracker mixture into cookies so it doesn't fall off. Place on ungreased cookie sheets. Bake for 10–14 minutes or until cookies are set and light golden brown. Cool on wire racks; store at room temperature.

Homemade Caramels

Homemade caramels are a fabulous treat. They're so inexpensive to make compared to candy shop caramels. And so much better!

INGREDIENTS | YIELDS 81 CARAMELS

1 cup sugar

½ cup brown sugar

½ cup light corn syrup

½ cup heavy cream

½ cup butter

½ cup whole milk

2 teaspoons vanilla

Hard Ball Stage

When making crystalline candy like caramels, a sugar syrup is cooked until some of the liquid evaporates. As the mixture concentrates, it will form shapes in cold water. Caramels are cooked to hard ball stage, or 248°F. Use a candy thermometer, or drop a bit of the candy in cold water. If it forms a ball that is hard but not brittle, the candy is done.

1. Grease a 9" × 9" square pan with unsalted butter and set aside. In large heavy saucepan, combine all ingredients except vanilla. Bring to a boil over high heat, then cover and let boil for 2 minutes to let steam wash down sugar crystals on sides of pan. Uncover, reduce heat to medium, and cook until mixture reaches 248°F, or hard ball stage.

2. Remove from heat and add vanilla. Immediately pour into prepared pan and let stand. When firm, cut into small squares and wrap individually in waxed paper.

Instant Oatmeal Bars

This easy bar cookie is perfect for summer because you don't have to bake them. The chewy chocolate and peanut butter mixture is layered over a buttery crumb crust.

INGREDIENTS | YIELDS 36 BARS

2 cups crushed graham cracker crumbs

¼ cup brown sugar

½ cup finely chopped peanuts

½ cup butter, melted

2 cups sugar

½ cup milk

½ cup butter

1 cup peanut butter

3 cups quick-cooking oatmeal

1 (11-ounce) package milk chocolate chips

Graham Cracker Crumbs

You can purchase graham cracker crumbs already crushed, but they are much more expensive. Thirty square graham crackers, crushed, will yield about 2 cups. To crush the crackers, break them into pieces and place them in a heavy-duty plastic bag. Using a rolling pin, crush the crackers into fine crumbs, turning the bag as you work.

1. In large bowl, combine graham cracker crumbs, brown sugar, and peanuts and mix well. Stir in ½ cup melted butter until crumbs are coated. Press into a 9" × 13" pan and set aside.

2. In heavy saucepan, combine sugar, milk, and butter and cook over medium heat, stirring frequently, until mixture boils. Boil, stirring constantly, for 2 minutes. Remove from heat and stir in peanut butter until smooth. Then stir in oatmeal until blended.

3. Pour over graham cracker crust. Chill until firm. In heavy saucepan, melt chocolate chips over very low heat, stirring until smooth. Spoon and spread over bars, then chill again until firm. Store covered in the refrigerator.

Soft Ginger Cookies

These cookies are soft, instead of hard like baked gingerbread men. The frosting adds a marvelous touch, plus you can decorate your cookies together for a wonderful family activity.

INGREDIENTS | YIELDS 48 COOKIES

½ cup butter, softened
1 cup brown sugar
½ cup sour cream
½ cup buttermilk
½ cup molasses
2½ cups all-purpose flour
¼ teaspoon salt
1 teaspoon ground ginger
½ teaspoon cinnamon
¼ teaspoon nutmeg
2 teaspoons baking soda
¼ cup butter
⅓ cup brown sugar
¼ cup milk
1 teaspoon vanilla
2–3 cups powdered sugar

Browned Butter

Browned butter adds great flavor to any recipe, but it can be tricky to make. The milk proteins in butter turn brown when they reach a certain temperature. The proteins break down and recombine to form the complex flavors and the brown color. Watch the butter carefully as it's cooking, because it goes very quickly from brown to black.

1. In large bowl, combine ½ cup butter with 1 cup brown sugar and beat well. Then add sour cream, buttermilk, and molasses and beat again. Stir in flour, salt, ginger, cinnamon, nutmeg, and baking soda until a dough forms. Cover dough and chill for at least 1 hour in the fridge.

2. Preheat oven to 375°F. Roll dough into 1" balls and place on ungreased cookie sheets. Flatten slightly with palm of hand. Bake for 8–13 minutes or until cookies are puffed and set. Let cool on baking sheet 2–3 minutes, then remove to wire racks to cool.

3. For frosting, in heavy saucepan melt ¼ cup butter over medium heat. Continue cooking butter, stirring frequently, until butter just begins to brown, about 7–9 minutes. Remove from heat and add ⅓ brown sugar and milk; stir with wire whisk. Then add vanilla. Stir in enough powdered sugar until spreading consistency. Frost cooled cookies.

Basic Pie Crust

Making your own pie crusts saves you more than 50 percent than buying pre-made crusts. Plus they taste so much better! These crusts can be used in both sweet and savory applications.

INGREDIENTS | **YIELDS 1 CRUST; SERVES 8**

¼ cup solid vegetable shortening

3 tablespoons cream cheese, softened

1¼ cups all-purpose flour

½ teaspoon salt

2 tablespoons water

1 tablespoon milk

Freezing Pie Crusts

You can make a large batch of pie crusts and freeze them so they're as easy to use as the purchased prepared kind. Just roll out each crust between two layers of waxed paper, then place in large freezer bags, label, seal, and freeze for up to 3 months. To use, just let each crust stand at room temperature for 30–40 minutes to thaw.

1. In small bowl, combine shortening and cream cheese and beat until combined. Cover and chill in refrigerator for 2 hours.

2. In medium bowl, combine flour and salt and mix well. Add shortening mixture and cut in, using pastry blender or two knives, until mixture looks like cornmeal. Sprinkle water and milk over all, tossing with fork until combined. Form into ball.

3. Wrap ball in plastic wrap and chill for at least 4 hours. When ready to bake, preheat oven to 400°F. Roll out dough between two sheets of waxed paper.

4. Remove top sheet of paper and flip into pie pan. Ease dough into pan. Turn edges under and flute. Prick bottom and sides of dough with fork. Bake for 10–15 minutes, pricking once during baking time, until crust is light golden brown.

Classic Apple Pie

This apple pie is livened up with the addition of a healthy amount of cinnamon. It's spicy and sweet at the same time, and your house will smell wonderful for days afterward!

INGREDIENTS | SERVES 8

½ cup solid shortening

⅓ cup butter, softened

2¼ cups all-purpose flour

½ teaspoon cinnamon

¼ cup sugar

¼ teaspoon salt

6 tablespoons apple juice, divided

3 pounds apples, peeled and sliced

1 tablespoon lemon juice

2 tablespoons all-purpose flour

1 teaspoon cinnamon

½ teaspoon nutmeg

⅔ cup brown sugar

3 tablespoons butter, divided

2 tablespoons sugar

½ teaspoon cinnamon

1. In small bowl, combine shortening and butter and mix well. Place in refrigerator for 1 hour to chill. In large bowl, combine 2¼ cups flour, ½ teaspoon cinnamon, ¼ cup sugar, and salt and mix well. Cut in chilled shortening mixture until particles are fine. Drizzle 4 tablespoons apple juice over mixture and work together until a dough forms. Form into a ball, wrap in plastic wrap, and chill for 1 hour.

2. Divide dough in half and roll each into a 12" circle on lightly floured surface. Fit one circle into a 9" pie plate, letting edges hang over.

3. Prepare apples and place in large bowl, sprinkling with 2 tablespoons apple juice and lemon juice as you work. Sprinkle with flour, cinnamon, nutmeg, and brown sugar and toss to coat. Pile into pie crust and dot with 2 tablespoons butter.

4. Preheat oven to 425°F. Top pie with second pie crust. Roll edges together to seal, then flute. Cut decorative holes in top to release steam. Melt 1 tablespoon butter and brush over pie. In small bowl, combine 2 tablespoons sugar and ½ teaspoon cinnamon; sprinkle over pie.

5. Bake pie for 15 minutes, then reduce heat to 350°F and bake for 35–45 minutes longer or until crust is browned and crisp and juices are bubbling in center of pie. Cool for at least 1 hour before serving.

Smooth Melon Parfait

This elegant dessert is perfect for company. If the gelatin mixture sets before you're ready, reheat it over low heat, then chill again until syrupy.

INGREDIENTS | SERVES 8

1 (0.25-ounce) package unflavored gelatin

½ cup cold water

½ cup sugar

1½ cups apricot nectar

1½ cups diced melon

1 (8-ounce) package cream cheese, softened

¼ cup powdered sugar

1 teaspoon vanilla

½ cup whipping cream

2 tablespoons powdered sugar

¼ cup chopped, toasted coconut

Chopping Coconut

There are a few ways to chop coconut. Combine the coconut with a teaspoon of flour in a food processor and process until finely chopped. Or put the coconut on a cutting board and cut with a chef's knife, stopping occasionally to gather coconut back into a mound. Continue until desired consistency is reached.

1. In small bowl, sprinkle gelatin over cold water and set aside. In large saucepan, combine sugar and nectar. Place over medium-high heat and cook until mixture simmers and sugar is completely dissolved.

2. Remove from heat and stir in softened gelatin; stir until gelatin is completely dissolved. Let cool for 30 minutes. Chill until mixture is syrupy, about 1 hour.

3. Fold in melon and chill while preparing cream mixture. In medium bowl, beat cream cheese until fluffy; beat in powdered sugar and vanilla. In small bowl, beat whipping cream until stiff; beat into cream cheese mixture. In 8 wine goblets, layer melon mixture and cream cheese mixture. Sprinkle with coconut and chill until firm, at least 4 hours.

Peach Spice Cake Crisp

This recipe lends itself well to substitutions. Consider changing the type of cake mix you use, as well as which fruits you choose.

INGREDIENTS | SERVES 8–10

1 (18-ounce) box spice cake mix

½ cup coconut

½ cup butter or margarine, softened

½ cup chopped walnuts

¼ cup brown sugar

1 teaspoon cinnamon

¼ teaspoon nutmeg

2 (15-ounce) cans sliced peaches, drained

Serving Crisps

Crisps, crumbles, grunts, and cobblers are all made of a fruit filling topped with a crunchy or cake-like topping. Serve them warm, placed in dessert dishes with whipped cream, ice cream, or hard sauce to melt onto the crisp. To make hard sauce, combine ½ cup butter with 1 cup powdered sugar, 1 teaspoon vanilla, and 2 tablespoons cream or rum, and beat well.

1. Preheat oven to 325°F. In large bowl, combine cake mix with coconut. Cut in butter until crumbs form. Add walnuts and mix well.

2. In small bowl, combine brown sugar with cinnamon and nutmeg and mix well.

3. Place drained peaches in glass 9" × 13" baking pan and sprinkle with brown sugar mixture. Sprinkle cake mix mixture over all. Using a straw or chopstick, poke holes in the topping down to the peaches. Bake for 50–60 minutes or until peach juices are bubbling and crumbs are golden brown. Let cool for 30 minutes, then serve.

Lemon White Chocolate Cake

This fabulous cake is a great choice for a celebration. It's sweet and tart, with a wonderful velvety texture.

INGREDIENTS | SERVES 12

1 (12-ounce) package white chocolate chips, divided

1 (18-ounce) package white cake mix

1 cup water

½ cup lemon juice, divided

⅓ cup oil

3 egg whites

1 (3-ounce) package cream cheese, softened

¼ cup butter, softened

2 tablespoons corn syrup

3 cups powdered sugar

¼ cup heavy whipping cream

3 tablespoons milk

1. Preheat oven to 350°F. Spray a 9" × 13" cake pan with nonstick cooking spray containing flour and set aside. Measure out 1 cup of the white chocolate chips and grind in a blender or food processor; set aside.

2. In large bowl, combine cake mix, water, ¼ cup lemon juice, oil, and egg whites and beat until combined. Beat for 2 minutes on high speed. Fold in the reserved ground white chocolate chips. Spoon into prepared pan. Bake for 35–40 minutes or until cake is light golden brown and pulls away from edges of cake pan. Place on wire rack to cool completely.

3. In small bowl, combine cream cheese, butter, ¼ cup lemon juice, and corn syrup and beat until fluffy. Alternately add powdered sugar and heavy cream, beating until fluffy.

4. In small microwave-safe bowl, combine remaining 1 cup white chocolate chips with the milk. Microwave on medium power for 1 minute, then remove and stir. Continue microwaving on medium for 30-second intervals, stirring after each time, until mixture is blended and smooth.

5. To assemble cake, pour melted white chocolate chip mixture over cake, spreading to cover. Let stand for 15 minutes, then frost with cream cheese mixture.

Dessert Crepes

With some frozen crepes in the freezer, you can whip up dessert in seconds.
Thaw and fill them with ice cream, pudding, or fresh fruit.

INGREDIENTS | YIELDS 8 CREPES

1¼ cups all-purpose flour

2 eggs

1 cup milk

¼ cup orange juice

½ teaspoon grated orange zest

1 teaspoon vanilla

2 tablespoons sugar

3 tablespoons butter, melted

Making Crepes

Making crepes takes some practice, but after one or two tries you'll be an expert. The tricks are to use a nonstick skillet, to quickly rotate the pan once the batter has been added, and to adjust the batter as necessary. The batter should be about as thick as heavy cream; any thicker and it will be difficult to manipulate.

1. In medium bowl, combine all ingredients. Beat at low speed until batter is smooth, about 1 minute. Cover and let stand for 30 minutes.

2. Heat a 6" nonstick skillet over medium heat for 1 minute. Lightly brush with oil, then pour in 3 tablespoons of batter, using a ¼ cup measure so you add the batter all at once. Swirl and tilt the pan so the batter evenly covers the bottom.

3. Cook crepe for 2–3 minutes or until bottom turns light golden brown. Using a fork, loosen the crepe from the pan and flip over; cook for 30 seconds on second side. Let cool on kitchen towels.

4. When crepes are completely cool, stack them with waxed paper or parchment paper between each crepe. Place in heavy-duty freezer bags, label, and freeze up to 3 months. To use, unwrap crepes and separate. Let stand at room temperature for 20–30 minutes.

Decadent Chocolate Cheesecake

This cheesecake gets a crumbled topping for even more wow factor!

INGREDIENTS | SERVES 10

1½ cups graham cracker crumbs

⅓ cup butter or margarine, melted

¼ cup finely chopped walnuts

2 (8-ounce) packages cream cheese, softened

½ cup sugar

½ cup brown sugar

⅓ cup cocoa powder

2 eggs

1 teaspoon vanilla

½ cup all-purpose flour

½ cup quick-cooking oatmeal

⅓ cup brown sugar

¼ cup butter, melted

½ cup semisweet chocolate chips

1. Preheat oven to 350°F. In medium bowl, combine graham cracker crumbs, ⅓ cup melted butter, and walnuts and mix well. Press into bottom and up sides of a 9" springform pan and set aside.

2. In large bowl, combine cream cheese with sugar and ½ cup brown sugar and beat until smooth. Add cocoa powder and beat just until combined. Then add eggs and vanilla and beat until smooth. Pour into crust.

3. In small bowl, combine flour, oatmeal, and ⅓ cup brown sugar and mix well. Add ¼ cup melted butter and mix until crumbly. Stir in chocolate chips and sprinkle over cheesecake, pressing in slightly.

4. Bake for 30–40 minutes or until filling is just set and crumbly topping is brown. Cool for 1 hour, then chill in refrigerator for at least 3 hours before serving.

About Cheesecakes

Cheesecakes aren't light and airy; they are creamy and dense. So when you make the filling, do not beat until fluffy; beat just until the ingredients are combined and the mixture is smooth. Too much air in the cheesecake will make the batter rise and fall, which creates cracks. But even if it cracks, it will still be good!

Orange Liqueur Sorbet

This is a classy, elegant sorbet that you can feel comfortable serving at a swanky party. If you want to adapt it for kids, just omit the alcohol.

INGREDIENTS | SERVES 6

1½ cups orange juice

¾ cup sugar

1 cup cranberry juice

1 teaspoon orange zest

2 tablespoons orange liqueur

Nips

Liqueurs are expensive! If you need just a little bit for cooking or baking, save money by purchasing "nips," or small presentation bottles that contain about 1 ounce, or 2 tablespoons, each. They are also a good way to try liqueur to see if you like it before investing in a larger bottle.

1. In medium saucepan, combine 1 cup of the orange juice with the sugar over medium heat. Cook and stir until sugar dissolves completely.

2. Remove pan from heat and stir in remaining orange juice, cranberry juice, and orange zest. Then blend in orange liqueur.

3. Pour mixture into a freezer-proof bowl and place in freezer. Freeze until firm, about 2 hours. Remove from freezer and beat with electric beater until smooth. Return to freezer and repeat process. Then transfer sorbet to a freezer container and freeze for at least 3 hours before serving.

Orange Cake with Vanilla-Caramel Drizzle

The oranges in this recipe keep the cake incredibly moist, and the sweet drizzled topping complements the fruit perfectly.

INGREDIENTS | SERVES 16

1 (18-ounce) box yellow cake mix

4 eggs

¾ cup vegetable oil

1 (11-ounce) can mandarin oranges, undrained

½ cup coconut

1¼ cups brown sugar

2 tablespoons dark corn syrup

6 tablespoons butter

6 tablespoons milk

2 teaspoons vanilla

1. Preheat oven to 350°F. Spray a 9" × 13" cake pan with cooking spray containing flour and set aside.

2. In large bowl, combine cake mix, eggs, oil, and undrained oranges. Beat on low speed until combined, then beat at medium speed for 3 minutes. Fold in coconut. Pour into pan. Bake for 25–35 minutes or until cake pulls away from sides of pan and top springs back when lightly touched. Place on wire rack.

3. While cake is cooling, make caramel topping. In medium saucepan, combine brown sugar, dark corn syrup, butter, and milk. Bring to a boil, stirring constantly with wire whisk. Boil for 3 minutes.

4. Using a chopstick, poke about 20 holes evenly in the warm cake. Add vanilla to caramel topping and slowly pour over cake, spreading evenly if necessary. Cool completely before serving.

Elegant Chocolate Soufflé

Contrary to popular belief, soufflés aren't difficult as long as you follow a few rules. Make the chocolate mixture ahead of time and refrigerate it to save time.

INGREDIENTS | SERVES 4

¼ cup butter or margarine

3 tablespoons all-purpose flour

⅛ teaspoon salt

¾ cup chocolate milk

⅓ cup cocoa powder

⅓ cup chocolate syrup

⅓ cup brown sugar

4 eggs, separated

2 teaspoons lemon juice

2 tablespoons sugar

Soufflé Rules

Be sure that the sauce that contains the egg yolks is cold before you fold in the egg whites. To fold, use a spatula and bring it down one side of the bowl, scrape the bottom, and up the other side, turning the mixtures together. And be sure to serve the soufflé as soon as possible. If it falls, it will still taste wonderful!

1. Up to 1 day ahead of time, make the chocolate mixture. In medium saucepan, melt butter over medium heat. Add flour and salt; cook and stir until bubbly, about 3 minutes. Then stir in chocolate milk and cook, stirring constantly with wire whisk, until mixture thickens.

2. Remove from heat and stir in cocoa, chocolate syrup, and brown sugar until blended. Then beat in egg yolks, cover, and refrigerate until cold. Place egg whites in medium bowl, cover, and keep refrigerated.

3. When ready to eat, preheat oven to 350°F. Grease a 6-cup soufflé dish with unsalted butter and set aside. Let egg whites stand at room temperature for 20 minutes. Add lemon juice and beat until foamy. Gradually add sugar and beat until egg whites are stiff but not dry.

4. With same beaters, beat chocolate mixture until smooth. Add a spoonful of egg whites and mix until combined. Then add remaining egg whites and fold together just until blended. Pour into prepared dish.

5. Bake for 30–40 minutes or until soufflé is puffed and just set. Serve immediately with ice cream.

Couponing Glossary

Blinkies: Coupons that you find in stores in machines that usually have a blinking light to get your attention.

BOGO: Buy-One-Get-One-Free. When you purchase an item and then get another one free. This can either be from a sale or a coupon.

Brand Loyal: When you only purchase a certain brand of a product and never try another brand.

Catalina: A coupon that is printed from a machine at the register called a Catalina machine.

Competitor Coupon: A coupon issued by a competing store.

Coupon Blogger: A blogger that blogs about coupons and sales.

Coupon Database: An online database that lists coupons, where to find them, and when they expire.

Coupon Etiquette: The wrong and right way to use coupons.

Coupon Policy: The rules a store has for using coupons in their store.

Double Coupons: When a store will give you double what the manufacturer coupon is offering.

E-Coupons: Coupons that you can load onto your store loyalty card, which are then deducted from your total when the cashier scans your loyalty card.

Extra Care Bucks: Store coupons from CVS that are triggered by specific purchases.

Extra Care Card: A loyalty card issued by CVS that you give to the cashier each time you shop to receive the weekly sales, Extra Care Bucks, and store incentives.

Filler: A product you purchase within your transaction to absorb any overage you may receive on a purchase.

Flash-Freeze: When you freeze fresh items at a very low temperature to preserve all the liquid inside.

General Mills (GM): A coupon insert that can be found in the weekend newspaper.

Grocery Price List: A list of the prices of all the grocery items that you buy on a regular basis. This is used to keep track of sales so you know you're getting a good deal.

Loss Leaders: The items that the stores put on deep discount to get you into the store.

Loyalty Program: Incentives that stores give you to get your business.

Manufacturer Coupon: A small piece of paper that is issued by the manufacturer that allows you a discount off a product or service.

Meat Markdowns: Meat that the grocery stores mark down in price because they can only sell it for one more day.

Overage: The balance that you receive when an item costs less than what the coupon is for.

Peelies: Coupons that are found on packages in the store that you peel off and present to the cashier.

Price Match: When one store matches the price of the same product from another store.

Printable Coupons: Coupons that you find online that can be printed in your home.

Proctor & Gamble (PG): A coupon insert that can be found in the weekend newspaper.

Produce Markdowns: Produce that the grocery stores mark down because they can only sell them for one more day.

Rain Check: A form that is given to you when a store sells out of a product and allows you to purchase it for the sale price at a later date.

Rebate: When you get your money back on a product that you purchased.

Redeem: Using a coupon in a store.

Red Plum (RP): A coupon insert that can be found in the weekend newspaper.

Regional Coupons: Coupons that have different values that are distributed in different regions of the United States.

Register Rewards: Store coupons from Walgreens that are triggered by specific purchases.

Rite Aid Video Values: Videos that you can watch on the Rite Aid website for which you receive store coupons after you watch them.

Rock-Bottom Prices: The price of a product that is the absolute lowest it will ever be.

Sales Ad: A list of the sales that are happening at a particular store for a certain length of time, which can be found in the newspaper, in the store, or mailed directly to your house.

Sales Cycle: A length of time or cycle in which items will go on sale.

Single Check Rebate: A rebate check that you will receive for purchasing certain items at Rite Aid. You must request the rebate to receive the check.

Smart Source (SS): A coupon insert that can be found in the weekend newspaper.

Stacking Coupons: A term for using more than one coupon on an item to help you save the most. For example, a store coupon with a manufacturer coupon.

Stockpile: Items you purchase at deep discount that you keep in your home for future use. The purpose of a stockpile is to avoid paying full price when you run out of an item.

Stockpile Budget: The amount of money you want to spend each time building or maintaining your stockpile.

Store Coupons: A small piece of paper that is issued by the store that allows you a discount off a product or service.

Store Incentive: An extra savings given to you by the store to get your business.

Store Loyalty Card: A card for a specific store that you apply for in order to receive the store sales and incentives.

Tear Pads: Pads of coupons that you tear off.

Triple Coupons: When a store will give you triple what the manufacturer coupon is offering.

+Up Rewards: Store coupons from Rite Aid that are triggered by specific purchases.

Weekly Store Match-Ups: A list of items that are on sale along with the coupons that can be used along with those sales to save you money.

Wellness+ Card: A loyalty card issued by Rite Aid that you give the cashier each time you shop to receive +Up Rewards and other store incentives.

Wine Tag: A coupon that is found on the neck of a bottle of wine.

Resources

E-Coupon Websites

www.shortcuts.com
www.cellfire.com
www.pgesaver.com
www.upromise.com
www.savingstar.com

Printable Coupon Websites

www.coupons.com
www.redplum.com
www.smartsource.com
www.couponnetwork.com
www.bettycrocker.com
www.pillsbury.com
www.eatbetteramerica.com
www.boxtops4education.com

Coupon Policies Online

www.cvs.com/CVSApp/cvscontent/faq/couponpolicy.pdf
http://walmartstores.com/7655.aspx
http://content.riteaid.com/stores/CustomerCouponAcceptancePolicyAugust2010.pdf
www.walgreens.com/topic/help/generalhelp/coupon_policy_main.jsp?erule=couponpolicy
http://sites.target.com/site/en/company/page.jsp?contentId=WCMP04-040400
www.bjs.com/help.content.help.E#sav

Places to Send Expired Coupons for the Troops

www.ocpnet.org

Free-Sample Websites

www.startsampling.com
www.vocalpoint.com
www.kraftfirsttaste.com

Koupon Karen Resources

www.kouponkaren.com/coupon-database
www.kouponkaren.com/category/printable-coupons
www.kouponkaren.com/category/free-stuff
www.twitter.com/kouponkaren
www.facebook.com/KouponKaren
www.kouponkaren.com/category/current-weeks-deals

Daily Deal Websites

www.groupon.com
www.eversave.com
www.livingsocial.com
http://deals.mamapedia.com

Designer Markdown Websites

www.onekingslane.com
www.zulily.com
www.modnique.com
www.beyondtherack.com
www.hautelook.com
www.ruelala.com

Index

We Have
EVERYTHING®
on Anything!

With more than 19 million copies sold, the Everything® series has become one of America's favorite resources for solving problems, learning new skills, and organizing lives. Our brand is not only recognizable—it's also welcomed.

The series is a hand-in-hand partner for people who are ready to tackle new subjects—like you!

For more information on the Everything® series, please visit *www.adamsmedia.com*

The Everything® list spans a wide range of subjects, with more than 500 titles covering 25 different categories:

Business	History	Reference
Careers	Home Improvement	Religion
Children's Storybooks	Everything Kids	Self-Help
Computers	Languages	Sports & Fitness
Cooking	Music	Travel
Crafts and Hobbies	New Age	Wedding
Education/Schools	Parenting	Writing
Games and Puzzles	Personal Finance	
Health	Pets	